cover to cover God's People

cover to cover God's People

Through the Bible **Character by Character**

365 daily readings

Selwyn Hughes and **Trevor J Partridge**

CWR

Waverley Abbey House, Waverley Lane, Farnham, Surrey GU9 8EP

CWR, Waverley Abbey House, Waverley Lane, Farnham, Surrey GU9 8EP

UK (and countries not listed below)
CWR, PO Box 230, Farnham, Surrey GU9 8XG Tel: 01252 784710 Outside UK (44) 1252 784710

AUSTRALIA: CMC Australasia, PO Box 519, Belmont, Victoria 3216 Tel: (03) 5241 3288

CANADA: CMC Distribution Ltd., PO Box 7000, Niagara on the Lake, Ontario L0S 1J0
Tel: 1 800 325 1297

GHANA: Challenge Enterprises of Ghana, PO Box 5723, Accra Tel: (21) 222437/223249

INDIA: Crystal Communications, Plot No. 83, Sesachalla Society, Entrenchment Road, East Marredpalli,
Secunderabad, Andhra Pradesh 500 026 Tel: (40) 7732511/7730577

KENYA: Keswick Bookshop, PO Box 10242, Nairobi Tel: (02) 331692/226047

MALAYSIA: Salvation Book Centre (M) Sdn. Bhd., 23 Jalan SS 2/4, 47300 Petaling Jaya, Selangor
Tel: (603) 78766411/78766797 Fax: (603) 78757066

NEW ZEALAND: CMC New Zealand Ltd., Private Bag, 17910 Green Lane, Auckland
Tel: 09 5249393 Fax: 09 5222137

NIGERIA: FBFM, (Every Day with Jesus), Prince's Court, 37 Ahmed Onibudo Street, PO Box 70952,
Victoria Island Tel: 01 2617721, 616832, 4700218, 2619156

PHILIPPINES: Praise Incorporated, 145 Panay Avenue, Cor Sgt Esguerra St, Quezon City
Tel: 632 920 5291 Fax: 920 5747

REPUBLIC OF IRELAND: Scripture Union, 40 Talbot Street, Dublin 1 Tel: (01) 8363764

SINGAPORE: Campus Crusade Asia Ltd., 315 Outram Road, 06-08 Tan Boon Liat Building,
Singapore 169074 Tel: (65) 222 3640

SOUTH AFRICA: Struik Christian Books (Pty Ltd), PO Box 193, Maitland 7405, Cape Town
Tel: (021) 551 5900

SRI LANKA: Christombu Books, 27 Hospital Street, Colombo 1 Tel: (1) 433142/328909

TANZANIA: City Christian Bookshop, PO Box 33463, Dar es Salaam Tel: (51) 28915

UGANDA: New Day Bookshop, PO Box 2021, Kampala Tel: (41) 255377

USA: CMC Distribution, PO Box 644, Lewiston, New York 14092-0644 Tel: 1 800 325 1297

ZIMBABWE: Word of Life Books, Shop 4, Memorial Bldg., 35 S Machel Ave., Harare.

Tel: 781305 Fax: 774739

Cover to Cover – God's People
Compiled by Selwyn Hughes and Trevor J Partridge
© CWR 2000
Previous editions published as *Character by Character* 1985, 1986, 1997
First published in 1985 as a bi-monthly six-part work, reprinted 1986
Revised single volume edition published 1997. Reprinted 1998, 1999.

Concept development, editing, design and production by CWR
Cover photograph: Roger Walker
Illustrations and diagrams: Happy House
Photographs: Corel Corporation, CWR Photo Library, Ed Pugh, PhotoDisc, Roger Walker, Sonia Halliday.
Printed by: Litografia Rosés, SA Barcelona, Spain.

ISBN 1 85345 160 6

Introduction

Dear Friend

Welcome to *Cover to Cover – God's People* in which we look at some of the well-known and not so well-known personalities in the Bible. Each character has been preserved by divine inspiration for a purpose. And what is that purpose? This: "These things happened to them as examples and were written down as warnings for us, on whom the fulfilment of the ages has come" (1 Corinthians 10:11).

God's method has always been to use people to achieve His purposes. He speaks to us best through people because we identify more easily with them than with events or situations. In the experiences of different Bible characters we can see ourselves – our victories and defeats.

As you study these different characters keep in mind that you should not attribute to them superhuman qualities. They were people "just like us" (James 5:17), ordinary people who became extraordinary by their submissiveness to the power of God. Watch how, at times, God chooses the weak instead of the strong, how sometimes He has to break people to get their attention, and how He takes the failures of men and women and uses them as a refining fire to bring about His ultimate purpose.

How wonderful it is to know that, just as in Bible times, God's present plans still involve people – and ordinary people like you and us. We are praying that the positive character traits which are held up to view by the Holy Spirit in these studies will become evident in your life and personality. And that prayer goes for ourselves too!

Have a wonderful year with the great personalities of the Bible.

Selwyn Hughes and Trevor J Partridge

Adam and Eve

Adam: "Of the ground – red earth" Eve: "The mother of all living"

DAY 1 — Made in the image of God

Genesis 1:26–27; 2:1–7

Although Adam and Eve were created at different times and from different materials (Adam from dust – Eve from Adam's rib) both were created in God's image and likeness, thus signifying their equality. "Image" means "representation", and "likeness" means "resemblance". Adam and Eve's likeness to God was not a physical one, but a spiritual one. They were like God in the sense that they could think like Him, feel like Him and love like Him. No other part of creation bore this likeness. It is because of the image of God in man that murder is such a heinous crime (see Genesis 9:6). Note also the first hint of the Trinity as seen in the plural expressions: "Let **us** make man in **our** image, in **our** likeness."

"He is the image of the invisible God, the firstborn over all creation. For by him all things were created: things in heaven and on earth, visible and invisible ... all things were created by him and for him." (Col. 1:15–16)

FURTHER THOUGHT

Through sin, the image of God in man has been damaged and defaced, but not destroyed. Every person you meet carries within them a likeness to their Creator. Learn to look at people from this point of view, and see if it doesn't add a new perspective to your relationships.

Adam and Eve

CREATION

2

"Be fruitful, and increase"

Genesis 1:28-31; 2:8-25

God's twofold command to Adam and Eve to (1) be fruitful and increase, and (2) to subdue the earth and have dominion over it, indicates the great privilege and authority with which God endowed the first human pair. **Privilege** because they were invited by God to become co-creators with Him in the task of perpetuating the human race, **authority** because they were given the task of ruling over the entire earth. If Adam and Eve had not sinned, then doubtless they would have produced offspring "in their own image" – children in whom there was no inherited sin, and who, under God, would have had dominion over the whole of creation.

"Every day they continued to meet together ... They broke bread in their homes and ate together with glad and sincere hearts, praising God and enjoying the favour of all the people. And the Lord added to their number daily those who were being saved." (Acts 2:46–47)

FURTHER THOUGHT

Although God's purpose of creating a people through whom He could reflect His love and oversee His creation was temporarily frustrated by sin, that purpose will yet be fulfilled. It will be achieved through God's redeemed people, the Church, who are destined not only to reflect His wisdom and grace, but also to rule the world.

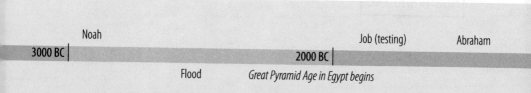

Noah		Job (testing)	Abraham
3000 BC	2000 BC		
Flood	Great Pyramid Age in Egypt begins		

DAY **3**   Temptation presents itself
Genesis 3:1–7; 1 Timothy 2:13–14

In the original temptation which Satan brought to Eve, we see a strategy which the devil uses, even to this very day. Firstly, he cast doubt upon the word of God: "Did God really say?" Secondly, he caricatured the word of God: "*None* of the fruit in the garden? God says you mustn't eat *any* of it?" (v. 1, TLB). Thirdly, he contradicted the word of God: "You will not surely die." Fourthly, he appealed to self-centredness and pride: "You will be like God, knowing good and evil." Despite the strength and power of Satan's temptation there was, however, a way of escape. God had given clear instructions concerning the tree of the knowledge of good and evil (see Genesis 2:16–17); if Eve had believed **God's** word instead of **Satan's** word, then the temptation would have been conquered and overcome.

"Jesus said to him, 'Away from me, Satan! For it is written: "Worship the Lord your God, and serve him only."' Then the devil left him ..." (Matt. 4:10–11)

FURTHER THOUGHT

Remember how Jesus dealt with Satan's temptations in the wilderness? He resisted them through God's Word. No matter what temptation faces you today, remember God's infallible way of escape is through His Word. Hide His Word in your heart, cling to it when under attack, and you will be more than a match for any of Satan's temptations.

Adam and Eve

Guilt and fear arise

Genesis 3:8–20; Job 31:33

After the Fall, Adam and Eve experienced for the first time the negative emotions of guilt and fear. In almost every instance, these negative emotions can be traced to a wrong belief and wrong behaviour. Eve believed Satan's lie – "You will be like God" (Gen. 3:5) – and then engaged in an act of disobedience: she took some of the forbidden fruit and ate it (Gen. 3:6). When this happened, guilt and fear were the natural consequence. Guilt arises within us when we believe that what God says is not in our interests, and we step outside His will to get what we want. Fear comes when we believe that God does not love us and no longer has our highest interests at heart.

"Therefore, there is now no condemnation for those who are in Christ Jesus, because through Christ Jesus the law of the Spirit of life set me free from the law of sin and death." (Rom. 8:1–2)

FURTHER THOUGHT

Feeling guilty or fearful about anything today? Then don't do as Adam and Eve did and run away from God; stop and see if you can trace those negative feelings to a wrong belief or wrong behaviour. When you have identified the culprits, confess them at once to God. This way you are sure of keeping the lines of communication open with Him.

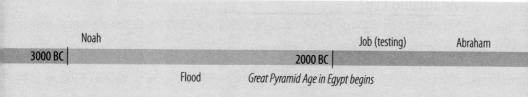

Noah		Job (testing)	Abraham
3000 BC		2000 BC	
Flood	Great Pyramid Age in Egypt begins		

5

DAY **5**

Separation results

Genesis 3:21–24; Romans 1:20–32

S in inevitably produces separation. When Adam and Eve sinned, they not only experienced a separation in their relationship with God by being expelled from the Garden of Eden, but their transgression adversely affected the whole of their posterity. At least four separations can be traced to Adam and Eve's fall. (1) Man is separated from God – a spiritual separation. (2) Man is separated from himself – a psychological separation. (3) Man is separated from others – a social separation. (4) Man is separated from nature – an ecological separation. Notice how God began at once to heal the breach that sin had made: He "made garments of skin" (Gen. 3:21). From the beginning of time, something had to die to cover sin.

"For I am convinced that neither death nor life, neither angels nor demons, neither the present nor the future, nor any powers, neither height nor depth, nor anything else in all creation, will be able to separate us from the love of God that is in Christ Jesus our Lord." (Rom. 8:38–39)

FURTHER THOUGHT

"We will never understand conversion," said someone, "until we see it in terms of relationships." Through the death of God's Son, we are not only rightly related to God, but to ourselves, to others and to the whole of creation. And that's not all – this new relationship will never know a separation. Hallelujah!

Adam and Eve

The family feud

Genesis 4:1-26

Then word "Genesis" means "beginning", and here we have the **beginning** of family life. Adam and Eve had no children prior to the Fall, but no sooner, so to speak, do they produce their offspring than the taint of their original sin can be seen. Cain, the firstborn, becomes jealous of Abel his brother, and in a fit of temper commits the world's first murder. Adam and Eve lost both their sons that day; one to death and the other to darkness and disillusionment: "So Cain went out from the Lord's presence" (Gen. 4:16). Adam and Eve had many other children, and presumably because the effects of sin had not yet taken their toll on the human frame, lived to a great age. Adam died at the age of 930 (Gen. 5:5)!

"Unless the Lord builds the house, its builders labour in vain. Unless the Lord watches over the city, the watchmen stand guard in vain." (Psa. 127:1)

FURTHER THOUGHT

As a result of Adam and Eve's original transgression, hardly a family has escaped the problems of jealousy, misunderstanding and suspicion. The root problem of disharmony in today's homes is the same as that which afflicted the first human family – a refusal to let God be God.

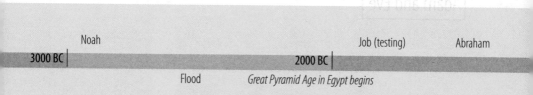

	Noah	Job (testing)	Abraham
3000 BC		2000 BC	
	Flood	Great Pyramid Age in Egypt begins	

Adam and Eve

DAY **7**

The first and last Adam

Romans 5:6–21

In the New Testament Christ is referred to as the last Adam, and many comparisons and contrasts are made between Him and His Old Testament counterpart (see 1 Corinthians 15:45–47). The most powerful contrast of all is the one drawn by Paul in Romans 5 in which he shows that the whole story of the human race can be summed up in terms of what happened, and will yet happen, because of Christ. There have been two federal heads of the human race – Adam and Christ. The first Adam, by reason of his sin, plunged us into ruin and despair; the last Adam, by virtue of His victory on Calvary, has given us an entrance into a new humanity.

"For since death came through a man, the resurrection of the dead comes also through a man. For as in Adam all die, so in Christ all will be made alive." (1 Cor. 15:21–22)

FURTHER THOUGHT

Dr Martyn Lloyd-Jones put it powerfully when he said: "Can there be any greater truth in Scripture than this – that as I was in Adam, I am now in Christ?" Let the truth which the hymnist wrote thrill and flood your whole being this day:
"In Him the tribes of Adam boast More blessings than their father lost."

Adam and Eve

The first Adam & The last Adam

Gen. 2:17	He introduced ... death	**Heb. 2:9**	He dealt with ... death
Gen. 3:7	He introduced ... nakedness	**John 19:23**	He dealt with ... nakedness
Gen. 3:14	He introduced ... curse	**Gal. 3:13**	He dealt with ... curse
Gen. 3:17	He introduced ... toil	**Matt 11:28**	He dealt with ... toil
Gen. 3:18	He introduced ... thorns	**John 19:5**	He dealt with ... thorns
Gen. 3:19	He introduced ... sweat	**Luke 22:44**	He dealt with ... sweat
Gen. 3:24	He introduced ... sword	**John 18:11**	He dealt with ... sword

Key Lesson – Adam and Eve

Adam and Eve are not mythical individuals, but real people. They appear in the opening pages of the Bible, not only to explain where and how the human race began, but to expose the strategy which lay behind Satan's temptations. The method used to tempt the first human pair is still part of Satan's present-day strategy. Understand how it works and you need never be at the mercy of satanic pressure again. Genesis 3:6 says that "the fruit of the tree was good for food and pleasing to the eye, and also desirable for gaining wisdom":

"Good for food" – "the lust of the flesh"; *"Pleasing to the eye"* – "the lust of the eyes"; *"Desirable for gaining wisdom"* – "the pride of life". Let God have control of your natural appetites. Make a pact with Him not to gaze on those things which are displeasing to Him. Surrender your pride and self-interest to Him and let Him be Lord. Follow this plan, and in His strength you can succeed where Adam and Eve failed.

Noah

DAY 8   A recipient of grace

Genesis 5:28–6:8

Little is known of Noah's early life except that he was from the line of Seth, was the son of Lamech, and the tenth man from Adam. He appears in Bible history at a time when there was great sin and wickedness on the earth. No catalogue of specific sins is to be found, but the Bible goes to the root of the matter by saying "every inclination of the thoughts of his heart was only evil all the time" (Gen. 6:5). The source of sin is shown to be not so much in deeds, but in the depths of man's heart. How was it possible for Noah to live a godly life in the midst of such wickedness? The answer is "grace". This was the power that not only supported him, but made him more than equal to his great task.

"The weapons we fight with ... have divine power to demolish strongholds. We demolish arguments and every pretension that sets itself up against the knowledge of God, and we take captive every thought to make it obedient to Christ." (2 Cor. 10:4–5)

FURTHER THOUGHT

Scripture tells us that "as it was in the days of Noah, so also will it be in the days of the Son of Man" (Luke 17:26). How comforting to know that as we draw nearer to Christ's coming, the same grace that made Noah equal to his task is available to us.

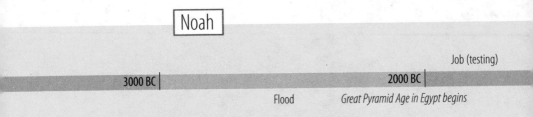

Noah

Job (testing)

3000 BC | 2000 BC |

Flood   *Great Pyramid Age in Egypt begins*

He walked with God

Genesis 6:9-22

Noah's personal relationship with the Almighty is described in four simple but meaningful words: "Noah walked with God." Moses encouraged the children of Israel to walk **after** God, and Abraham was said to walk **before** God, but only of Noah and Enoch was it said that they walked **with** God. To walk **after** God implies a willingness to follow Him in all the ways He leads; to walk **before** God suggests a consciousness of His abiding presence; to walk **with** God is to be constantly at His side and in the closest possible communion with Him. The only other time that this phrase occurs in the Old Testament is in Malachi 2:6, when it is applied to the priests who stood in a closer relationship to God than the rest of the people.

"Trust in the Lord with all your heart and lean not on your own understanding; in all your ways acknowledge him, and he will make your paths straight."
(Prov. 3:5–6)

FURTHER THOUGHT

How would you describe your daily walk with God? Do you walk before Him, after Him or with Him? Check on your relationship with the Lord today, and do whatever is necessary to bring your life alongside His.

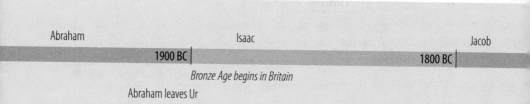

Abraham	Isaac	Jacob
1900 BC		1800 BC

Bronze Age begins in Britain

Abraham leaves Ur

DAY **10**

A man of faith

Genesis 7:1-16; Hebrews 11:6-7

lthough Noah was surrounded by a generation which was engaged in impiety, impurity and lawlessness, he believed, nevertheless, that God was in charge of history. He **believed** when God told him that a great flood was about to engulf the earth – even though he had never before seen rain (Gen. 2:5). He **believed** when God told him to build a gigantic boat – miles from the nearest ocean! And he kept on **believing** even though the flood did not actually come for over a hundred years. There are many definitions of faith, but basically faith is acting on what God says. Doubtless many of the things God said to Noah would have caused him some surprise; but it was enough for him that God said it.

"Now faith is being sure of what we hope for and certain of what we do not see." (Heb. 11:1)

FURTHER THOUGHT

Ready for a challenge? If faith is acting on what God says – how much of a man or woman of faith are you? If the answer makes you feel unworthy, then don't despair. List the things in which you have not obeyed, then focus on one thing you have not done – and do it. Then move on quietly to the others – and deal with them one by one.

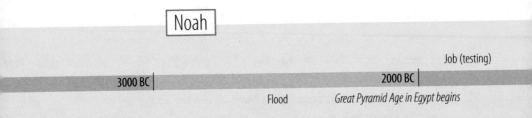

Noah

Job (testing)

3000 BC

2000 BC

Flood

Great Pyramid Age in Egypt begins

A preacher of righteousness

Genesis 7:17-24; 2 Peter 2:5; Luke 17:26-27

Although the age in which Noah lived was exceedingly wicked and sinful, he did not withdraw from it but became a preacher of righteousness right in their midst. What agony of soul he must have endured as he beheld the scenes of wild disorder and sinfulness, but he made his righteous protest nevertheless. In a sense his preaching seemed to be unsuccessful, for ultimately only he and his family were saved. Noah's mission, however, was not to save the world – that prerogative belongs only to God – but to faithfully witness to what God had told him, and thus make sure that the generation in which he lived would hear God's warning and be without excuse.

"But you will receive power when the Holy Spirit comes on you; and you will be my witnesses in Jerusalem, and in all Judea and Samaria, and to the ends of the earth." (Acts 1:8)

FURTHER THOUGHT

How important it is to recognise that our primary task in life is not to save our generation, but to witness to it. And understood correctly, this should not diminish our evangelistic zeal and passion, but increase it.

Abraham

Isaac

Jacob

1900 BC

1800 BC

Bronze Age begins in Britain

Abraham leaves Ur

DAY **12**

Remembered by God

Genesis 8:1–22; 1 Peter 3:20

The flood swept away every living person and animal on the earth except Noah and his family, who were "remembered" by the Lord. Noah was obedient to the letter in following God's instructions: he built the ark according to God's design, witnessed to the coming flood and selected pairs of every living creature for the preservation of the species. Thus because of his obedience he and his family – eight in all – were saved. Those who remember God are remembered by God. When Noah emerged from the ark approximately a year after he had entered it, his first task was to build an altar. Note that the first foundation in the new world was not a house but a church!

"Therefore, I urge you, brothers, in view of God's mercy, to offer your bodies as living sacrifices, holy and pleasing to God – this is your spiritual act of worship." (Rom. 12:1)

FURTHER THOUGHT

Some people's first reaction to the dramatic deliverance from God, such as a healing or a miracle, is to focus on how to get on with their lives. But not Noah; his first concern was to give God the honour that was due to His Name – a principle we would all do well to follow!

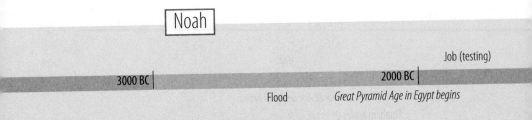

| Noah |

Job (testing)

3000 BC | 2000 BC |

Flood   *Great Pyramid Age in Egypt begins*

Noah's family prophecy

"Then God blessed Noah and his sons, saying to them, 'Be fruitful and increase in number and fill the earth.' " **(Gen 9:1)**

Concerning HAM & CANAAN

General servitude to seed of Shem and Japheth.
"THE LOWEST OF SLAVES"
- Joshua, David, and Solomon subdued them.
- Alexander the Great subdued them.
- The Romans subdued them.

TECHNICAL PROFICIENCY
The famous Christian anthropologist Arthur C. Custance states that all the earliest civilisations of note were founded and carried to the highest technical proficiency by Hamitic peoples.

Concerning JAPHETH

"May God extend the territory of Japheth; may Japheth live in the tents of Shem."
"MAY GOD EXTEND THE TERRITORY OF JAPHETH"
- Since 539 BC, with the defeat of the Babylonians by Cyrus the Great, no Semitic or Hamitic race has succeeded in breaking the world supremacy of the Japhetic race.

"MAY JAPHETH LIVE IN THE TENTS OF SHEM."
This glorious prophecy is fully explained by Paul in Romans 11:13–25.

Concerning SHEM

"May Canaan be his slave."
"BLESSED BE THE LORD, THE GOD OF SHEM!"
- Here is obviously a reference to the special favour bestowed upon Shem's descendants, beginning with Abraham, and ending in a Bethlehem manger.

The threefold contribution of NOAH'S SONS

HAM
- Technical proficiency.
- Responsible for man's physical well-being.

JAPHETH
- Application of philosophy.
- Development of the scientific method.
- Responsible for man's mental well-being.

SHEM
- Religious insights.
- Responsible for man's spiritual well-being.

DAY 13   The rainbow covenant

Genesis 9:1–17; Isaiah 54:9

The flood distinctly marks the end of one order of things, and the beginning of another. It was expedient that one generation should die for all generations, and that generation having been removed from the earth, fresh provision is made for the co-operation of man and God. On man's part there was the acknowledgement of God by sacrifice, and on God's part there was a renewed gift to man of the world and all its fullness. God's covenant with Noah, and through him to every living creature (v. 17), that never again would the earth be engulfed by a flood was dramatically ratified by a rainbow.

"This is the covenant I will make with the house of Israel after that time, declares the Lord. I will put my laws in their minds and write them on their hearts. I will be their God, and they will be my people." (Heb. 8:10)

FURTHER THOUGHT

Did you know that there is a rainbow in heaven? You can read about it in Revelation 4:3. It is God's pledge that when this fleeting dispensation is ended, and all things have reached their consummation, never again will sin rise up to spoil God's fair and beautiful universe. Hallelujah!

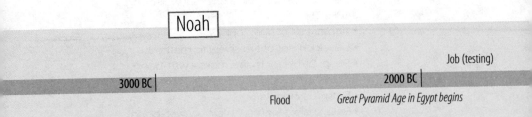

Noah

Job (testing)

3000 BC

2000 BC

Flood   Great Pyramid Age in Egypt begins

A blessing and a curse

Genesis 9:18–29

The flood had swept away many things, but not the evil tendency that is resident in the human heart – as Noah's drunkenness clearly shows. This lapse became the occasion of the blessing upon Shem and Japheth, but the curse upon Ham. Most scholars believe that Ham not only saw his father's nakedness, but looked upon it with lewdness and told his brothers about the problem in a disrespectful manner. The situation brought to light the character of the three sons – the coarse irreverence of Ham in contrast with the dignified sensitivity and honour of Shem and Japheth. These three sons of Noah repopulated the earth as commanded by the Lord in Genesis 9:1.

"Your boasting is not good. Don't you know that a little yeast works through the whole batch of dough? Get rid of the old yeast that you may be a new batch without yeast – as you really are. For Christ, our Passover lamb, has been sacrificed." (1 Cor. 5:6–7)

FURTHER THOUGHT

How sad that Noah, a man who when all the world was against him was able to face single-handed both scorn and violence, fell prey to the sin of drunkenness. It underlines the fact that it is the smaller temptations that are often most effectual, and that it is not over the mountains that we trip, but over the mat!

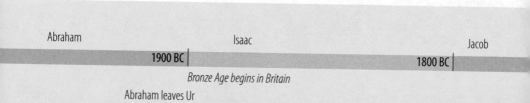

Abraham

Isaac

Jacob

1900 BC

1800 BC

Bronze Age begins in Britain

Abraham leaves Ur

Key Lesson
– Noah

Noah's life and witness illustrate the importance of maintaining a consistent witness in the face of abounding scorn and ridicule, and never giving up even though one's message seems to be falling on deaf ears. His resource, according to the writer to the Hebrews, was faith – the foresight of a better future. The qualities that spring from such faith are moral integrity, vision of God's plans and purposes, and an inner conviction that releases us from the pressure to perform. Great though Noah was, the Scripture has no hesitation in revealing that he fell into sin. It shows how alert we must be in recognising that our accomplishments for God do not, in themselves, insulate us from the power or possibility of temptation.

Abraham

A great call

Genesis 12:1-9

DAY **15**

Although Abraham was born in Ur of the Chaldees, he was a descendant of Shem and thus is in the line of Christ (Gen. 11:10–26). Little is known of his family, but we do know that his father was Terah, and that he married his half-sister Sarai. When God called him to leave the land where he lived and make his way to an unknown destination – "the land I will show you" (v. 1) – Abraham obeyed God without question and without hesitation. Although Abraham did not have a clear destination, he did have a clear promise: "I will bless you; I will make your name great" (v. 2). Doubtless it was this promise which fired his faith and started him out on a march which, with hindsight, is one of the greatest marches of history.

"... being confident of this, that he who began a good work in you will carry it on to completion until the day of Christ Jesus." (Phil. 1:6)

FURTHER THOUGHT

When God calls us to do a new work or to accomplish something special for Him, His call is not always accompanied by a reason, but it is always accompanied by a promise. It is always easy to understand a promise, but not always easy to understand a reason.

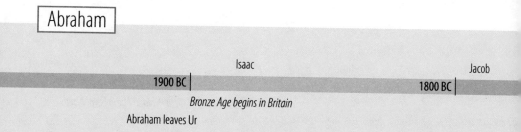

Abraham

Isaac

Jacob

1900 BC

1800 BC

Bronze Age begins in Britain

Abraham leaves Ur

DAY **16**

A great decision

Genesis 12:10–13:18

Abraham's journey into Egypt, which some think was done under his own volition and not by divine guidance, was shot through with heartache and failure. He lied about Sarai his wife to Pharaoh, saying she was his sister. Eventually Abraham returned from Egypt in company with his nephew, Lot, and returned to the place where he had first built an altar (Gen 13:4). Strife between the herdsmen of Lot and the herdsmen of Abraham led to the decision to separate. Abraham gave Lot the first choice, whereupon he chose the rich plain of Jordan. After Lot and Abraham separated, God chose for Abraham and gave him the title deeds of all the land he could see.

"'For my thoughts are not your thoughts, neither are your ways my ways,' declares the Lord. 'As the heavens are higher than the earth, so are my ways higher than your ways and my thoughts than your thoughts.'"
(Isa. 55:8–9)

FURTHER THOUGHT

When called upon to make a choice, do you first think of what God may want, or do you resort to the way of Lot who "chose for himself" (Gen. 13:11). As one wag said: "Lot went for a lot and got a little." Abraham finished up with the Promised Land. God always gives the best to those who leave the choice to Him.

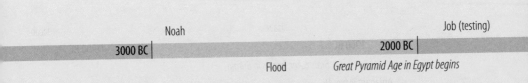

Noah

Job (testing)

3000 BC

2000 BC

Flood

Great Pyramid Age in Egypt begins

A great rescue

Genesis 14:1–15:21; Hebrews 7:1–28

Lot, who is now living in the city of Sodom (Gen. 14:12), is taken captive as a non-fighting civilian in the battle between King Kedorlaomer and Bera, the king of Sodom. When Abraham heard of his nephew's plight, he mounted a rescue operation which resulted not only in Lot's deliverance, but in the acquisition of much wealth and possessions. As Abraham and Lot returned from defeating Kedorlaomer, Melchizedek, a priest of God Most High, came to meet him. This priest, who was also the king of Salem, gave him refreshment and blessed him. Immediately Abraham took a gift of his own (a tenth of everything) and gave it to the man of God. Here was established the principle of tithing which Abraham's physical and spiritual descendants would follow.

"We have this hope as an anchor for the soul, firm and secure. It enters the inner sanctuary behind the curtain, where Jesus, who went before us, has entered on our behalf. He has become a high priest for ever, in the order of Melchizedek." (Heb. 6:19–20)

FURTHER THOUGHT

How do you feel about tithing? Do you regard it as something that was "under the law"? Well, here you can see that the principle was established long before the law was given. Tithing is a Biblical principle, and Scripture encourages us to follow it.

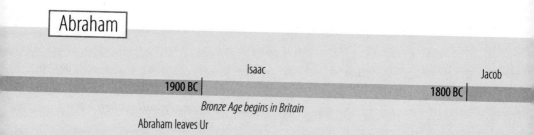

Abraham

Isaac

Jacob

1900 BC

1800 BC

Bronze Age begins in Britain

Abraham leaves Ur

DAY **18**

A great mistake

Genesis 16:1–16; 20:1–18

After God had reconfirmed His promises to Abraham, all seems ready for him to be installed as the head of a new covenant with the promise of many descendants. His marriage to Sarai, however, does not produce a child, and he begins to entertain the idea of an adopted heir. God responds to this by saying, "A son coming from your own body will be your heir" (Gen. 15:4). These words left no doubt that Abraham would become a father, but they gave no definite indication that Sarai would be the mother. Perhaps this may be one reason why Abraham responded so easily to Sarai's suggestion to become intimate with her servant Hagar. When Ishmael is born, the home which before was a scene of bliss, sadly becomes a house of discord.

"... the testing of your faith develops perseverance. Perseverance must finish its work so that you may be mature and complete, not lacking anything." (James 1:3–4)

FURTHER THOUGHT

The delay that often occurs between God revealing His purposes and actually bringing them to pass is one of the greatest testing times in life. How careful we must be that we do not attempt to interfere with or "speed up" the plans of God. That way is always a short cut to disaster.

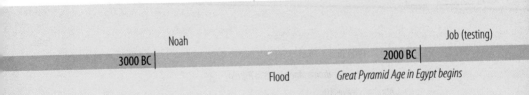

Noah

3000 BC |

Flood

2000 BC |

Job (testing)

Great Pyramid Age in Egypt begins

A great change

Genesis 17:1–18:15; 21:1–8

When Abraham is ninety-nine years old, God appears to him and announces Himself under a new name: "I am God Almighty" (Hebrew, El-Shaddai – the nourisher of His people) (Gen. 17:1). This announcement is followed by the news that Abraham's name is to be changed – from Abram to Abraham. Sarai's name is to be changed also – from Sarai to Sarah – and the first direct intimation is given that she is to be the mother of the promised seed, whose name is to be Isaac. These new revelations are accompanied by the announcement that every male child must be circumcised. Sarai's response to the news that, at ninety, she is to become a mother, is one of incredulous laughter. Nevertheless, what God promised twenty-five years previously comes to pass, and Isaac is born.

"For the revelation awaits an appointed time; it speaks of the end and will not prove false. Though it linger, wait for it; it will certainly come and will not delay." (Hab. 2:3)

FURTHER THOUGHT

Did you notice that when God breathed His divine life into Abram and Sarai, thus enabling them to have a child, the letter He introduced into their names was the letter "h"? How wonderfully things change when God breathes into them. Take the word "impossible", for example. See what it becomes – Him-possible.

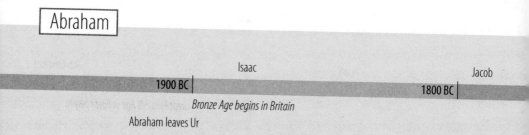

Abraham

Isaac

Jacob

1900 BC

1800 BC

Bronze Age begins in Britain

Abraham leaves Ur

DAY 20

A great intercession
Genesis 18:16–19:38

Once before Abraham had saved Lot by rescuing him from the hands of King Kedorlaomer. On that occasion he went and personally brought him out of difficulty; this time he prays him out. Abraham's intercession for Lot contains the ingredients that are common to all great intercessors: (1) boldness (18:23); (2) pleading (18:24); (3) argument (18:25); (4) humility (18:27); and (5) perseverance (18:32). As a result of Abraham's powerful intercession, God sent two angels to Sodom to rescue Lot and his family, but unfortunately Lot's wife disobeyed the command not to look back and was turned into a pillar of salt.

"... pray in the Spirit on all occasions with all kinds of prayers and requests. With this in mind, be alert and always keep on praying for all the saints." (Eph. 6:18)

FURTHER THOUGHT

How effective are you in your intercessions? Do your prayers for others contain the characteristics which show up time and time again in the great prayers of the Bible? Look up, for example, Isaiah's great prayer in Isaiah 63 and see if you can spot these same five characteristics.

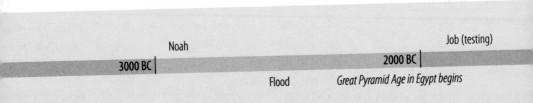

Noah

3000 BC

Flood

2000 BC

Great Pyramid Age in Egypt begins

Job (testing)

A great test of faith

Genesis 22:1-23:20; 25:1-8; Hebrews 11:17

Isaac is already a young man when Abraham receives a command from God to offer him up as a sacrifice. Obedient and devoted Abraham makes the necessary preparations and climbs to the top of Mount Moriah – the appointed place of sacrifice. His hand is raised to kill his son when he hears the divine voice loud and clear saying that God does not desire the completion of the act but is satisfied with Abraham's proved willingness. The animal which is to be substituted in his son's place stands ready by divine providence and is sacrificed for him. Without doubt this was the greatest test of faith which Abraham ever endured, and is seen by commentators as the most significant act of his life.

"Dear friends, do not be surprised at the painful trial you are suffering, as though something strange were happening to you. But rejoice that you participate in the sufferings of Christ, so that you may be overjoyed when his glory is revealed." (1 Pet. 4:12–13)

FURTHER THOUGHT

Have you ever considered that the theme of the Old Testament can be summed up in Isaac's question on Mount Moriah: "The fire and wood are here, but where is the lamb?" (Gen. 22:7)? And that question is wonderfully answered in the New: "Look, the Lamb ... who takes away the sin of the world!" (John 1:29).

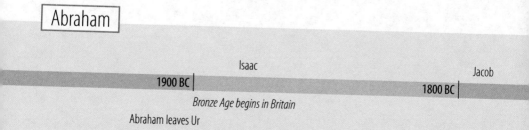

Abraham

Isaac

Jacob

1900 BC

1800 BC

Bronze Age begins in Britain

Abraham leaves Ur

God's sevenfold promise *to Abraham*

1. I will make you into a great nation
2. I will bless you
3. I will make your name great
4. You will be a blessing
5. I will bless those who bless you
6. I will curse those who curse you
7. Through you shall all peoples on earth be blessed
   (a reference to Christ; see Matthew 1:1)

 # Key Lesson – Abraham

Abraham's life, as one commentator puts it, "defines the difference between a true pilgrim and a mere pedestrian". Everything about this illustrious patriarch says that he delighted to be a sojourner (literally, "here for the day"), the archetypal pilgrim, alienated, disengaged and a stranger on the earth. He lived in the world but his heart was set on another country, his treasure was in another currency and his citizenship in another realm. Like Abraham, we live in the world, but the direction of our lives must always be *forward*.

Abraham made for a place he would afterwards receive, and seeing the promise from afar he greeted it as present and sure. A true pilgrim realises that he has struck camp and is going places with God, adventuring, searching beyond the distant horizons. Faith, detachment, hope: these are the qualities which are evidenced in Abraham's life and which God still seeks to cultivate in His present-day pilgrims.

The submissive son

DAY 22

Genesis 21:1–8; 22:1–14

Isaac, as we have seen, was the product of a miracle, born when his father Abraham was 100 years old and his mother Sarah 91 years old. Isaac is one of the few men in the Bible whose name was selected and announced by God prior to his birth. Commentators believe that Isaac was between twenty-five and thirty years of age when his father prepared to offer him as a sacrifice on Mount Moriah. If Abraham's attitude was outstanding in this situation, so also was Isaac's. He meekly allowed himself to be placed upon the altar, and lay there unresisting until the sacrificial knife was about to be plunged into him. It was an ordeal for the father, but no less for the son.

"We all, like sheep, have gone astray, each of us has turned to his own way; and the Lord has laid on him the iniquity of us all. He was oppressed and afflicted, yet he did not open his mouth; he was led like a lamb to the slaughter ..." (Isa. 53:6–7)

FURTHER THOUGHT

Question: Where do you find another instance of a Son voluntarily surrendering His life and laying Himself on an altar at His Father's bidding? Answer: It was less than a mile from Mount Moriah – at the place called Calvary. Eternal praise be to His wonderful Name!

Isaac

Abraham

Jacob

1900 BC

1800 BC

Bronze Age begins in Britain

Abraham leaves Ur

Isaac

DAY 23   The selected spouse

Genesis 24:1–51

ow that Isaac is about forty years of age, Abraham concludes that it is time that a bride is found for his beloved son. Realising that marriage to an idolater might interfere with God's future purposes, he commissions his servant Eliezer to travel to Mesopotamia in the hope of bringing back a fitting bride from among his own people. Worldly ambitions might have suggested that marriage to a Canaanite girl would be likely to result in the possession of territory by his grandchildren, but the spiritual considerations outweighed this. Abraham is not stated to have even consulted Isaac when he dispatched his servant to visit his homeland, and here again is evidence of Isaac's complete confidence in his father's faith and wisdom.

"Do not be yoked together with unbelievers. For what do righteousness and wickedness have in common? Or what fellowship can light have with darkness?" (2 Cor. 6:14)

FURTHER THOUGHT

The principle of not being "yoked together with unbelievers" is often sacrificed on the altar of expediency. How do you feel about this issue? Is it a principle that guides you in all your relationships?

Isaac

Abraham

Jacob

1900 BC

1800 BC

Bronze Age begins in Britain

Abraham leaves Ur

The gentle groom

Genesis 24:52-67

Abraham's servant, Eliezer, performed his task of finding a bride for Isaac to perfection. Having prayed for divine guidance, he was led to a beautiful young girl by the name of Rebekah who instantly struck him as being a suitable choice for his master's son. After making all the necessary arrangements, he returns to Abraham's household with the bride-to-be under his charge. It seems, by this time, that Abraham has informed Isaac concerning Eliezer's mission, and as the servant is spotted returning to the homestead, Isaac goes out to meet him. He accepts Rebekah as a gift from God, takes her into his mother's tent and gives her his mother's place in his heart.

"... Christ loved the church and gave himself up for her to make her holy ... and to present her to himself as a radiant church, without stain or wrinkle or any other blemish, but holy and blameless." (Eph. 5:25–27)

FURTHER THOUGHT

What better thought to hold in mind than that expressed by Richard Wilton:

"Thus while to Heaven thought after thought was rising,
The fair Rebekah step by step drew nigh,
With life's chief joy the prayerful saint surprising:
For those who think of Him, God still is thinking."

Joseph

1700 BC

ISRAEL IN EGYPT

1600 BC

Jacob's family settle in Egypt

Isaac

DAY 25   The praying husband
Genesis 25:1-23

Isaac's marriage, though happy and promising at the start, brought new trials and difficulties into his life. Rebekah went through the same experience as her mother-in-law, Sarah – childlessness. This second barrenness in the prospective mother of the promised seed was of great concern to Isaac, and caused him to intercede with God on Rebekah's behalf. The prayer which he uttered was filled with deep intensity and concern: "Isaac prayed [Hebrew: "agonised"] to the Lord on behalf of his wife, because she was barren." God heard Isaac's prayer, and in due course the barren Rebekah became the mother of twin sons who, even in the womb, foreshadowed the long fierce struggle of the races that would spring from them.

"Sing, O barren woman, you who never bore a child ... because more are the children of the desolate woman than of her who has a husband ... Enlarge the place of your tent, stretch your tent curtains wide, do not hold back ... For you will spread out to the right and to the left; your descendants will dispossess nations ..." (Isa. 54:1–3)

FURTHER THOUGHT
How intriguing are the ways of the Lord, who arranges events and situations so that His people are constantly dependent upon Him. Have you lost your dependence on God? Then don't be surprised if He holds up the fulfilment of His promises until that truth fastens itself upon your heart.

Isaac

Abraham

Jacob

1900 BC

1800 BC

Bronze Age begins in Britain

Abraham leaves Ur

Like father, like son

Genesis 26:1-11

The land in which Isaac lived became stricken with famine and, seeking food for his cattle, he makes his way to Gerar but is warned by God not to go down into Egypt. It is in Gerar that Isaac imitated the ruse which his father practised on two previous occasions (see Genesis 12:10–20 and Genesis 20:1–18), and evasively declared Rebekah to be his "sister". His lie, however, was discovered by Abimelech, the king of Gerar, who rebuked him for his deceitfulness, and then instructed his people not to molest him. Isaac, a circumcised member of a chosen race, stood rebuked by an uncircumcised Philistine, and gave the enemies of Jehovah an occasion to blaspheme.

"Then you will know the truth, and the truth will set you free." (John 8:32)

FURTHER THOUGHT

Can a lie ever be justified? Some moralists say that a falsehood that is motivated by love is not a falsehood. But what does God say? "Do not lie to each other, since you have taken off your old self with its practices ..." (Col. 3:9).

Joseph
1700 BC

ISRAEL IN EGYPT

1600 BC

Jacob's family settle in Egypt

DAY 27

The willing worker

Genesis 26:12-33

Isaac eventually settles in the Valley of Gerar, where he found a number of wells which had been dug in the days of Abraham, but which had been filled up by the Philistines with rubbish and earth. Isaac sets himself the task of re-opening the wells, calling them by the very names that his father had called them. He thus not only honoured his father's memory, but also claimed his rights as his father's heir. The ill-feeling of the Philistines prompted Abimelech to ask Isaac to depart from this land, but God continues to bless him, which in turn leads the Philistines to recognise that, despite his failures, God is with the man whose heart is disposed toward Him.

"... I do not consider myself yet to have taken hold of it. But one thing I do: Forgetting what is behind and straining towards what is ahead, I press on towards the goal to win the prize for which God has called me heavenwards in Christ Jesus." (Phil. 3:13–14)

FURTHER THOUGHT

Feeling spiritually jaded at the moment? Does some memory of a past failure or sin continue to lacerate your soul? Confess it to God and put it behind you. Then go out as Isaac did, and do a great new work for God.

Isaac

Abraham

Jacob

1900 BC

1800 BC

Bronze Age begins in Britain

Abraham leaves Ur

A deceived father

Genesis 27:1-40

Isaac feels he is approaching the end of his days and, according to custom, desires to bestow his blessing upon his firstborn son – Esau. He is aware that God had said that the older would serve the younger (Gen. 25:23), but he decides to go ahead nevertheless. Rebekah, hearing Isaac's instructions to Esau that he should bring him some wild game, decided to trick the old man into believing that her favourite son, Jacob, was the firstborn. The deception resulted in Jacob being given the blessing of the firstborn, and Esau receiving the blessing of the secondborn. Actually Isaac lived many years after this incident, and died at the age of 180 (Gen. 35:27–29).

"The heart is deceitful above all things and beyond cure. Who can understand it?" (Jer. 17:9)

FURTHER THOUGHT

What a train of evils follows in the wake of deceit. The poet was right when he wrote:
"Oh what a tangled web we weave, When first we venture to deceive." Trickery and worldly schemes bring only heartache to any family.

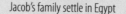

Joseph

1700 BC

ISRAEL IN EGYPT

1600 BC

Jacob's family settle in Egypt

God provides for Isaac

In the lone field he walks at eventide,
To meditate beneath the open sky,
Where borne on lighter wings prayers upward fly,
And down from Heaven sweet answers swiftly glide.
But as he glanced around the landscape wide,
Far off a train of camels meets his eye,
And as they nearer come he can descry
A maiden veiled – his unseen, God-sent bride.
Thus while to Heaven thought after thought was rising,
The fair Rebekah step by step drew nigh,
With life's chief joy the prayerful saint surprising:
For those who think of Him God still is thinking,
With tender condescension from on high,
Some comfort ever to some duty linking.

Richard Wilton

Key Lesson - Isaac

Most Bible scholars agree that Isaac's life is far nearer to the level of ordinary humanity than that of his father, Abraham's. He seems to have started well but, as he grew older, trends appeared in his personality which blemished the record of his early days. He is regarded by many as being too fond of "creature comforts", and unduly favouring the son who provided them for him. No formal eulogy is bestowed upon Isaac in the Scriptures; he is like his son, Jacob – "a quiet man" (Gen. 25:27). Despite the negatives, however, Isaac had many virtues and graces: faith (Heb. 11:20), obedience (Gen. 22:6-9), affection (Gen. 24:67; 25:28; 27:27-33), as well as gentleness and marital fidelity. Without doubt the outstanding characteristic of his life is self-effacement. He taught the men and women of his day that "a servant of the Lord must not quarrel" – not be aggressive, taking things from people without their consent – but gentle, patient, self-effacing and humble (2 Tim. 2:24-25).

The schemer

Genesis 25:27-34; 27:1-29

Jacob's parents were Isaac and Rebekah, and Esau was his twin brother. God spoke to Rebekah before the birth of the twins, saying, "Two nations are in your womb ... and the older [Esau] will serve the younger [Jacob]" (Gen. 25:23). As soon as Jacob makes his appearance in Scripture, we find him manipulating his brother Esau into surrendering his birthright. Esau was so hungry that he gave up his birthright, which he did not really care about (Gen. 25:32). Later, Jacob tricked his father into giving him the blessing of the firstborn, and is thus called "the supplanter", or "one who takes the place of another".

" ... he who doubts is like a wave of the sea, blown and tossed by the wind ... he is a double-minded man, unstable in all he does." (James 1:6;1:8)

FURTHER THOUGHT

When the realisation of our ambitions has been clearly shown and pledged by the Almighty, our task is to wait for the Lord to bring about His purposes in His own way and in His own time. God is well able to perform what He has promised – without the aid of human schemes.

Jacob

Isaac

1900 BC

Bronze Age begins in Britain

Abraham leaves Ur

1800 BC

DAY **30**

The dreamer

Genesis 28:1-22

Driven from his home by Esau's threats, Rebekah's fears and Isaac's demand, Jacob sets out on the long, dangerous journey from Beersheba to Haran. As he journeys northward, he comes to the hill country of Bethel where, tired and weary, he falls asleep with a stone for his pillow. There, he dreams of a ladder which stretches from heaven to earth with angels ascending and descending upon it. God has often spoken to people through dreams – from Abimelech to Paul – and in Jacob's dream the Almighty confirms to him the covenant He made with his grandfather, Abraham. The promise is given that his seed will be "like the dust of the earth". He anoints the pillow of stone and calls the name of the place "Bethel" (house of God), which previously had been called "Luz" (a place of separation).

"In the last days, God says, I will pour out my Spirit on all people. Your sons and daughters will prophesy, your young men will see visions, your old men will dream dreams." (Acts 2:17)

FURTHER THOUGHT

Has God ever spoken to you in a dream? It's encouraging to know that God can always find a secret stairway to our souls. If He can't get to us when we are awake, He will get to us when we are asleep. Day or night makes no difference to Him.

Jacob

Isaac

1900 BC

Bronze Age begins in Britain

Abraham leaves Ur

1800 BC

The suitor

Genesis 29:1-35

The experience that Jacob went through at Bethel was most definitely a turning-point in his life, and he proceeds toward the east with confidence and joy, little knowing, however, that he is soon to reap what he has sown. Jacob meets Rachel and falls deeply in love with her, but her father Laban requires him to serve seven years for her. On the wedding night, Laban tricks Jacob into believing that Rachel is in his tent, while all the time it is Leah, his older daughter. Laban later gives Rachel to Jacob, at the cost of another seven years of service – so Jacob now has two wives. Leah had many children while Rachel had only two – Joseph and Benjamin.

"This is love: not that we loved God, but that he loved us and sent his Son as an atoning sacrifice for our sins."
(1 John 4:10)

FURTHER THOUGHT

Love has a way of taking the drudgery out of work, making long and hard service short and easy. How deep is your love for the Lord? Are you truly in love with Him? An age of work will seem as nothing if love, and not merely a sense of duty, burns at the centre of your soul.

Joseph

1700 BC | ISRAEL IN EGYPT 1600 BC |

Jacob's family settle in Egypt

DAY **32**

The enterpriser
Genesis 30:1–31:55

After many years in Laban's service, Jacob longs to return to his own country, but his discipline is not yet complete. He must wait and serve for even longer. Laban entreats Jacob to stay, acknowledging that Jacob's abilities have contributed to his own prosperity. Jacob continues to serve Laban, claiming just a small wage, but Jacob cleverly outwits his father-in-law and becomes extremely prosperous. Eventually God speaks to Jacob, indicating that he must return to the land of his fathers, and so without notice he leaves Laban's house. He is soon pursued by his father-in-law, but God intervenes to protect Jacob from Laban's revenge and a covenant of friendship is set up between them which they call "Mizpah" – "May the Lord keep watch ... when we are away from each other."

"He said to another man, 'Follow me.' But the man replied, 'Lord, first let me go and bury my father.' Jesus said to him, 'Let the dead bury their own dead, but you go and proclaim the kingdom of God.'" (Luke 9:59–60)

FURTHER THOUGHT
Question: What do we do when, like Jacob, we feel on the one hand, the pull of the divine purpose and on the other, the varied claims of relations and friends? Answer: We must keep all our relationships open, but give God's call the highest priority.

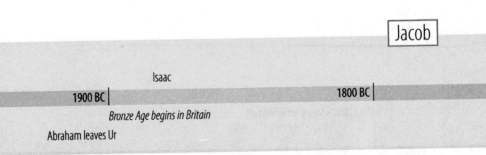

Jacob

Isaac

1900 BC

Bronze Age begins in Britain

Abraham leaves Ur

1800 BC

The wrestler

Genesis 32:1-32

After twenty years away from the land of Canaan, Jacob is on his way home. There is, however, one thing that he fears – the displeasure of his brother Esau. Sending messengers ahead of him to acquaint Esau with the news of his return, Jacob learns that Esau intends coming out to meet him accompanied by 400 men. Fear strikes into his heart and he cries out to God. In answer to his prayer, God sends an angel to wrestle with him, and Jacob is finally subdued when the angel dislocates his thigh. God's intention, however, was not to kill Jacob but to conquer him. Once Jacob is brought to a place of helplessness, his name is changed to Israel – a prince with God – and he becomes a changed man.

"But he said to me, 'My grace is sufficient for you, for my power is made perfect in weakness.' ... That is why, for Christ's sake, I delight in weaknesses ... For when I am weak, then I am strong." (2 Cor. 12:9–10)

FURTHER THOUGHT

How sad that in order to overcome our self-centredness, God sometimes has to not only wrestle with us, but cripple us. When will we learn that the key to spiritual power lies not in our strength, but in our weakness?

Joseph

1700 BC

ISRAEL IN EGYPT   1600 BC

Jacob's family settle in Egypt

Jacob

Jacob: "Supplanter"

DAY 34

The restorer

Genesis 33:1-20

After a night of wrestling with the angel, "Jacob looked up and there was Esau, coming with his four hundred men." Jacob, still somewhat apprehensive, approached his brother and "bowed down to the ground seven times". Jacob had the birthright and therefore, according to custom, was superior, but this action of humility deeply impressed Esau and they become fully reconciled. Esau offers to escort Jacob to his destination, Canaan, but Jacob declines. Eventually Jacob crosses the Jordan, buys a plot of ground in Shechem and for the first time on the sacred soil of Canaan, erects an altar. At that spot he calls God his God; not the God of Jacob, but the God of Israel – his new name.

"Him who overcomes I will make a pillar in the temple of my God ... I will write on him the name of my God and the name of the city of my God, the new Jerusalem ... and I will also write on him my new name." (Rev. 3:12)

FURTHER THOUGHT

Have you noticed that, more often than not, when something happens to us, something happens to those around us? A changed Jacob resulted in a changed Esau. Many, though not all, of our problems are problems in ourselves which we project on to others. When we change – others change.

Jacob

Isaac

1900 BC

1800 BC

Bronze Age begins in Britain

Abraham leaves Ur

The worshipper

Genesis 35:1-29

Once again God speaks to Jacob, this time instructing him to establish his home in Bethel and build there an altar to Jehovah. Idols obviously defiled Jacob's house so, before leaving Shechem, he issues the command: "Get rid of the foreign gods" (v.2). When Jacob eventually arrives at Bethel, he builds an altar, calling it "El Bethel", which means "the God of the house of God" (vv. 6, 7). At Bethel, Jacob moves into a more worshipful relationship with God than ever before – but his life is beset with more trials and difficulties than ever before. First, Rachel's nurse dies, and then he suffers the bereavement of Rachel, who dies giving birth to Benjamin. Jacob's twelve sons are all listed in this chapter (vv. 23–26).

"... he restores my soul. He guides me in paths of righteousness for his name's sake." (Psa. 23:3)

FURTHER THOUGHT

How far have you wandered away from your "Bethel" – the place where you first met with God? Have you allowed the things of the world to disrupt your relationship with the Lord? Then today God is calling you back to "Bethel". Don't wait until tomorrow – respond now.

Joseph

1700 BC

ISRAEL IN EGYPT

1600 BC

Jacob's family settle in Egypt

The peaks and troughs in *Jacob's spiritual life*

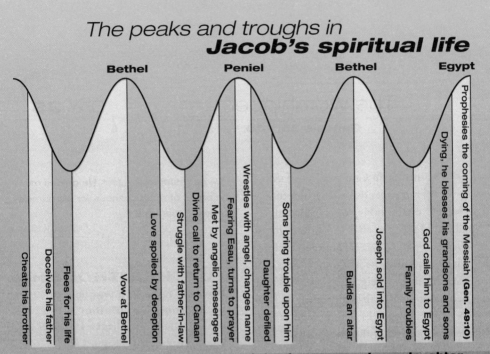

Bethel   **Peniel**   **Bethel**   **Egypt**

- Cheats his brother
- Deceives his father
- Flees for his life
- Vow at Bethel
- Love spoiled by deception
- Struggle with father-in-law
- Divine call to return to Canaan
- Met by angelic messengers
- Fearing Esau, turns to prayer
- Wrestles with angel, changes name
- Daughter defiled
- Sons bring trouble upon him
- Builds an altar
- Joseph sold into Egypt
- Family troubles
- God calls him to Egypt
- Dying, he blesses his grandsons and sons
- Prophesies the coming of the Messiah (Gen. 49:10)

These four women would bear Jacob twelve sons and one daughter

Leah – 1.Reuben 2.Simeon 3.Levi 4.Judah 9.Issachar 10.Zebulun, Dinah (daughter)

Bilhah (Rachel's handmaid) – 5.Dan 6.Naphtali

Zilpah (Leah's handmaid) – 7.Gad 8.Asher

Rachel – 11.Joseph 12.Benjamin

Key Lesson – Jacob

The outstanding lesson of Jacob's life is that God never fails to discipline those who resist, or who are slow to conform to His purposes. If we do not rise to the level which God purposes for us through gentle entreaties and persuasion, then we will be obliged to rise to it through the firm hand of discipline. Jacob's life shows, too, that it never pays to cheat or deceive – for, as the Scripture so clearly states: "A man reaps what he sows" (Gal. 6:7). Three great milestones can be seen in Jacob's life: (1) the dream at Bethel; (2) the long discipline at the hands of Laban; and (3) the night when the angel of the Lord wrestled with him and overcame him. That night, a new humility was stamped upon Jacob's character.

Favoured by his father

DAY **36**

Genesis 37:1-17

The story of Joseph is unquestionably one of the most thrilling in the whole of Scripture, and records his life in more detail than that of the lives of other great patriarchs, such as Abraham and Isaac. Most scholars believe this is because Joseph typifies, more than any other Bible personality, the life and character of our Lord Jesus Christ. The likenesses between Joseph and Christ are so compelling that we cannot help but build our outline around these parallels. Joseph, the son of Jacob and Rachel, was born in Haran before the family returned to Canaan. He was Jacob's favourite child – an affection due not just to the fact that he was the son of Jacob's old age, but also to the innate charm and winsomeness of his personality.

"Dear friends, now we are children of God, and what we will be has not yet been made known. But we know that when he appears, we shall be like him, for we shall see him as he is."
(1 John 3:2)

FURTHER THOUGHT

God delights in having many sons. Adam, for example, was described as a "son of God", and all those who have entered by faith into Christ's redemption are called children of God (1 John 3:1). No one, however, has brought such delight to the Father's heart as His "own beloved Son", for only in Him has no flaw or imperfection been found.

Joseph

Joseph
Joseph: "May he add"

Rejected by his brothers
Genesis 37:18-36

The favouritism which Jacob showed toward Joseph sparked off in the hearts of his brothers a desire to get rid of him. One day when Jacob sends Joseph to look after his brothers' welfare, they decide to take advantage of this opportunity to plot against him. Although Reuben tries to save him, the other brothers, led by Judah, arrange to sell him to some Ishmaelites who are passing by on their way to Egypt. Joseph is taken from the pit in which they had put him, and sold for the sum of twenty pieces of silver. The brothers then take the fine robe which had been worn by Joseph, sprinkle it with the blood of an animal and carry it to their father with the deceptive story that Joseph, his beloved son, has been killed.

"He came to that which was his own, but his own did not receive him." (John 1:11)

FURTHER THOUGHT

Jesus, too, was rejected by His kinsmen – the Jews – who were His brothers according to the flesh (Luke 20:13-14). But there is an even more dramatic parallel: Joseph was sold by Judah for twenty pieces of silver; Jesus was sold by Judas (Judah) for a similar but slightly larger amount.

Isaac

Jacob

1900 BC

1800 BC

Bronze Age begins in Britain

Abraham leaves Ur

44

Tested by adversity

Genesis 39:1-20

Joseph is carried by the Ishmaelites into Egypt and is purchased in the slave market by Potiphar, a captain of the guard. If he was to be a slave, Joseph was determined to be the best of slaves, and to do what he was required to do with a glad and willing heart. So well, in fact, does he do his duties that soon he becomes an overseer in his master's house. One day, however, Potiphar's wife attempts to seduce him and although he refuses to agree to her suggestion, he is falsely accused and brought before the master of the house for punishment. Yet despite the pressures that were upon him, no self-pity arises in his heart and his spirit remains unbowed and unbroken.

"In bringing many sons to glory, it was fitting that God, for whom and through whom everything exists, should make the author of their salvation perfect through suffering." (Heb. 2:10)

FURTHER THOUGHT

Comb the record of Christ's days with the most scrupulous care, and what do you find? Though rejected, slandered, tempted, and falsely accused, not once is His sensitive soul ever ensnared into self-pity. Only a heart occupied with love for others is secure against self-pity.

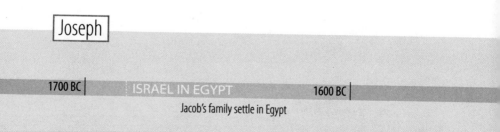

Joseph

1700 BC

ISRAEL IN EGYPT

1600 BC

Jacob's family settle in Egypt

Joseph

Joseph: "May he add"

DAY 39 — Honoured by God

Genesis 39:21–40:23

Joseph is unable to refute the slander of Potiphar's wife, and is thrown into prison. Once again he refuses to give way to despondency and looks for a way to use his many talents and abilities. And just as previously his conduct as a slave had approved itself to his master, so now his conduct as a prisoner approves itself to his warder. Joseph's integrity and godliness take a stronger hold on the prison warder's mind than they did on Potiphar's – so much so that he commits to Joseph the security of the prison. While in prison, Joseph is able to interpret the dreams of Pharaoh's cupbearer and butler, and events come about exactly as Joseph predicts.

"If God is for us, who can be against us?" (Rom. 8:31)

FURTHER THOUGHT

Although Jesus was rejected and outlawed by the religious leaders of His day, on three separate occasions God honoured His Son by speaking from heaven in words of the highest commendation. Why not look up those three references right now? You'll find them in Matthew 3:17, Luke 9:35 and John 12:28

Isaac

1900 BC

Jacob

1800 BC

Bronze Age begins in Britain

Abraham leaves Ur

Exalted by example

Genesis 41:1-57

I n a dramatic turn of events, Joseph is transported from prison to become prime minister of Egypt. The events that led to this change in Joseph's destiny have to do with the restored cupbearer who, when he hears that Pharaoh has had a dream which the wise men of his household cannot interpret, remembers how Joseph interpreted his own while he was in prison. He communicates this fact to Pharaoh who, in turn, invites Joseph into his palace and bids him interpret his dream. This Joseph does to the immense satisfaction of Pharaoh, whose joy is so great that he elevates Joseph to the highest position in the kingdom. Joseph is married to Asenath and has two sons, Manasseh and Ephraim.

"... he humbled himself and became obedient to death - even death on a cross! Therefore God exalted him to the highest place and gave him the name that is above every name, that at the name of Jesus every knee should bow ..." (Phil. 2:8–10)

FURTHER THOUGHT

Just as Joseph was raised from the prison house of darkness and despair to the highest place in Pharaoh's kingdom, so, too, was Jesus raised from the grave and given the highest place in the universe. "Hallelujah! What a Saviour!"

Joseph

1700 BC | ISRAEL IN EGYPT   1600 BC |

Jacob's family settle in Egypt

DAY **41**   Unrecognised by his family

Genesis 42:1–43:34

The distressing effects of the famine are soon felt. Jacob, hearing that there is plenty of corn in Egypt, at once sends his sons – with the exception of Benjamin – to the favoured nation. When at last the brothers meet with Joseph, they fail to recognise him, and bow low before him. Little do they realise that in that action, they are fulfilling a dream which Joseph told them about many years before. Joseph's treatment of his brothers from this point on seems greatly uncharacteristic – especially the pain which he brought to his favourite brother Benjamin – but doubtless he embarked upon this strategy under the guidance of God.

"He was in the world, and though the world was made through him, the world did not recognise him." (John 1:10)

FURTHER THOUGHT

Occasionally in the Gospels, Jesus seemed to pursue a course that brought pain and consternation to those who were close to Him, but He, too, like Joseph, knew what it was to be guarded and guided by the hands of a loving God.

Isaac

Jacob

1900 BC

1800 BC

Bronze Age begins in Britain

Abraham leaves Ur

Identified by his forgiveness

Genesis 44:1–45:28

One of the most moving scenes in the whole of Scripture is the moment when, in response to Judah's appeal for Benjamin's release, Joseph reveals himself to his brothers. It is impossible to imagine the stunning effect the words, "I am Joseph", must have had upon the assembled group. Remembering their cruelty to him, what terror and remorse would have arisen within their hearts. Joseph shares with them the secret of his own perfect peace and poise: "You sold me ... but God sent me." He saw the whole of his life as divinely guided, and had been supported by the fact that everything that had happened to him had furthered the wonderful purposes of God.

"When he was at the table with them, he took bread, gave thanks, broke it and began to give it to them. Then their eyes were opened and they recognised him ..." (Luke 24:30–31)

FURTHER THOUGHT

Ponder the parallel between the words, "I am Joseph", and similar words spoken by the Son of God to Saul on the Damascus road: "I am Jesus" (Acts 9:5). Both were revelations that could have struck terror, but instead brought salvation.

Joseph

Jacob's family settle in Egypt

Joseph foreshadows the Saviour

	JOSEPH	JESUS
Beloved by their fathers	Gen 37:3	Matt 3:17
Sent by their fathers to their brothers	Gen 37:13,14	Lk 20:13; Heb 2:12
Hated by their brothers without a reason	Gen 37:4,5,8	Jn 1:11; 7:5; 15:25
Severely tempted	Gen 39:7	Matt 4:1
Taken to Egypt	Gen 37:28	Matt 2:14,15
Stripped of their robes	Gen 37:23	Jn 19:23,24
Sold for the price of a slave	Gen 37:28	Matt 26:15
Remained silent and offered no defence	Gen 39:20	Isa 53:7
Falsely accused	Gen 39:16-18	Matt 26:59, 60
Respected by their guards	Gen 39:21	Lk 23:47
Placed with two prisoners, one of whom was later lost, the other saved	Gen 40:2,3	Lk 23:32
Both around thirty at the beginning of their ministry	Gen 41:46	Lk 3:23
Both highly exalted after their sufferings	Gen 41:41	Phil 2:9-11
Both took non-Jewish brides	Gen 41:45	Eph 3:1-12
Both forgave and restored their repentant brothers	Gen 45:1-15	Zech 12:10-12
Both visited and honoured by all earthly nations	Gen 41:57	Isa 2:2,3; 49:6

Key Lesson – Joseph

Joseph is one of the most inspiring characters in the whole of Scripture. Unlike his often-erring father, Jacob, the errors and mistakes of Joseph are so insignificant as to remain unrecorded. He was one of the few people who were able to maintain their spiritual poise at the peak of success as well as in the midst of trouble. Even though his tremendous organisational ability, his patience through tribulation, his faithfulness in fame and success and his forgiving spirit are all tributes to his character, what stands out above all else is his conviction that God had a specific purpose for his life, and neither his brothers nor Potiphar's wife could interfere with that purpose. He moved forward in the quiet conviction that his life was not merely a succession of coincidences, but was being directed by a loving God.

Moses the murderer

DAY **43**

Exodus 2:1-25

Moses was born under the sentence of death – an edict given by the Pharaoh who ruled at that time. He was placed by his mother in a papyrus basket, however, cast upon the waters of the Nile, and eventually saved by Pharaoh's daughter. Moses' sister, who was watching nearby, suggested a nurse for Moses – his real mother, Jochebed. Though educated and brought up in Pharaoh's household, Moses learned from his true mother of his real identity and family history. At the age of forty, seeing an Egyptian striking a Hebrew, he turns on the oppressor and kills him. Now the die is cast, and Moses has committed himself to the task of relieving the hard lot of his fellow Israelites.

"...'This is the word of the Lord to Zerubbabel: "Not by might nor by power, but by my Spirit," says the Lord Almighty.'" (Zech. 4:6)

FURTHER THOUGHT

It was natural that Moses should want to do something for the relief of his kinsmen, but it was an act done in the pride of his own strength. Moses was too strong. God can only entrust His power to men who are humbled and emptied and conscious, not of their power, but of their helplessness.

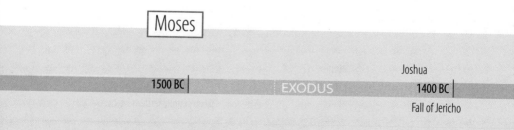

Moses

1500 BC	EXODUS	Joshua
		1400 BC
		Fall of Jericho

DAY **44**   Moses the mumbler
Exodus 3:1–4:31

Moses' life can be divided into three forty-year periods: (1) Forty years in Pharaoh's palace (Acts 7:23); (2) Forty years in Midian (Acts 7:29–30); and (3) Forty years in the wilderness (Acts 7:36). At the end of Moses' time in Midian, God called and commissioned him to lead Israel out of bondage. Moses' initial response to this call is to offer one excuse after another. First: "Who am I, that I should go?" (Ex. 3:11). Second: "What shall I say Your name is?" (see Ex. 3:13). Third: "What if they do not believe me?" (Ex. 4:1). Fourth: "I have never been eloquent ... I am slow of speech and tongue" (Ex. 4:10). Even after God answered his excuses, Moses still asks that someone else should be sent instead (Ex. 4:13).

"But God chose the foolish things of the world to shame the wise; God chose the weak things of the world to shame the strong. He chose the lowly things of this world and the despised things ... to nullify the things that are."
(1 Cor. 1:27–28)

FURTHER THOUGHT
When God prepares us and calls us to a specific task, it is pointless to fall back on excuses – for one of God's principles is that when His finger points the way, His hand then opens to supply our every need. Do not forget that the task ahead of us is never as great as the power behind us.

Joseph
| 1700 BC | ISRAEL IN EGYPT | 1600 BC |

Jacob's family settle in Egypt

Moses the messenger

Exodus 5:1–6:12; 7:1–11:10

After receiving God's call, Moses and Aaron return to Egypt and, on God's behalf, issue the command to Pharaoh: "Let my people go." Pharaoh responds by increasing the workload of the children of Israel. Again the Lord reassures Moses that despite the obstacles, He will do what He has promised (see the seven "I wills" in Exodus 6:6–8). The contest between God and Pharaoh becomes extremely fierce, and the nation is beset with ten serious plagues. These plagues were not just the result of God's wrath, but were designed to reveal God's power and holiness (Ex. 9:16), His judgement upon the gods of Egypt (Ex. 12:12), to uphold and honour Israel (Ex. 8:22–23), and as a testimony to future generations (Ex. 10:1–2).

"God is not a man, that he should lie, nor a son of man, that he should change his mind. Does he speak and then not act? Does he promise and not fulfil?" (Num. 23:19)

FURTHER THOUGHT

How easily we forget that when God decrees a thing, no matter who or what stands against Him, His purposes are always fulfilled. Has God decreed something in your life? Then be encouraged, for even though the timing of His purposes may not coincide with yours, He will most certainly bring them to pass.

Moses

1500 BC

EXODUS

Joshua

1400 BC

Fall of Jericho

DAY **46**

Moses the marcher

Exodus 12:1–14:31

The death of the firstborn in Egypt and the institution of the Passover mark the end of Pharaoh's resistance to God's commands, and Moses and the nation take the first steps on their exodus from Egypt. No sooner have the children of Israel left Egypt than Pharaoh and the Egyptians say to themselves: "What have we done? We have let the Israelites go and have lost their services!" (Ex. 14:5). Pharaoh pursues them with his horses and chariots, and catches up with them at the Red Sea. Miraculously God opens up the Red Sea, and when Israel is safely across He causes the waters to return and drown the armies of Pharaoh.

"Jesus looked at them and said, 'With man this is impossible, but with God all things are possible.'" (Matt. 19:26)

FURTHER THOUGHT

Are you facing a "Red Sea" experience at this moment – difficulties ahead, danger behind? Then remember God's word through Moses: "Stand firm and you will see the deliverance the Lord will bring you today" (Ex. 14:13). Stop struggling, stop striving – and EXPECT A MIRACLE!

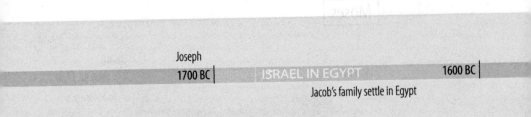

Joseph

1700 BC

ISRAEL IN EGYPT

1600 BC

Jacob's family settle in Egypt

Moses the mediator

Exodus 15:1–18:27

After the marvellous deliverance from Egypt and the opening up of the Red Sea, the children of Israel begin their pilgrimage toward the Promised Land with optimism and hope. Three days later, however, they find themselves dying of thirst, and are filled with indignation when they discover that the water at Marah is impure. Moses intercedes before God and he is shown how to make the water pure. Later, they complain that they have no food, but once again, Moses intercedes for them before God which results in the miraculous supply of manna. While at Rephidim, they complain because they have no water. Moses, in anger, strikes the rock. Finally Jethro, Moses' father-in-law, persuades Moses to delegate some of his responsibilities.

"The end of a matter is better than its beginning, and patience is better than pride. Do not be quickly provoked in your spirit, for anger resides in the lap of fools." (Eccl. 7:8–9)

FURTHER THOUGHT

How did Moses, who was described as being very humble (see Numbers 12:3), become so irritable and lose his temper? There may be a clue in the fact that Jethro suggested Moses might be doing too much and that he should delegate some of his responsibilities. Is God saying something through this to you?

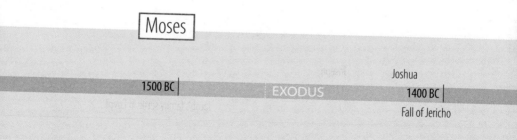

Moses

1500 BC	EXODUS	Joshua
		1400 BC
		Fall of Jericho

DAY **48**

Moses the minister

Exodus 19:1-20:21; 32:1-34:28

Without doubt the greatest event in Moses' life was receiving from God the Ten Commandments – the laws which were to inspire and shape the moral and religious life of mankind. While Moses is on the mountain top with God, the children of Israel slip into idolatry. Moses is so angry that he breaks the two tablets containing the law. He later intercedes for the people and ascends again to Sinai where he receives a new copy of the law. Moses then instructs the children of Israel to build and assemble the tabernacle, a portable building in which God would dwell and have fellowship with His people.

"...'Now the dwelling of God is with men, and he will live with them. They will be his people, and God himself will be with them and be their God.'" (Rev. 21:3)

FURTHER THOUGHT

As you reflect on the beauty and wonder of the ancient tabernacle today, let your thoughts focus also on the Son of God, who tabernacled (John 1:14) among us, took on our flesh, ate with tax collectors and sinners, and was swift to forgive.

Joseph		
1700 BC	ISRAEL IN EGYPT	1600 BC
	Jacob's family settle in Egypt	

Mission unfulfilled

Numbers 20:1–29; Deuteronomy 31:1–32:52; 34:1–12

As a consequence of his sin (Num. 20:1–12), Moses is forbidden to lead the children of Israel into the Promised Land, and eventually Joshua is chosen to be his successor. God allows Moses, however, to view the Promised Land from Mount Nebo. When, at the age of 120 years, Moses dies, a great and final honour is bestowed upon him. No human hands bore the dead lawgiver and prophet to his grave; God buried him, and "to this day no-one knows where his grave is" (Deut. 34:6). That is a fitting crown to such a life, for the memory of Moses lives on, not in a sepulchre, but in the hearts of men.

"For what the law was powerless to do ... God did by sending his own Son in the likeness of sinful man ... in order that the righteous requirements of the law might be fully met in us, who do not live according to the sinful nature but according to the Spirit." (Rom. 8:3–4)

FURTHER THOUGHT

Although Moses, because of his sin, was forbidden to enter the Promised Land, he did eventually arrive there – in company with Elijah on the Mount of Transfiguration! The law kept him out, but grace – as expressed in Jesus – brought him in!

Moses

1500 BC

EXODUS

Joshua

1400 BC

Fall of Jericho

Plagues sent under *Moses' leadership*

Nature	Egyptian god defeated	
1. Water into blood	OSIRIS	Exodus 7:20
2. A frog invasion	HEKT	8:6
3. Gnats	SEB	8:17
4. Flies	HATKOK	8:24
5. Cattle disease	APIS	9:6
6. Boils	TYPHON	9:10
7. Hail with lightning	SHU	9:24
8. Locusts	SERAPIA	10:13
9. Three-day darkness	RA	10:22
10. Death of firstborn	ALL gods	12:29

Key Lesson – Moses

There is not a single character in the Old Testament who can bear comparison with Moses – his powerful reasoning with Pharaoh, his courageous journey through the wilderness, his amazing patience with the complaining, his magnanimity toward rivals, and his unfailing confidence in God's promises. One commentator says of him: "He is awesome and endearing, a maker of history and a friend of God." Perhaps the greatest lesson that comes out of his life is that we should pay as much attention to our strengths as we do to our weaknesses. Moses was noted for his meekness and humility (Numbers 12:3), but it was in this – an area of strength – that he was tempted and gave way. Because of that particular lapse, he was shut out of Canaan.

God speaks to Joshua

DAY 50

Joshua 1:1-18

We know very little about Joshua's early life, except that he was born in Goshen, in the land of Egypt; he was the son of Nun, an Ephraimite; he was in the twelfth generation from Joseph; and he was about forty years old at the time of the exodus. He is styled as "Moses' assistant" and following Moses' death is appointed by God to lead the children of Israel into the Promised Land. In the call and commission of Joshua, God gives him two promises: (1) that he would possess the land of Canaan, and (2) that God would be with him and would never forsake him. The Lord directs him (Josh. 1:8) to the secret of success – meditation on the Word of God. It was this more than any other single thing that made Joshua the great leader he proved to be.

"Be diligent in these matters; give yourself wholly to them, so that everyone may see your progress."
(1 Tim. 4:15)

FURTHER THOUGHT

Doubtless, you know how to read the Bible, study the Bible and even memorise the Bible – but do you know how to meditate on it? Research shows that only 1 in 10,000 Christians understand and practise the principles of meditation. Take a moment to turn to page 72 and see what meditation is all about.

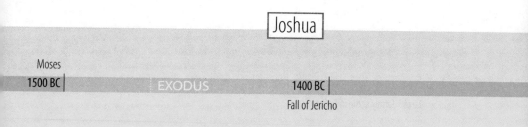

Joshua

Moses
1500 BC

EXODUS

1400 BC

Fall of Jericho

DAY **51**   The reins of leadership taken up

Joshua 2:1-24

Although Joshua is a man of faith, he is also a military strategist. Before setting out to invade Canaan, he dispatches two of his men on a special reconnaissance mission. Joshua himself had taken part in a similar spying mission many years prior to this, but he now wanted an up-to-date report of the condition of the inhabitants, and especially of the defences that surrounded the city of Jericho. While in Jericho, the two spies stay in the home of Rahab the prostitute, who informs them that because of the news that the Israelites are about to invade the land, the morale of the inhabitants is extremely low. In response to Rahab's plea for protection and safety, the spies give her the promise that she and her family will be saved.

"In the same way, faith by itself, if it is not accompanied by action, is dead." (James 2:17)

FURTHER THOUGHT

Some feel that Joshua's act of sending in spies to view the land of Canaan was an action that sprang from doubt - but this is hardly so. Faith is a partnership between us and God: we do the possible - He does the impossible.

ISRAEL IN EGYPT

1600 BC

Jacob's family settle in Egypt

A man of faith emerges

Joshua 3:1-4:24

ithout doubt, one of the greatest tests of Joshua's faith was the crossing of the Jordan. After forty years of wandering in the wilderness, Israel arrived at the Jordan when it was in flood! Six months earlier – in the dry season – the crossing would have been much simpler, but now it was obvious they needed divine help. However, as soon as the feet of the priests who were carrying the ark touched the river's edge, the waters rolled back, allowing the whole of Israel to cross over into Canaan – dry-shod. The miracle served to set God's seal of approval on Joshua, and demonstrated once more to the nation of Israel that God was with them. Later God commands Joshua to raise a memorial in stones at Gilgal so that they have a permanent reminder of God's faithfulness in bringing them into the land.

"... everyone born of God overcomes the world. This is the victory that has overcome the world, even our faith." (1 John 5:4)

FURTHER THOUGHT

If the priests had waited for the waters to recede before stepping out, they would never have experienced a miracle. They had to get their feet wet! Whatever may be your "Jordan" at the present moment, walk right up to it in simple faith. Then - watch it recede.

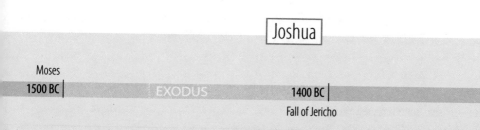

Joshua

Moses

1500 BC

EXODUS

1400 BC

Fall of Jericho

DAY 53   A divine plan for God's man
Joshua 5:1-6:27

Now that the Israelites were in Canaan, it would have made good military sense to move straight ahead and take immediate possession of the key city of Jericho. But God had another plan. First, all the males had to be circumcised, and having done this, God tells Israel that the reproach of Egypt is now rolled away (Josh. 5:9). When the Israelites have recovered from the act of circumcision, some days later, Joshua leads them toward Jericho. The priests carry the ark around the city for seven days, and on the seventh day they blow a blast on their trumpets while the people give a loud shout, and the great walls of Jericho come tumbling down. Only one part remains intact – the part which contains Rahab's house. As promised by the spies, she and her family were miraculously saved.

"... He has sent me to ... provide for those who grieve in Zion – to bestow on them a crown of beauty instead of ashes, the oil of gladness instead of mourning, and a garment of praise instead of a spirit of despair. They will be called oaks of righteousness ..."
(Isa. 61:1, 3)

FURTHER THOUGHT

An important key to victorious Christian living is the necessity of learning to shout, not after the walls of difficulty have come down, but before. If you are in need of some deliverance from the power of Satan, then, as well as praying, try the shout of praise. Things happen when God's people praise Him.

Facing the issues of defeat

Joshua 7:1-8:35

The success at Jericho is followed by a great defeat at Ai. After hearing the report of the spies, Joshua decided to send only 3,000 men to conquer the city of Ai, but the army was outnumbered and routed. Joshua is devastated by the news, and as he pleads with God for an explanation, he is told that there is sin in the midst of the camp. One of the soldiers of Israel – Achan – had kept for himself some of the treasure which had been forbidden by God, and it is only when he and his family are put to death that God's anger is appeased. The sin now put away, Joshua is told by the Lord that he can go forward and Ai will be given into his hands. At the close of this victorious expedition, Joshua holds a great service of thanksgiving on Mount Ebal.

"If we confess our sins, he is faithful and just and will forgive us our sins and purify us from all unrighteousness."
(1 John 1:9)

FURTHER THOUGHT

If only we could deal as drastically with our own sin as God dealt with Achan's, what a transformation it would bring about in our lives – as well as that of our local churches and fellowships. One thing is sure: if we do our part in confessing, God will do His part in forgiving.

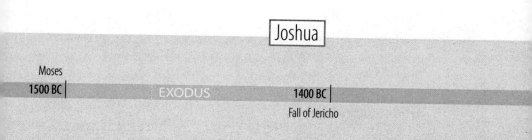

Joshua

Moses
1500 BC

EXODUS

1400 BC

Fall of Jericho

DAY 55 — Diplomacy in dividing the land

Joshua 13:1-33

The result of Joshua's southern and northern campaigns was that it became possible to settle in Canaan, even though the Philistines remained in the coastal area and the Canaanites still controlled many inland cities. He invites the Israelites to send representatives from each district of Canaan, and the division of the land is settled by the casting of lots in a special assembly at Shiloh. We do not know for sure what each one's portion was, but when Joshua had allotted territory to all the tribes, he kept for himself a modest piece of land among the hills of Ephraim. Joshua is thought to have been about ninety years of age when the land was divided, although he lived for a number of years at Timnath Serah – which means "the portion that remains".

"For the Son of Man is going to come in his Father's glory with his angels, and then he will reward each person according to what he has done." (Matt. 16:27)

FURTHER THOUGHT
There are many on this earth who, after doing a great work for God, seem to get little reward. Someone has put that truth in these words: "First in service; last in reward." Is that true of you? Then take heart – a day of reward is come, and then you will be paid in full.

ISRAEL IN EGYPT — 1600 BC

Jacob's family settle in Egypt

His charge to Israel

Joshua 23:1-24:33

Prior to his death, Joshua hears that not everywhere is the Lord the uncontested King of Israel. The great soldier returns to fight once more – this time with words instead of a sword. He calls together a great assembly at Shechem and there, in a tremendously moving speech, rehearses for them the plan of God. He reminds them how God brought them out of Egypt and fulfilled His promises to them, and brings them finally to a point of decision: "Choose for yourselves this day whom you will serve" (Josh. 24:15). To ratify the decision which the people then made, Joshua writes the words, "We will serve the Lord our God" in a book and then, taking a stone, sets it up under an oak tree as a memorial of their recommitment to God. This was the last recorded act of Joshua, who died at the age of 110 years.

"As God's fellow-workers we urge you not to receive God's grace in vain. For he says, 'In the time of my favour I heard you, and in the day of salvation I helped you.' I tell you, now is the time of God's favour, now is the day of salvation." (2 Cor. 6:1–2)

FURTHER THOUGHT

One of the great certainties of life is that we will constantly be called upon to choose. And the choice of one thing often involves the putting away of another. Are you being half-hearted in living for Christ? Then choose now – this day – whom you are going to serve!

Joshua

Moses
1500 BC

EXODUS

1400 BC

Fall of Jericho

After Joshua - decline

Note the total contrast between these two periods

Joshua	Judges
Victory	Defeat
Freedom	Slavery
Faith	Unbelief
Progress	Declension
Obedience	Disobedience
Heavenly vision	Earthly emphasis
Joy	Sorrow
Strength	Weakness
Unity among tribes	Disunity among tribes
Strong leader	No leader

 **Key Lesson - Joshua**

Joshua, the son of Nun, began his ministry for God as the assistant, or minister, of Moses, and although he was overshadowed by the great leader, he functioned happily in the role which God had designed for him. C.H. Spurgeon once said:"It takes more grace than I can tell, To play the second fiddle well."
Joshua, in his willingness to play "second fiddle", showed his true strength of character, for before one can rule well, one must know how to serve well. When the time came for him to become the leader of Israel, he showed himself to be a great soldier and diplomat. He showed, however, not only the valour of a warrior, but the justice, gentleness, forbearance and humility of a great ruler. Probably the most outstanding characteristic of his life – and one that we ought to emulate – is his unselfishness. It was his utter indifference to all selfish considerations – as evidenced by his willingness to leave himself to the last in division of the land – that marked him out as being what someone described as a "soldier-saint".

Deborah the judge

DAY **57**

Judges 3:12–4:5

The years of comparative spiritual prosperity which Israel enjoyed during the leadership of Ehud came to an end with his death. In order to discipline His people, God allowed them to be overwhelmed by Jabin, the king of Hazor and his commander-in-chief, Sisera. In response to the cry of the Israelites, the Lord raised up a woman by the name of Deborah – the wife of Lappidoth – who functioned in the nation as a judge. Her great ability and razor-sharp mind drew many to her "counselling room" – a palm tree halfway between Ramah and Bethel. As well as being a fine judge, Deborah was also a prophetess, with a passionate desire to elevate the spiritual vision of her people.

"... the Lord disciplines those he loves, and he punishes everyone he accepts as a son." (Heb. 12:6)

FURTHER THOUGHT

From the Old Testament we learn that whenever God's people became disobedient, He disciplined them by allowing them to fall into the hands of their enemies. Could that be why today's Church is overwhelmed by the twin evils of secularism and humanism? Makes you think – doesn't it!

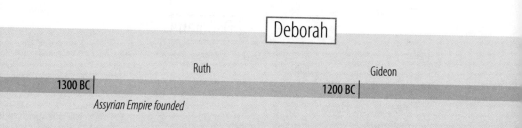

Deborah

Ruth

Gideon

1300 BC

1200 BC

Assyrian Empire founded

Deborah
Deborah: "A bee"

Deborah the deliverer
Judges 4:6-24

The threat and intimidation that Jabin and Sisera brought upon the Israelites who lived in the northern part of Canaan was of great concern to Deborah, who devised a plan to bring about her people's freedom and deliverance. Deborah's high reputation can be seen by the fact that when she shared with Barak, one of Israel's military leaders, her plan to overcome Jabin and Sisera, he refused to engage in the campaign unless Deborah was present to counsel and to guide. Deborah gave the word for battle to commence, and the Israelites, with God's help, overcome the great army of Sisera. Although Sisera escaped, he was later killed by Jael who, after giving him milk and butter attacked him with a tent-peg and a workman's hammer.

"It is better to take refuge in the Lord than to trust in man." (Psa. 118:8)

FURTHER THOUGHT
How easily does the thing in which we put our confidence become the means of our own undoing. Sisera's 900 iron chariots were his pride and gave him confidence – yet he was put to death with just one peg!

Deborah

Ruth

Gideon

1300 BC

1200 BC

Assyrian Empire founded

Deborah and Barak
defeat Sisera and the Canaanites

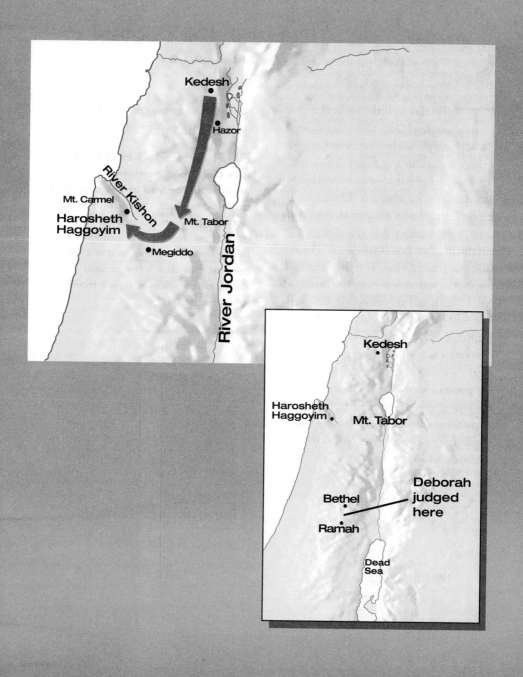

Deborah

Deborah: "A bee"

DAY 59 — Deborah the poetess

Judges 5:1–31

There can be little doubt that the words of Deborah's song were written within hours of the great victory over Jabin and Sisera. The sense of common danger, the joy of united action, the exultation in Jehovah's deliverance are felt and described with a vividness which could only come in the immediate aftermath of such an experience. The song falls into three divisions: an introduction (vv. 2–11); a description of the battle (vv. 12–22); and the sequel (vv. 23–31). The first part tells of God being the Deliverer of His people. The second part contains a magnificent description of the battle, witnessed, as it were, from a bird's eye point of view. The third part contrasts the courageous devotion of Jael with the unpatriotic selfishness of Meroz – a nearby community of people who failed to come to the aid of Israel.

"Give thanks to the Lord, for he is good; his love endures for ever." (Psa. 118:1)

FURTHER THOUGHT

Has God done something wonderful for you in the past few days or hours? Then don't wait until next week to praise Him – do it now. No time should be lost in returning thanks to the Lord for His mercies – for praise flows best when it flows from a full heart.

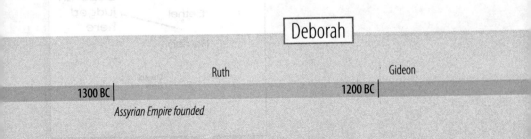

Deborah

Ruth   Gideon

1300 BC   1200 BC

Assyrian Empire founded

Key Lesson
- Deborah

It is difficult to find another woman in the Old Testament with such dauntlessness and determination as Deborah. Her faith, energy, confidence, character, intellect and clear-sightedness mark her out as a woman who was God's gift to the age in which she lived. The most outstanding lesson we learn from her life is that to the degree that a passion for freedom and deliverance burns in the heart, to that degree one is able to rouse and stir others to rise up and claim their freedom. Deborah felt so strongly about her nation's predicament that she fired the faith and hope of even such fighting men as Barak. Although Deborah's life and witness has a message for both men and women, there can be little doubt that she stands as an encouragement to all those women whose prayerful concern for the times in which we live and the needs of the nation causes a passionate and prayerful desire for deliverance to rise up like a flame within them. Deborah reminds us that women have a great and important role to play in the hour through which our world is passing – and not the least, the stirring up of the hearts of men.

Meditation

The words used in the Hebrew for meditation
– *hagah* and *siyach* – mean to ponder,
imagine, contemplate, reflect, pray,
commune, murmur, mutter and converse
with oneself.

In other words, meditation means to roll a
word, thought or phrase around in the mind,
continually contemplating, pondering and
dwelling upon it, viewing it from every angle,
weighing it, and considering it carefully. Do
this, not just once, but over and over again
until you begin to talk to yourself about it,
allowing it to penetrate, permeate and
saturate your thinking.

Scripture meditation, then, is the digestive
system of the soul, and is of vital importance
to spiritual development. It is the process by
which we apply, absorb and internalise truth
as a working principle into our daily lives.
Just as natural food is taken into our bodies,
and the digestive system absorbs it, so, as
we take God's Word into our minds through
the process of meditation, spiritual food is
absorbed into our spirits and transformed
into spiritual faith and energy, making biblical
principles working realities in our daily lives.

2

Gideon

Gideon: "A great warrior"

A call received

Judges 6:1-24

At the time Gideon appears on the pages of Scripture, the nation of Israel was being invaded year after year by hordes of nomadic Midianites who deprived them of both crops and livestock. This greatly discouraged the Israelites and caused them to cry out to the Lord for help (v. 6). God, in answer to their plea, spoke to them through a prophet who challenged them to recognise their disobedience, then sent an angel to commission Gideon to be Israel's deliverer. When the angel met Gideon, he found him secretly threshing wheat in a wine press – to hide it from the marauding Midianites – and greeted him with the words: "The Lord is with you, mighty warrior" (v. 12). Despite Gideon's blunt query as to whether God could really be with Israel when they were so overwhelmed by their enemies, God's call still sounded out.

"With God we shall gain the victory, and he will trample down our enemies." (Psa. 60:12)

FURTHER THOUGHT

How reassuring it is to know that when our response to God's call is one of uncertainty and disbelief, He never allows our innate pessimism and gloom to divert Him from His purposes. The Almighty seems to believe in us more than we believe in ourselves.

Gideon

	Ruth	Deborah and Barak	
1300 BC			1200 BC

Assyrian Empire founded

A doubt emerges

Judges 6:25-40

As a result of God's call, Gideon mobilises some of the local tribes to confront the marauding Midianites, but despite this clear call, a strong doubt emerges. He ponders on the fact that he is an untried soldier, ignorant of the methods of warfare: "My clan is the weakest in Manasseh, and I am the least in my family" (6:15). Suddenly invested with the responsibility of leading Israel into battle, he therefore seeks a confirmatory sign from the Lord. His first request is that a fleece he spreads out overnight should be wet, while the ground around it stays dry. When this is granted, he asks for a more convincing sign – namely that the fleece should remain dry, while the ground around becomes wet. This, too, is granted, and never again does Gideon doubt his commission from the Lord.

"...'I do believe; help me overcome my unbelief!'" (Mark 9:24)

FURTHER THOUGHT

Many have criticised Gideon for the fact that, even though God had spoken to him and commissioned him to be Israel's deliverer, he still sought a confirmatory sign. But how unlike men is God: the Almighty accommodates Gideon's doubts and makes him not only assured, but doubly assured.

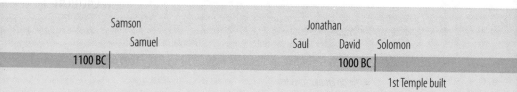

	Samson			Jonathan		
		Samuel		Saul	David	Solomon
1100 BC					1000 BC	
						1st Temple built

Gideon

DAY 62　　　A strategy develops
Judges 7:1-18

Gideon succeeds in recruiting an army of 32,000 men, but God tells him that granting victory to so many could lead to the boast that they had overcome the enemy without His aid. Sending home the faint-hearted left 10,000 brave men, but an alertness test – watching the way in which they drank from the river – resulted in the 10,000 being whittled down to just 300 men. On a night visit to the enemy camp, Gideon overhears a conversation anticipating success (v. 14), and returns to inspire his men and organise a surprise attack. He equips his army, not with swords or staves, but with the strangest military equipment an army has ever known – trumpets, earthenware jars and, inside each jar, a lighted torch.

"Now it is required that those who have been given a trust must prove faithful." (1 Cor. 4:2)

FURTHER THOUGHT

If you had been a member of Gideon's 32,000, would you have made it into the final 300? You might have passed the test of fearfulness - being unafraid of a fight - but would you have passed the test of faithfulness? Faithfulness means always keeping one eye on the enemy.

Gideon

	Ruth	Deborah and Barak	
1300 BC			1200 BC

Assyrian Empire founded

A victory results

Judges 7:19-22

When darkness fell, Gideon divided his 300 men into three companies who were deployed silently around the enemy and gave them instructions that, at a given signal, they should copy his actions with military precision. When the moment for action came, the 300 blew a blast on their trumpets and shattered their earthenware jars, thus causing the light to shine out, and shouted loudly: "A sword for the Lord and for Gideon!" (v. 20). These surprise tactics brought great consternation to the enemy, who fought amongst themselves and finally fled in disorder and disarray. Gideon and his men stood and watched the Lord defeat the Midianites without having to strike a blow! It was obvious to all that the Lord's strategy, although strange and unusual, was nevertheless the cause of their great victory.

"... Do not be afraid or discouraged because of this vast army. For the battle is not yours, but God's ... Take up your positions; stand firm and see the deliverance the Lord will give you ..." (2 Chron. 20:15, 17)

FURTHER THOUGHT

How our lives would be transformed if we could learn the lesson that God delights to be given the credit for our conquests and victories. Pride and egotism want to say, "I did it", but humility and dependence delight in saying, "God did it". Which of these two attitudes is uppermost in you?

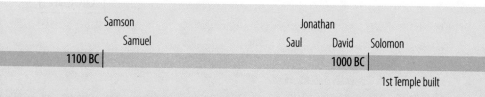

Samson
Samuel

Jonathan
Saul   David   Solomon

1100 BC

1000 BC

1st Temple built

Gideon

DAY 64

A pursuit ensues
Judges 7:23–8:21

To bring about lasting peace, the Midianites must not only be scattered, but expelled from the land of Israel. Gideon sends messengers to the Ephraimites to intercept the retreating Midianites at the River Jordan who, when they arrive, put to death two Midianite leaders. The Ephraimites express great anger toward Gideon for not having called in their assistance earlier, but Gideon appeases their anger by a shrewd speech. He points out that although he and his army had dispersed the Midianites, it was the Ephraimites who had put their two leaders to death. Later, he is faced with another problem when the local inhabitants refuse to supply his famished troops with food. But he surmounts this, too, and presses on to capture and personally execute the kings of Midian.

"A man of many companions may come to ruin, but there is a friend who sticks closer than a brother." (Prov. 18:24)

FURTHER THOUGHT

Gideon seemed to meet with more opposition from those who were supposed to be his friends than from those who were his enemies. Isn't that also true of the Christian Church? Nevertheless, we must not allow ourselves to be discouraged by those who are Israelites in name, but Midianites in heart.

Gideon

Ruth   Deborah and Barak

1300 BC | 1200 BC |

Assyrian Empire founded

A promotion resisted

Judges 8:22-27

Upon his triumphal return, the Israelites proposed that because Gideon had delivered them from the Midianites, he should become their king and found a family dynasty (v. 22). He firmly rejects this offer, saying that the Lord alone must rule over Israel (v. 23). Three hundred men under the Lord's leadership had routed 135,000 Midianites, and Gideon believed that God's rule over the nation was superior to kingship. Instead, Gideon requested from his fellow Israelites some of the spoils of war in order that he might make an ephod, a priestly garment to which a breastplate was attached. This breastplate was associated with the casting of lots to obtain God's guidance in ruling the nation (see Exodus 28:30).

"He chose the lowly things of this world and the despised things – and the things that are not – to nullify the things that are, so that no-one may boast before him." (1 Cor. 1:28–29)

FURTHER THOUGHT

How sad it is when God's people are so taken up with the way things happen that they fail to give credit to God's hand which is at work bringing everything about. Pause for a moment and think of something "unusual" that has happened to you recently. Done that? Now give God the praise.

	Samson			Jonathan		
		Samuel		Saul	David	Solomon
1100 BC				1000 BC		
					1st Temple built	

DAY 66

A peace follows

Judges 8:28-35

Gideon's perseverance in exploiting the God-given victory in the valley of Jezreel ushered in forty years of peace for Israel. It is interesting to note that the Midianites, as enemies, are never mentioned again in Scripture. Gideon sets up a religious centre at his seat of judgement in Ophrah and, by use of his new ephod, seeks to implement his declared policy that the Lord, not himself, should rule over Israel. The ark of the covenant, however – the symbol of God's presence in Israel – was at Bethel, and Gideon's rival shrine becomes a snare to him and his fellow Israelites, causing them to fall into idolatry. No sooner does Gideon die than the Israelites turn to worship a heathen deity, forgetting all that the Lord had done for them through Gideon (vv. 33–35).

"...'Love the Lord your God with all your heart and with all your soul and with all your mind.' This is the first and greatest commandment." (Matt. 22:37–38)

FURTHER THOUGHT

It has been said that although an idol is "nothing at all in the world" (1 Cor. 8:4), there is nothing in the world more real than an idol. Putting something else in God's place, making a god of something other than God – is that not a very real transaction? Take care it doesn't happen to you.

Gideon

Ruth   Deborah and Barak

1300 BC   1200 BC

Assyrian Empire founded

Gideon's fleece

Some Christians resort to the metaphorical use of a fleece to determine the will of God, basing this on the experience of Gideon. A close examination of the incident reveals, however, that the fleece was used not to determine the will of God, but to confirm it. Although God honoured Gideon's fleece-prayer, it was nevertheless unnecessary as Gideon already knew what he should do. It was also an unprofitable exercise as he needed further reassurance (Judges 7:10).

Judges 6	
14–16:	God clearly assured Gideon of what he should do
17–21:	God gave Gideon the sign he requested
36–37:	Gideon puts out the fleece for the first time
39:	Gideon puts out the fleece for the second time
38 & 40:	God graciously confirms His purposes

Key Lesson – Gideon

Although the angel of the Lord hailed Gideon as a "mighty warrior", this description seems to stand out in sharp contrast with his initial statements and demands. Gideon appears at first as pessimistic, argumentative, demanding and unbelieving. But it was not unbelief that lay behind his moods – it was insecurity. In time God overcomes this deep insecurity in his nature, after which Gideon never again asks God for a sign.

The main lesson we learn from his life is that once we face up to the challenges which God gives us, our weaknesses can become strengths. Gideon's insecurity gave way to a sublime confidence in the sovereignty of God, and although his life ends on an extremely sad note, we should not overlook the fact that he had earlier learned how to simply and humbly accept God's help – an attitude which transforms every insecure struggler into a "mighty warrior".

Samson
Samson: "Sunny"

DAY **67**   Selected in birth
Judges 13:1-25

Like Isaac, Samuel and John the
Baptist, Samson was a special gift of
God to a barren woman. The angel
of the Lord appears to the wife of Manoah,
a Danite of Zorah in Judah, promising
that though barren, she will conceive and
bear a son who must be set apart to God
from the moment of his birth. A person
who was set apart in this way was called a
Nazirite – "one separated to the Lord".
When Manoah's wife informs him of the
appearance of the angel, he prays that the
angel will appear to them both – a request
which God answers. The angel repeats the
instructions given to Manoah's wife that
the child that will be born must be
separated to God from birth, abstain from
wine and refrain from having his hair cut.
Manoah and his wife offer a burnt offering
to the Lord and bow down in reverence
and worship.

"For my thoughts are not your thoughts,
neither are your ways my ways ... As
the heavens are higher than the earth,
so are my ways higher than your ways
and my thoughts than your thoughts."
(Isa. 55:8–9)

FURTHER THOUGHT
Did you notice how, when Manoah
asked for instruction in his duty,
he was readily told (v. 12), but
when he sought to gratify his
curiosity (v. 17), his request was
denied? God pledges to tell us all
we need to know to perform our
Christian duty, but He never
promises to satisfy our curiosity.

| Samson |

Deborah and Barak   Gideon   Samuel
            1200 BC| 1100 BC|

Foolish in choice

Judges 14:1–10

Samson grew up in the belief that he was consecrated to God and that there was a definite, God-appointed work for him to do. He experienced great movings of the Holy Spirit in his life, at which time he became conscious of having unusual physical strength. Attracted by a Philistine woman at Timnah, he insists on his parents obtaining her as his wife. They protest, but Samson will not be thwarted and goes to Timnah with them to arrange the marriage. On the way there, Samson meets a young lion, and promptly proceeds to demonstrate his supernatural strength by killing the lion and tearing it apart. When he later returns to Timnah, he discovers a swarm of bees have taken possession of the lion's carcass, prompting Samson to devise his famous riddle.

"And I will ask the Father, and he will give you another Counsellor to be with you for ever – the Spirit of truth." (John 14:16–17)

FURTHER THOUGHT

Have you ever considered that the ministry of the Holy Spirit in Old Testament days was temporary and occasional? The Spirit of God moved Samson "at times in the camp of Dan" (Judg. 13:25, AV). How reassuring that in New Testament times, His ministry is not temporary but permanent, not occasional but continuous. Hallelujah!

Jonathan

Saul   David   Solomon

Rehoboam

1000 BC

Jeroboam I

1st Temple built

DAY 69 — Deceived in love

Judges 14:11–15:5

The feast which accompanied Samson's marriage lasted seven days, during which he put before his guests the riddle which he had devised. The riddle proved impossible to answer, but the Philistine guests, by the use of intimidation and threats, persuaded Samson's bride to extract the answer from her husband. Samson, unaware of the evil plan that lay behind his wife's deception, finally gave in to her pleadings and revealed the answer to the riddle which she, in turn, passed on to the guests. When they reveal that they know the answer, Samson realises he has been tricked. In anger he goes to the town of Ashkelon, twenty-three miles away, where he slaughters thirty Philistines, taking their clothes with which he redeems his pledge. Later, in a further burst of anger, Samson sets the Philistine crops and olive orchards ablaze.

"Do not be yoked together with unbelievers. For what do righteousness and wickedness have in common? Or what fellowship can light have with darkness?" (2 Cor. 6:14)

FURTHER THOUGHT
Have you ever been deceived by someone whom you thought really loved you? It hurts, doesn't it? How refreshing it is to know, however, that in the love relationship that exists between a believer and Christ, our Lord will never deceive us.

Samson

Deborah and Barak   Gideon   Samuel
1200 BC | 1100 BC |

Mighty in strength

Judges 15:6–20

The Philistines react to Samson's destruction of their crops in an extremely gruesome fashion – by burning his former bride and her father. Samson retaliates by viciously attacking and slaughtering many of them, and then goes to ground at Etam, a natural rock fortress in Judah. The conflict between Samson and his enemies escalates further when a band of men from Judah storm the fortress where Samson is hiding and demand his surrender. These men are deeply afraid of the Philistines, and persuade Samson to give himself up. Samson is bound with two new ropes and taken to his captors, but the Spirit of God falls upon him and he breaks the ropes that hold him. Then, seizing an ass's jawbone, he kills a thousand Philistines single-handed.

"This is the word of the Lord to Zerubbabel: 'Not by might nor by power, but by my Spirit,' says the Lord Almighty." (Zech. 4:6)

FURTHER THOUGHT

It's quite amazing what a small and seemingly insignificant item like a jawbone can achieve when it is taken up and used for a divine purpose and in the power of the Holy Spirit. Take you own jawbone, for example. Ever thought what miracles of speech and witness come from it when it is surrendered to the Holy Spirit?

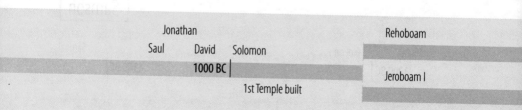

Jonathan

Saul   David   Solomon

1000 BC

1st Temple built

Rehoboam

Jeroboam I

DAY 71 — Weak in temptation

Judges 16:1-17

Although endued with great physical strength, it is obvious that Samson is morally and spiritually weak. When visiting a prostitute in Gaza, he is surrounded by hostile Philistines and escapes at night by uprooting the heavy gates which bar his way out of the city. Once again he falls in love with a Philistine woman – Delilah. She, too, is persuaded to extract from Samson the secret of his strength, although at first her wiles were unavailing. Three times she pleads with Samson to reveal the secret of his strength, and three times he resists her temptations by telling her a lie. With unholy persistence, Delilah makes a supreme attempt to accomplish her ends, and after wearing down Samson's resistance, finally learns the secret of his great strength.

"No temptation has seized you except what is common to man. And God is faithful; he will not let you be tempted beyond what you can bear. But when you are tempted, he will also provide a way out so that you can stand up under it." (1 Cor. 10:13)

FURTHER THOUGHT

Want a challenging thought with which to come to grips during the day that lies ahead? Then consider this – in the day of his power Samson first became prayerless, then careless, then powerless. Take steps now to make sure that same deterioration doesn't happen in your life.

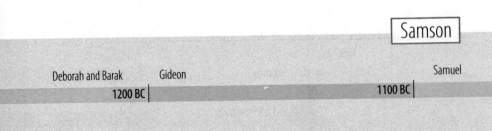

Samson

Deborah and Barak   Gideon

1200 BC

Samuel

1100 BC

Fettered in failure

Judges 16:18-21

In response to Delilah's persistent nagging, Samson reveals that the secret of his supernatural strength lies in his Nazirite vow, and explains that if his hair is cut he will be no different from any other man. The secret gained by deceit is then sold to the Philistines and, lulling Samson to sleep, Delilah gives orders for his hair to be shaved off. Samson awakes, expecting to shake himself free from the restraints put on him by Delilah, but he discovers that his strength has gone and thus he becomes an easy prey for the Philistines. He handles himself as at other times but nothing comes of it. Cruelly, the Philistines gouge out Samson's eyes, and he is imprisoned at Gaza and made to grind corn like an ox.

"Be self-controlled and alert. Your enemy the devil prowls around like a roaring lion looking for someone to devour." (1 Pet. 5:8)

FURTHER THOUGHT

All who indulge their appetites in ways which God prohibits will see themselves surrounded and waylaid by their spiritual enemies. If we fall asleep in the lap of Delilah, then we must not complain if we wake in the hands of the Philistines.

Jonathan

Saul   David   Solomon

Rehoboam

1000 BC

Jeroboam I

1st Temple built

Samson

Samson: "Sunny"

DAY **73**

Retribution in death

Judges 16:22-31

The Philistines attribute Samson's capture to the intervention of their god, Dagon, and hold a great sacrifice in his honour. Prior to this, however, Samson's hair has started to grow again, and at the time of the festivities his strength has partly returned. The temple of Dagon is filled to capacity with 3,000 people on the roof who have come not only to celebrate their victory over Samson, but to make sport of him in his weakness. Samson prays that God will give him back the fullness of his supernatural strength so that he can bring retribution on the Philistines. His prayer is answered, and he is able to pull down the support pillars of the temple, bringing about not only his own death, but the deaths of thousands of his enemies.

"So I say, live by the Spirit, and you will not gratify the desires of the sinful nature." (Gal. 5:16)

FURTHER THOUGHT

Samson's afflictions were the means of bringing him to deep repentance; through the loss of his physical sight, the eyes of his understanding were opened. How sad, however, that sometimes God has to allow us to be overtaken by tragedy in order that we might really "see".

Samson

Deborah and Barak   Gideon

1200 BC

Samuel

1100 BC

Samson – a reflection of his time

'Every man did what was right in his own eyes' **Judges 17:6, AV**

NAZARITE VOW	Not to touch wine	Num 6:2-3
BROKEN	Drank wine	Judg 14:10
	Hair to remain untouched by razor	Num 6:5
	His hair was cut	Judg 16:19
	Not to touch a dead body	Num 6:6
	He touched the carcass of a lion	Judg 14:8-9

Key Lesson – Samson

The story of Samson is one of the most pathetic accounts in the whole of God's Word. One commentator says of him:

"The sight of Samson, fighting himself, putting his defunct forces into line only to find himself utterly beaten and wholly ruined is a sight to stir the pity of God and men." Some believe that the meaning of Samson's name - "sunny" – indicated that he had a bright and attractive temperament – a man of wit, charm, humour, faith and deep spiritual insight who could impress and control others by his disposition and brilliance. Unfortunately, though Samson could master others, he never learned how to master himself. This leads us to the conclusion that the main lesson to be learned from his life is that gifts and talents without self-discipline amount to very little. Samson controlled part of his nature but not the whole; while going about the task of overcoming the enemies without, he never learned how to conquer the enemy within. What good is it if we focus on outward victories yet, in the meantime, allow the enemy to creep in and take the citadel?

DAY **74**

Ruth renounces

Ruth 1:1–17

Bethlehem being in the grip of famine, Elimelech, Naomi, and their two sons cross the Jordan into the land of Moab in search of food. After a period of time in the new country, Elimelech dies and his sons, Mahlon and Kilion, who had married two local girls, also die. Destitute and helpless, the three childless widows set out for Bethlehem, but on the way Naomi decides that it would be more prudent for her two daughters-in-law to return to their childhood homes and find new husbands. One of them, Orpah, responds to Naomi's suggestion, bids her mother-in-law farewell, and returns to her native people. Ruth, however, refuses to return, preferring to stay with Naomi – expressing this in words of matchless beauty.

"Jesus replied, 'No-one who puts his hand to the plough and looks back is fit for service in the kingdom of God.'" (Luke 9:62)

FURTHER THOUGHT

What a magnificent picture this is of true conversion. Orpah draws back to end her days in idolatry; Ruth moves on to become part of the line from which Jesus Himself descended. How sad that some can travel for a time with God's people, yet fail to make that "leap of faith" that entrusts all to the Saviour. Are you such a one?

Ruth

Joshua

1400 BC

Fall of Jericho

1300 BC

Assyrian Empire founded

Ruth resolves

Ruth 1:18-22

Ruth not only renounces her heathen past, but embraces her new future with a firm faith in the God of Israel, in whom, under Naomi's instruction, she had come to trust. When Naomi sees the depth of her resolve, she gives up trying to persuade Ruth to return to her native land and allows her to accompany her to Bethlehem. They arrive in the little town at the time of harvest, and their presence causes quite a stir. Many old friends and acquaintances of Naomi greet her by name. Naomi feels that God has brought calamity upon her (v. 21) and that her name should no longer be Naomi ("pleasant"), but Mara ("bitter"), because of the tragic experience she had gone through while in the land of Moab. In Bible days, remember, names were not just designations, but definitions.

"And we know that in all things God works for the good of those who love him, who have been called according to his purpose." (Rom. 8:28)

FURTHER THOUGHT

Naomi's judgement on herself, though understandable, seems punitive and harsh. Had she known the truth of Romans 8:28-29 - that God takes all things and works them for good - she might have viewed things differently. Through God, negative experiences work to make us not bitter - but better.

Deborah and Barak | Gideon | Samson | Samuel
1200 BC | 1100 BC

DAY 76

Ruth's redeemer

Ruth 2:1-12

Ruth had no difficulty in finding a task to gainfully occupy her attention. At harvest time there was always work to be found in the fields clearing up after the reapers. Ruth decides on a certain field, not by chance, but under the controlling providence of God. There she meets for the first time the owner of the field, Boaz – a relative of her late father-in-law and the man who would later redeem her and become her husband. When Boaz discovers who Ruth really is, he shows a personal interest in her and says: "Don't go and glean in another field ... Stay here with my servant girls" (v. 8). His protective care and concern prompts Ruth to ask: "Why are you doing this for me?" He explains that the story of her devotion to Naomi has touched him deeply, and this is his way of showing appreciation.

"Trust in the Lord with all your heart and lean not on your own understanding; in all your ways acknowledge him, and he will make your paths straight." (Prov. 3:5–6)

FURTHER THOUGHT

Did Ruth find herself in the field owned by Boaz just by chance? Hardly. She might not have been conscious of divine guidance – but it was there nevertheless. How thrilling it is to know that God is working for our highest good – even when we are not conscious of it!

Ruth

Joshua

1400 BC

Fall of Jericho

1300 BC

Assyrian Empire founded

Ruth reaps

Ruth 2:13-23

Although Ruth was involved in the overall task of reaping, her specific work was that of gleaning. When the reapers worked their way through the fields, they would, because of the speed at which they worked, leave some parts of the field unreaped. This was then picked up by people called "gleaners" who came behind them, picking up the grain that was still standing, which then became their own property under Jewish law (see Leviticus 19:9–10 and Deuteronomy 24:19). Boaz, obviously greatly attracted to Ruth, sets about doing everything possible to help her. He invites Ruth to join him in a meal and afterwards, sensing her need of encouragement, instructs his workers to "pull out some stalks from the bundles" (v. 16) and leave them for her to glean.

"A bruised reed he will not break, and a smouldering wick he will not snuff out, till he leads justice to victory."
(Matt. 12:20)

FURTHER THOUGHT

Has there been a time when, deeply discouraged and about to give up, God has let drop some "handfuls on purpose" for you? Perhaps it was a word in a sermon, a smile, a gift of money arriving at the right time.
Thank Him for the many encouragements He places across your path.

Deborah and Barak   Gideon   Samson   Samuel

1200 BC | **1100 BC** |

DAY **78**

Ruth rests
Ruth 3:1-18

When Ruth returns to Naomi with a large quantity of grain and some roasted barley, Naomi realises that her daughter-in-law has been the recipient of special privileges and enquires: "Where did you glean today?" (2:19). Ruth replies that she has been working in Boaz' field, whereupon Naomi, recognising the Lord's guidance and direction, praises Him for His goodness. Naomi explains that Boaz is a close relative and, as such, can redeem the family inheritance by marrying Ruth, as required by the laws of Israel (see Deuteronomy 25:5–6). Naomi instructs her to claim the right of redemption in a tactful and seemly manner, and Ruth dutifully complies. Boaz commends her for her action, and promises to marry her if a closer relative's claim is not taken up. Ruth rests in this glad assurance.

"Be still, and know that I am God; I will be exalted among the nations, I will be exalted in the earth." (Psa. 46:10)

FURTHER THOUGHT

How often do our lives become tangled by precipitate and premature action. Naomi's advice to "wait" (v. 18) may well be God's Word for you today. "Wait" – for a higher hand than yours is leading, and a purpose far more wonderful than you can ever conceive will open up in the days that lie ahead.

Ruth

Joshua

1400 BC

Fall of Jericho

1300 BC

Assyrian Empire founded

Ruth rewarded

Ruth 4:1-12

As Naomi had predicted, Boaz moves swiftly to settle the matter of Ruth's redemption. He hurries to the town gate – the place where legal matters were transacted – and waits for the next-of-kin to appear. There, in the presence of the elders of Bethlehem, Boaz asks him if he proposes to purchase Elimelech's inheritance, and hears that this is his intention. However, when Boaz tells the next-of-kin that he must also marry Ruth the Moabitess, he changes his mind and renounces his prior claim, which then devolves upon Boaz. The agreement is ratified publicly, and the way is now open for Boaz to announce his forthcoming marriage to Ruth. When he does this, he is showered with the good wishes of all present.

"It is because of him that you are in Christ Jesus, who has become for us wisdom from God – that is, our righteousness, holiness and redemption." (1 Cor. 1:30)

FURTHER THOUGHT

A redeemer in ancient Israel had to fulfil three conditions:
(1) he must be a close relative;
(2) he must be able to pay the redemption price;
(3) he must do it willingly. Pause for a few moments and think how beautifully our Saviour, the Lord Jesus Christ, meets these conditions as the Redeemer of the human race.

Deborah and Barak   Gideon

Samson

Samuel

1200 BC |

1100 BC |

DAY **80**

Ruth rejoices

Ruth 4:13–22

Remember that when Boaz first met Ruth, he prayed that she should be repaid by the God of Israel for her care and concern for Naomi (2:11–12)? This prayer, it seems, is abundantly answered, for now Ruth not only becomes Boaz' wife, but she is rewarded with a son, whose name was Obed – an ancestor of David, on whose throne Jesus the Messiah would one day sit (Luke 1:26–33). It is worthy of note, too, that the day came, hundreds of years later, when the little town of Bethlehem displayed greater wonders than those recorded in the story of Ruth, when the outcast babe of another forlorn woman appeared, and drew princes and wise men from the East to place treasures at His feet. And in that Seed shall all the nations of the earth be blessed.

"Rejoice in the Lord always. I will say it again: Rejoice!" (Phil. 4:4)

FURTHER THOUGHT

One thing, and one thing only, brought Ruth into the position of blessing which she enjoyed – her redemption by Boaz. Remember that the next time you are tempted to think that you are accepted by God because of your own virtue. You are what you are because Jesus is what He is.

Ruth

Joshua

1400 BC

Fall of Jericho

1300 BC

Assyrian Empire founded

Ruth 4:21-22

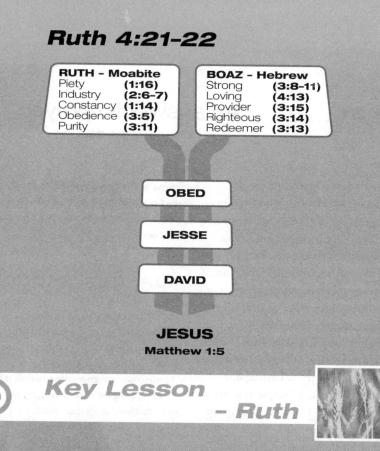

RUTH – Moabite		BOAZ – Hebrew	
Piety	(1:16)	Strong	(3:8-11)
Industry	(2:6-7)	Loving	(4:13)
Constancy	(1:14)	Provider	(3:15)
Obedience	(3:5)	Righteous	(3:14)
Purity	(3:11)	Redeemer	(3:13)

OBED

JESSE

DAVID

JESUS
Matthew 1:5

Key Lesson – Ruth

One commentator points out that the book of Ruth – coming, as it does between Judges and 1 Samuel – books which are full of wars, violence and intrigue – is like a "beautiful valley full of flowers and fertile fields set between two rugged mountain ranges". There can be little doubt that the story of Ruth brings to this part of the Old Testament a beauty and a fragrance which is greatly needed. Ruth is the kind of woman who draws the world after her, not just because of her beauty but by the lasting qualities of unselfish devotion and lowly service.

The main lesson we learn from Ruth's life is the importance and value of disinterestedness. Ruth's concern was for others more than for herself, and as a result she experienced great rewards, one of which was being part of the genealogy of none other than our Lord Jesus Christ. The less of bargain or condition we put into our service for God, the more likely we are to receive special rewards in the end.

Samuel
Samuel: "Heard of God"

DAY 81 — An answered prayer

1 Samuel 1:1-28

Samuel was the firstborn son of Elkanah and Hannah who lived in the province of Ramah, somewhere around 1000 BC. Elkanah was a Levite who followed the common custom of polygamy. Peninnah, his other wife, had borne him several sons and daughters, but Hannah, his favourite wife, was childless. Every year the family visited Shiloh to sacrifice to the Lord, and Peninnah used to taunt Hannah because of her barrenness, reducing Hannah to tears. During one visit, Hannah enters the Temple and prays earnestly and silently for a son, promising to dedicate him to the Lord. She is so distraught that Eli the priest considers her drunk and rebukes her. When he hears the truth, however, his rebuke turns to a blessing. In due time, Samuel is born, and when he is about two or three years old is presented to Eli for training in the work of the Lord.

"Now instead, you ought to forgive and comfort him, so that he will not be overwhelmed by excessive sorrow." (2 Cor. 2:7)

FURTHER THOUGHT

How do you respond when you become the victim of spitefulness, misunderstanding and contempt? Hannah refused to let either the taunting of Peninnah, or the misconceptions of Eli goad her into anger or retaliation. A good model to follow – today, and every day.

Samuel
Samson

Deborah and Barak   Gideon
1200 BC | 1100 BC |

A servant's heart

1 Samuel 2:1-36

Having fulfilled her vow to dedicate Samuel to the work of the Lord, Hannah breaks forth into joyful prayer (vv. 1–10). In future her annual visits to Shiloh will not be made with sadness, but with joy and expectation to see her growing son, Samuel, and supply him with new clothes. Samuel seems to have slept within the holiest place, having the duties of keeping the lamp of God burning and opening the Temple doors at sunrise. Eli's two sons, though acting as priests in the Lord's Temple, have no real respect for the Almighty, whereupon a man of God visits Eli and prophesies the death of his two evil sons and the downfall of his household. He announces also that God will, in due time, raise up a faithful priest who will carry out His will, and bring honour and glory to the Lord.

> "... the Lord disciplines those he loves, and he punishes everyone he accepts as a son." (Heb. 12:6)

FURTHER THOUGHT

Most commentators believe that one of the reasons why Eli's sons turned out to be failures was due to lack of loving and corrective discipline. In Deuteronomy 21:18–21 are contained clear steps of action which Eli, as a priest and a judge, should have known. Where there is no discipline, there can be no disciples.

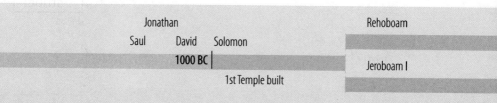

Jonathan

Saul   David   Solomon

Rehoboam

1000 BC

Jeroboam I

1st Temple built

DAY 83   A call from God

1 Samuel 3:1–21

Like Samson, whom we have already studied, Samuel was a Nazirite. He was promised to God by his mother prior to birth, and this promise constituted the Nazirite vow (see Numbers 6:1–8). Samuel was called to the prophetic office (that is, to be a special spokesman for God) when he was very young. One night, while Samuel is fast asleep, he is awakened by a voice calling his name. Thinking the voice to be that of Eli, he immediately presents himself to the old man, but Eli assures Samuel that he did not call. After this happens three times, Eli realises that God is calling Samuel, and instructs him how to respond if he hears the voice again. Samuel obeys and receives a message for Eli – a message which repeats an earlier prophecy (1 Sam. 2:27–36). As Samuel grows up, he is acknowledged by everyone in Israel to be a prophet sent from God.

"Instead, speaking the truth in love, we will in all things grow up into him who is the Head, that is, Christ." (Eph. 4:15)

FURTHER THOUGHT

Can you imagine how hard it must have been for Samuel to have reported to Eli the message which God had given him about the judgement that was to come upon his family? Yet Samuel does not hesitate. How good are you at passing on the messages the Lord gives you for others?

Samuel

Samson

Deborah and Barak   Gideon

1200 BC   1100 BC

An intercessor's prayer

1 Samuel 7:1-14

The prophecies given to Eli concerning Hophni and Phinehas, his two sons, come true when they are killed during a fierce battle with the Philistines in which the ark of God is captured. On hearing the terrible news, Eli falls from where he is sitting and dies of a broken neck (1 Sam. 4:10–18). Later the ark is miraculously returned to Israel from the hands of the Philistines, and is safely housed at Kiriath Jearim. Twenty years pass before Israel is ready to respond to Samuel's call to show the reality of their repentance by putting away heathen gods and serving the Lord. When finally they obey, Samuel offers a burnt sacrifice and takes up the work of intercession for his people. As a result, Israel gains a great victory over the Philistines and a period of peace and prosperity begins.

"After Job had prayed for his friends, the Lord made him prosperous again and gave him twice as much as he had before." (Job 42:10)

FURTHER THOUGHT

Have you ever realised that a refusal to pray for others could constitute a sin? Turn to 1 Samuel 12:23 and you will see what we mean. Perhaps this is an appropriate moment to check on your personal prayer life. How much time do you give to praying for others? Seconds? Minutes? Hours?

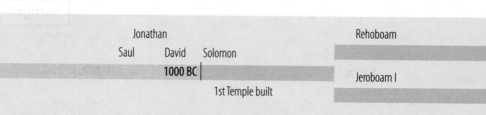

Jonathan

Saul   David   Solomon

Rehoboam

1000 BC

Jeroboam I

1st Temple built

DAY **85**   A judge in Israel
1 Samuel 7:15-8:22

At this juncture in the history of Israel, Samuel is established not only as a prophet and a priest, but also as a judge. His home is at Ramah, where he builds an altar and administers justice on an annual circuit which takes in Bethel, Gilgal and Mizpah. Samuel's style of justice is firmly based on godliness, fairness and good organisation. In his old age, Samuel appoints his two sons to be judges in Israel but, regrettably, they fall prey to the evil of bribery and pervert the course of justice. The elders of Israel, concerned that Samuel's sons are not following in their father's footsteps, approach Samuel and ask for a king. Their request greatly displeases Samuel, but he seeks God's guidance and is told to grant their request, at the same time solemnly warning them of the outcome.

"Therefore, I urge you, brothers, in view of God's mercy, to offer your bodies as living sacrifices, holy and pleasing to God – this is your spiritual act of worship." (Rom. 12:1)

FURTHER THOUGHT
Ready for a challenge? Then here it is: it was never God's perfect will for Israel to be ruled by a king, but only His permissive will. In settling for a king, Israel settled for second best. How about you? Are you settling for second best in your spiritual life? If so, then decide to do something about the issue - today.

Samuel

Samson

Deborah and Barak   Gideon

1200 BC   1100 BC

A prophet's mantle

1 Samuel 9:1-27

A long and unsuccessful hunt for his father's lost donkeys brings about a meeting between Samuel and Saul – the future king of Israel. Saul and his servant are on the point of giving up their fruitless search when the servant suggests they should consult a local seer whose words always come true (1 Sam. 9:6; 3:19). As Saul and his servant enter the town, they meet Samuel, who has been prepared by God for the meeting. Samuel knows Saul by divine intimation as soon as he sees him, but Saul does not know Samuel. The prophet tells him that he need no longer be concerned for the donkeys as they have been found, and then invites the two men back to his house for a specially prepared feast. Saul is given a place of honour, and eats the meat which is normally reserved for priests.

"Your word is a lamp to my feet and a light for my path." (Psa. 119:105)

FURTHER THOUGHT

How different are the Lord's purposes from our individual and personal intentions. Saul went out looking for some donkeys and instead found a kingdom. How grateful we ought to be for the fact that our lives are guided by an unseen, but benevolent hand.

Jonathan

Saul David Solomon

Rehoboam

1000 BC

Jeroboam I

1st Temple built

Samuel

Samuel: "Heard of God"

DAY 87 · A priestly role

1 Samuel 10:1-27

After the celebration feast given in Saul's honour is over, both he and his servant stay at Samuel's home for the night, and in the morning Samuel sets them on their way home. With simple courtesy, the prophet accompanies his guests down the hill to the last house of the city, and then sends Saul's servant on ahead in order that he might have a private moment with the future king. Samuel informs Saul that he is chosen by God to be king over Israel and pours over Saul's head the consecrated anointing oil, announcing him to be the ruler and deliverer of Israel. God gives Saul a new heart (v. 9), and the farmer's son becomes a national leader and a warrior. Later Samuel presides over Saul's coronation at Mizpah when the Israelites shout: "Long live the king!" (v. 24)

"Do not touch my anointed ones; do my prophets no harm." (Psa. 105:15)

FURTHER THOUGHT

Despite Samuel's personal dislike of Israel's desire to appoint a king, he nevertheless treated Saul with respect and courtesy. This was because he saw and understood the principle of submission to God-ordained authority. If you are not familiar with Romans 13:2, then look it up right now. You may be in for a surprise.

Samuel

Samson

Deborah and Barak   Gideon

1200 BC   1100 BC

Horns

In primitive times the horn of a ram or cow, with a mouth-piece cut at the narrow end, was used as a trumpet. They were also used as containers for precious substances. They were hollowed out and decorated. Samuel used one for his anointing oil (1 Sam. 10:1; 1 Kings 1:39). The shepherd carried oil in a horn for bathing cut sheep (Psa. 23:5).

The word "horn" also came to be used to describe power or might (Psa. 75:4–5; 92:10; 112:9). Horned animals like the rhinoceros or bull were the strongest animals known. So the horn came to be a symbol of strength.

 ## Key Lesson – Samuel

In terms of moral stature, historical significance and devotion to God, Samuel stands head and shoulders above most other Old Testament personalities. Samuel was selfless, prayerful, strong and discreet, but the main lesson to be learned from his life is the power and importance of loyalty. He supported and attended Eli. He remained to counsel and support Israel even though they chose to go contrary to God's desires. What is loyalty? Loyalty is refusing to abandon someone who has let you down, opposing mistaken policies without losing fellowship. But loyalty is not blind or weak or silent – Samuel did not support Saul in his wrongdoing, yet how loyal he was to him is shown by the words: "Until the day Samuel died, he did not go to see Saul again, though Samuel mourned for him." (1 Sam. 15:35). Samuel learned his loyalty from God. So must we!

Saul

Saul: "Asked" or "Demanded"

DAY 88   Chosen to be king

1 Samuel 8:1-22

Little is known about Saul's family, except that he was the son of Kish, who was of the tribe of Benjamin. It is interesting to note that Saul of Tarsus, whose story is recorded for us in the New Testament, was also a Benjamite (see Romans 11:1 and Philippians 3:5). We have already seen how Saul met Samuel, and something of the circumstances in which he was chosen and anointed to be king of Israel, but now we examine some of these details again – this time from Saul's point of view. Although Saul turned out to be a disappointment to both God and Israel, when we first meet him he appears to have some excellent character traits. Look them up for yourself: obedience (1 Sam. 9:3), respect (9:7), politeness (9:18) and modesty (9:21).

"... add to your faith goodness ... knowledge ... self control ... perseverance ... godliness ... brotherly kindness ... love. For if you possess these qualities in increasing measure, they will keep you from being ineffective and unproductive in your knowledge of our Lord Jesus Christ." (2 Pet. 1:5–8)

FURTHER THOUGHT

What do you think is the prime quality which God looks for in those He selects to do a special work for Him? Courage? Faith? Ability? All of these are important, but the prime quality is character. As someone once said: "No character – no consequences."

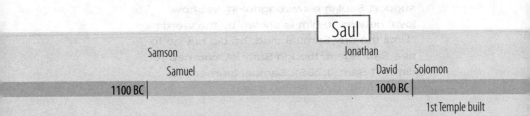

	Saul	
Samson		Jonathan
Samuel		David Solomon
1100 BC		1000 BC
		1st Temple built

The preparation for kingship DAY **89**

1 Samuel 10:1-27

Before Saul was presented to the people as the king of Israel, God took care to prepare him for the task in a number of ways. First He dealt with any doubts Saul may have had about his divine calling by inspiring Samuel to anoint him and give him several signs (vv. 2–6). The three signs which are given to Saul all take place on his way home, thereby convincing him of God's calling and election. Secondly, He moves within the depths of Saul's personality and changes his heart (v. 9). Later, an assembly is convened at Mizpah and lots are cast – a common practice at that time – to find the family which is to produce the king. When Saul is named, he is overcome with diffidence and hides among the baggage. God shows the people, however, where he is hiding – thus confirming him to be the man of His choice.

"... obey your earthly masters ... not only to win their favour when their eye is on you, but like slaves of Christ, doing the will of God from your heart." (Eph. 6:5–6)

FURTHER THOUGHT

Did you notice that although most of the people gave their allegiance to Saul, there were some who disliked him (v. 27)? It should not be expected that when God calls you to do His work, everyone is going to applaud you and pat you on the back. This principle, if recognised, can save you from a good deal of heartache. Have you learned it yet?

Rehoboam		Jehoshaphat	Obadiah	Joel	
	900 BC		JUDAH		800 BC
Jeroboam I		Ahab	Elijah	Elisha	
			ISRAEL		
	Homer's epics written				

Saul

Saul: "Asked" or "Demanded"

DAY 90 — The king is crowned

1 Samuel 11:1–12:25

After Saul has been appointed as the first king of Israel, he returns to the quiet and humble task of tending the cattle, but soon an incident takes place which thrusts him into prominence. Returning from the fields, he hears that the Ammonites have come against the men of Jabesh, and instantly Saul's patriotism is aroused. The Spirit of God comes upon him, and cutting into pieces two of his oxen he sends some of his men throughout the length and breadth of Israel with the message: "This is what will be done to the oxen of anyone who does not follow Saul and Samuel" (11:7). The fear of the Lord falls upon the people and they rise up as one man to overcome and defeat the Ammonites. In the joy of their great victory the tribes gather at Gilgal, between Jericho and the Jordan, where Saul is made king, after which Samuel gives the coronation speech.

"... anyone who serves Christ in this way is pleasing to God and approved by men." (Rom. 14:18)

FURTHER THOUGHT

How did you get on with the thought we left with you yesterday? Did it dampen you somewhat? Then take heart: when the men who previously despised Saul saw the Spirit of God at work in him, they completely changed their attitude (11:7). Look up Proverbs 16:7 and take it as the Lord's word to your heart today.

Saul

Samson
Samuel
Jonathan
David   Solomon

1100 BC

1000 BC

1st Temple built

1 Samuel 13:1–22

For two years Saul prospered as king over Israel – then difficulties begin to occur. Saul recruits a small standing army of 3,000 men, considering them to be more effective than the much larger militia which is at his disposal. He places 1,000 men under the command of his son, Jonathan, who succeeds in overrunning the Philistine garrison at Geba. This sparks off a massive retaliation, and once more a general mobilisation is necessary to meet the Philistine invasion. Saul waits for Samuel at Gilgal, as arranged, but seeing his army beginning to disperse, Saul usurps Samuel's priestly office by offering sacrifices in his absence. Arriving soon after this event, Samuel rebukes Saul for his presumption and announces that he will be replaced by a king after God's own heart.

"If we confess our sins, he is faithful and just and will forgive us our sins and purify us from all unrighteousness." (1 John 1:9)

FURTHER THOUGHT

Notice that Samuel called sin – sin, and did not cover it up as we often tend to do. We live dangerously when we allow an act of disobedience to pass as an act of prudence. Learn to see every sin for what it is – a violation of God's principles – and confess it without delay.

Rehoboam		Jehoshaphat	Obadiah	Joel	
	900 BC		JUDAH		800 BC
Jeroboam I		Ahab	Elijah	Elisha	
			ISRAEL		
	Homer's epics written				

Saul

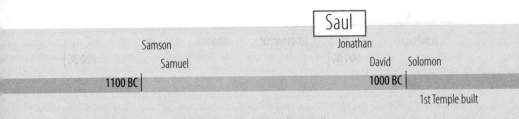

Saul: "Asked" or "Demanded"

DAY 92   A disobedient heart

1 Samuel 14:47–15:35

King Saul demonstrates his spiritual and moral deterioration, not only by his sin of presumption and impatience, but also by his disobedience and rebellion. Sent by God to exterminate the Amalekites – a warring tribe who had fought against the Israelites on their way into the Promised Land – he listens to the voice of the people and only partially obeys the Lord's instructions. He keeps the best sheep and oxen for himself and although he destroys the Amalekites, he spares Agag, the king. Later, when accused by Samuel of disobedience, Saul attempts to justify himself, but Samuel affirms that he is no longer fit to be king and that he is to be rejected by God. Samuel calls for Agag and carries out the death sentence upon him.

"If you love me, you will obey what I command." (John 14:15)

FURTHER THOUGHT

Ever heard of "selfism"? It's the desire to have one's own way and ignore what anyone else does or says. Unfortunately Saul was plagued with it – and so are many modern-day Christians. "Selfism" is a downward path, and one which leads away from God. Make sure you are not on it.

Saul

Samson   Jonathan

Samuel   David   Solomon

1100 BC   1000 BC

1st Temple built

The Spirit departs

1 Samuel 16:14–23; 18:1–12; 19:1–24

Saul's rebellion and subsequent rejection by God results in the Spirit of God departing from him, and it is not long before an evil spirit takes hold of Saul and begins to control his life. The presence of the evil spirit produces in Saul periods of deep depression and frenzied outbursts of rage. David ministers to Saul during his times of depression and is able to bring him some relief. Later, when Saul hears the women singers placing David's exploits above his own, he becomes insanely jealous and tries to kill Israel's anointed king (1 Sam. 18:9–11;19:9–10). Twice David spares Saul's life. Because of Saul's jealousy and hostility, David becomes an outlaw but gathers around him a loyal band of men (1 Sam. 22:1–2; 23:13).

"But now that you have been set free from sin and have become slaves to God, the benefit you reap leads to holiness, and the result is eternal life." (Rom. 6:22)

FURTHER THOUGHT

According to Scripture, every human being is a slave to something. Look up Romans 6:16, and you will see what we mean. We can choose to let God and grace rule over us – or allow sin and Satan to dominate us. Whose slave are you?

Rehoboam		Jehoshaphat	Obadiah	Joel	
	900 BC	JUDAH			800 BC
Jeroboam I		Ahab Elijah Elisha			
		ISRAEL			
	Homer's epics written				

Hebrew Universe –

this is how the Hebrews believed the universe was made:

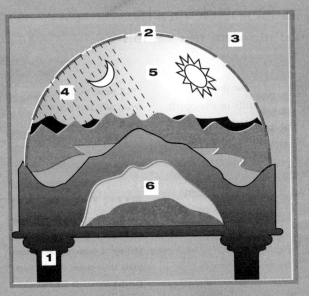

1.	Pillars, like foundations, supported the earth which was round and flat **(1 Sam. 2:8; Job 9:6; Psa. 104:5)**
2.	The arch of the heavens (the firmament) rested like a dome on the mountain tops **(Job 26:11; 37:18)**
3.	Waters, under the earth and over the dome, had been separated by God at the creation **(Gen. 1:6-7; Psa. 24:2; 148:4)**
4.	Floods came from the waters of the Great Deep below and rain came through the "windows" in the dome **(Gen. 7:11; 8:2)**
5.	The sun, moon and stars moved across the dome **(Psa. 19:4,6)**
6.	"Sheol", the home of the spirits of the dead, lay within the earth **(Num. 16:30-33; Isa. 14:9; 14:15)**

Now you can see why Saul went to the witch of Endor to "bring up" the spirit of Samuel from the kingdom of the dead *(1 Sam. 28:7-25)*:
And Saul said: "Bring up Samuel."

Saul's sad end

DAY **94**

1 Samuel 26:1-25; 28:1-25; 31:1-13

Now that Saul is bereft of divine guidance – the Spirit of the Lord having departed from him – he turns to another supernatural source for instruction. Disguising himself, he consults a medium – an act strictly forbidden by Jewish law (Lev. 19:31). To Saul's and the medium's surprise, God allows his request to consult Samuel (now dead) to be granted. Samuel appears before Saul and pronounces imminent doom upon him, and the following day this prediction is fulfilled. The Philistines go to battle with the Israelites and rout them, overtaking Saul and his sons. Saul is badly wounded and, rather than surrender to the Philistines and suffer the ignominy of defeat and torture, chooses to kill himself by falling on his sword.

"And lead us not into temptation, but deliver us from the evil one." (Matt 6:13)

FURTHER THOUGHT

Few people take a leap into spiritual degeneration; they usually move down the slope a step at a time. And what are those steps? They are egotism, pride, abuse of power, jealousy and self-will. Saul trod them and finished up a failure. Pause right now and ask God to protect you from placing your feet on any one of these slippery steps.

Samson
Samuel
Saul
Jonathan
David   Solomon

1100 BC | 1000 BC |

1st Temple built

Key Lesson – Saul

However much we try to sympathetically understand the life of Saul, we cannot help but view him as one of the most disappointing of all the characters in Scripture. He appears at first to be every inch a king and is polite, prudent, respectful and modest. He ends up, however, being disobedient and jealous, and is finally rejected by God. There are many lessons to be learned from the life of Saul – one being that obedience to the Lord is far more important than achieving success in any other realm. The main lesson that we learn from his life, however, is that of the evil of selfism. He refused to obey God, set about having his own way and, as a result, fell from the highest position in the land to finish up as a suicide.

Jonathan
Jonathan: "The Lord gave"

Heroic faith

1 Samuel 14:1-14

Jonathan was the oldest son of King Saul, and in human terms the heir apparent to Israel's throne. He was endowed with great mental ability, high and noble morality, a handsome appearance and a heart of love. That God should have other plans than to bring Jonathan to the throne of Israel is accepted with grace by this man of great courage, fidelity and unselfishness. These winsome characteristics all find their source in his unwavering faith in the God of Israel. Caught up in the perpetual skirmishing between the Israelites and the Philistines, Jonathan prepares to attack one of the enemy outposts, and says to his armour bearer: "Nothing can hinder the Lord from saving, whether by many or by few" (v. 6). Although just two lonely fighters, they emerge unscathed from a fight in which twenty Philistines are killed.

"The salvation of the righteous comes from the Lord; he is their stronghold in time of trouble." (Psa. 37:39)

FURTHER THOUGHT

Here's an exercise that should do you a lot of spiritual good. Take Jonathan's statement in the passage you have read today – "Nothing can hinder the Lord from saving, whether by many or by few" – and meditate upon it until you have drained it of every precious drop of spiritual refreshment. We'll be surprised if it doesn't change your day.

			Jonathan		
	Samson				
		Samuel		Saul	David	Solomon
1100 BC			1000 BC		
					1st Temple built

115

Jonathan

Jonathan: "The Lord gave"

DAY 96 — Undaunted courage

1 Samuel 14:15-46

Having demonstrated his faith in God and his great physical courage, Jonathan's standing is now high among the Israelites – but he must demonstrate moral courage too, for he has to serve under a very unstable father. A confusing battle follows Jonathan's initial attack upon the Philistines, and again the Philistines are routed. Saul issues a rash order that none of his men should eat that day while pursuing the enemy. Jonathan, unaware of this order, eats some of the honey which is readily available. When told of Saul's order that no food should pass their lips during the foray, he bravely speaks out against it. By the casting of lots, Jonathan is then singled out as the one who has disobeyed the king's order, and Saul sentences him to death. Popular support for Jonathan, however, prevents the execution.

"Now the Lord is the Spirit, and where the Spirit of the Lord is, there is freedom." (2 Cor. 3:17).

FURTHER THOUGHT

Why did Jonathan disapprove of his father's order to fast? Quite simply, because he sensed that on this particular occasion it was not a divine command, and was therefore unnecessary. Much legalism would be emptied out of the Church if we could emulate Jonathan's dedicated and sensitive spirit.

	Jonathan
Samson	
Samuel	Saul David Solomon
1100 BC	1000 BC
	1st Temple built

A covenant relationship

1 Samuel 18:1-15

Jonathan and David first meet in Saul's presence when the shepherd boy is presented to the king after the defeat of Goliath. An immediate bond of love is forged between David and Jonathan – a love which endures right up to the moment of Jonathan's untimely death in battle. Jonathan presents his robe, military dress and weapons to David as a public mark of honour and respect. David behaves wisely at court, and rises rapidly in the army and in popular esteem. This, as we have seen, causes Saul to become exceedingly jealous of him. While David plays to him, Saul twice hurls his spear at him but David escapes unharmed. Jonathan quickly realises that he faces a conflict of loyalties, and that he will require all the skill and diplomacy of which he is capable to maintain his loyalty to his father and his friendship for David.

"Blessed are the peacemakers, for they will be called sons of God." (Matt. 5:9)

FURTHER THOUGHT

Not many can stand between two people who are distanced by strife, and retain a loyalty and love for both. But Jonathan was such a person. In New Testament language, he would be described as a "peacemaker". Could this description be given of you?

Rehoboam		Jehoshaphat		Obadiah	Joel		
	900 BC			JUDAH		800 BC	
Jeroboam I		Ahab	Elijah	Elisha			
			ISRAEL				
	Homer's epics written						

Jonathan

DAY 98

A faithful friend

1 Samuel 19:1-7; 20:1-42

Saul instructs Jonathan and the courtiers to kill David, but Jonathan warns him to go into hiding while he reasons with his father. Jonathan points out to Saul that David has done nothing but good for the king, and that he had risked his life to kill Goliath. Saul heeds the words of his son and swears that David will not be put to death. Through Jonathan's intercession, David is able to return to the court, but it is not long before Saul's jealousy is aroused yet again, causing David to flee for his life. David seeks out Jonathan's help in overcoming the problem, but Jonathan does not really believe that David's life is in danger. He agrees to speak to his father once again, but Jonathan's public defence of David at a feast results in Saul hurling a spear at his son also. David and Jonathan decide with great sorrow that they must part, and together they reaffirm their oath of friendship.

"And I pray that you, being rooted and established in love, may have power, together with all the saints, to grasp how wide and long and high and deep is the love of Christ, and to know this love that surpasses knowledge ..." (Eph. 3:17–19)

FURTHER THOUGHT

The friendship of David and Jonathan is one of the most beautiful and pure relationships the world has ever seen. But how it pales beside the love of Christ for His redeemed people. Can you think of a few comparisons? Here's one to start you off: their love had a beginning – His love is from everlasting. Now think up some more.

Jonathan

Samson

Samuel

Saul   David   Solomon

1100 BC

1000 BC

1st Temple built

An encouraging word

1 Samuel 23:1–18

David is forced to become an outlaw, and gathers to himself in the cave of Adullam a band of faithful men. One of their exploits is to save Keilah from a Philistine attack. When Saul hears of this, he prepares to descend on Keilah, intending to trap David in the walled city. David, however, has enquired of the Lord, and has learned that the inhabitants of the city will hand him over if it is besieged. David and his men then take to a nomadic existence in the desert of Ziph, and Jonathan seeks him out to encourage him in the Lord. The message that Jonathan gives to David is one that is very simple, but heartening: "Don't be afraid ... My father Saul will not lay a hand on you. You shall be king over Israel ..." (v. 17). David and Jonathan again renew their covenant of friendship as they part for the last time.

"A word aptly spoken is like apples of gold in settings of silver."
(Prov. 25:11)

FURTHER THOUGHT

What a difference a word of encouragement makes when someone is caught up in the midst of doubt and uncertainty. Ask God to help you come in contact today with someone who needs a special word of encouragement. And when you meet them, be sure to pass it on. May God guide you to the right person at the right time.

Rehoboam		Jehoshaphat	Obadiah	Joel	
900 BC		JUDAH		800 BC	
Jeroboam I	Ahab	Elijah	Elisha		
		ISRAEL			
	Homer's epics written				

Key Lesson – Jonathan

It has been said of Jonathan that "he is the most chivalrous figure in the whole of the Old Testament, the flower and crown of Hebrew history, a knight without reproach". The Scripture, which we know to be open and honest concerning the lives of its personalities, has nothing negative to say about Jonathan. From first to last, there is not one crooked line or dark spot in his conduct. Jonathan is the perfect example of a good and godly friend, and this, no doubt, is the main lesson that we observe from his life. He could take second place without jealousy or a spirit of rivalry, and maintain his love and loyalty for David despite everything that worked to the contrary. No wonder when David looks back and remembers the friendship of Jonathan, that he weeps and cries out: "Your love for me was wonderful, more wonderful than that of women" (2 Sam. 1:26). Have you a friend like that? Then consider yourself greatly blessed. But perhaps what is more important is this – are you a friend like that?

The shepherd

1 Samuel 16:1-13

David was the youngest of the eight sons of Jesse. Nothing is said in Scripture about David's mother, but we know that the family came from Bethlehem, which means "the house of bread". At the time David appears on the pages of Scripture, Saul and Samuel are estranged (1 Sam. 15:34). Samuel is instructed by God to anoint one of the sons of Jesse as the second king of Israel – a command which, because of possible reaction from Saul, causes Samuel to fear for his life. Samuel obeys, however, and invites Jesse and his sons to a sacrificial feast. Seven of the sons are examined by Samuel, but there is no divine confirmation until David is hastily called in from the fields, whereupon the Lord speaks to Samuel and says: "Rise and anoint him; he is the one" (v. 12).

"But God chose the foolish things of the world to shame the wise ... the weak things of the world to shame the strong. He chose the lowly things of this world and the despised things – and the things that are not – to nullify the things that are." (1 Cor. 1:27–29)

FURTHER THOUGHT

How unlike human ways are the ways of the Lord. The Almighty overlooks the seven stalwart sons of Jesse, and alights on a mere stripling. We can tell how men look, but only God can tell how men are. Keep this in mind the next time you are puzzled about the way God goes about His choices.

David

Samson

Samuel

Jonathan

Saul

Solomon

1100 BC

1000 BC

1st Temple built

DAY **101**

The singer
1 Samuel 16:14-23

After Samuel anoints David as the second king of Israel, the young lad returns to his task of looking after his father's sheep, where he develops some skill as a musician. It appears that he has fighting skills too, for he is described as "a brave man and a warrior" (v. 18). When Saul is possessed with an evil spirit, his servants suggest that he be brought to soothe the king with his music. The courtiers hope that his ministry in music will bring relief to Saul during his periods of depression, and David's playing has the desired effect. Saul is taken with David and grows to admire and love him. The musical ability which David shows opens a way for him into the king's presence and the daily life of the court, which one day will become his own.

"Speak to one another with psalms, hymns and spiritual songs. Sing and make music in your heart to the Lord ..." (Eph. 5:19)

FURTHER THOUGHT

Modern research shows that music is one of the greatest influences in human life. It can influence us for good, or bad. Learn to shut your ears to the raucous music of the world and concentrate instead on making "music in your heart to the Lord".

David

Samson

Jonathan

Samuel

Saul

Solomon

1100 BC

1000 BC

1st Temple built

1 Samuel 17:1–58

When the Philistines and the Israelites face each other across the Valley of Elah for another round in their never-ending conflict, the Philistines produce a nine-foot champion named Goliath. He calls for an Israelite to step forward and face him in a one-to-one combat and thus settle the war. The Israelites, including Saul, cower in fear in the camp. David arrives on the scene, and is outraged that Goliath's challenge – eighty times repeated – should remain unanswered. He responds to Goliath's challenge in the Name of the Lord and, refusing to wear Saul's armour, fells the giant with one well-directed stone from his sling. The craven army is thus inspired with fresh courage to enter into battle and eventually overthrow and defeat the Philistines.

"Jesus Christ is the same yesterday and today and for ever." (Heb. 13:8)

FURTHER THOUGHT

Do you have a "Goliath" in your life at this moment? Someone – or something – that causes you to cower in terror and fear? Then rise up in the Name of the Lord and hurl your faith at the problem. Remember, the God who lived in David's time is just the same today.

Rehoboam		Jehoshaphat	Obadiah	Joel	
	900 BC	JUDAH			800 BC
Jeroboam I		Ahab Elijah Elisha			
		ISRAEL			
	Homer's epics written				

David

DAY **103**

The sovereign

2 Samuel 5:1-6:23

Although David was anointed to be king, he could not be enthroned as king until after Saul's death. When eventually David ascends the throne of Israel he is about thirty years of age, and one of his first exploits is to capture Jerusalem from the Jebusites. Having made Jerusalem his capital city, David decides that the ark of the covenant, which had remained in Kiriath Jearim as a half-forgotten religious relic for close on eighty years, should be brought to Jerusalem. He appears, however, to have been ignorant of the law which governed the transportation of the ark – namely that it should be borne on the shoulders of consecrated men – and loads it on to a new cart. When the oxen drawing the cart stumble and the ark looks as if it might topple, Uzzah puts out his hand to steady it – with fatal results.

"Then I heard the voice of the Lord saying, 'Whom shall I send? And who will go for us?' And I said, 'Here am I. Send me!'" (Isa. 6:8)

FURTHER THOUGHT

Someone once said: "The Church is looking for new methods, new machinery, and new modes of operation, but God is looking for new men." We ought not to forget that God has designed His Church to move forward, not on the "new carts" of human achievement, but on the shoulders of men and women whose lives are devoted to Him. Worth pondering?

David

Samson

Samuel

Jonathan

Saul

Solomon

1100 BC

1000 BC

1st Temple built

The sinner

2 Samuel 11:1-27

David dispatches his army to fight the Ammonites, but he himself remains in safety in his palace. One afternoon while sitting on the flat roof of his home he sees, close by, a beautiful woman – Bathsheba, the wife of Uriah the Hittite – washing herself. Overcome with lust, he sends for the woman and seduces her. Later, when it is discovered that Bathsheba is expecting David's child, he sets up a carefully contrived plan to make it appear that the baby really belongs to Bathsheba's husband. David summons Uriah from the front and, after some polite conversation, suggests that he spends the night with his wife before returning to the war. Uriah refuses to do this, and thus David's plan to avoid a public scandal is foiled. David sends Uriah back to the front with a letter instructing General Joab to arrange his death in battle.

"The heart is deceitful above all things and beyond cure. Who can understand it?" (Jer. 17:9)

FURTHER THOUGHT

There can be little doubt that the greatest deception is self-deception. Take a moment right now to examine your conscience and ask yourself: Am I walking about with a drugged conscience, calling evil harmless until I really believe it myself? David did, but what is more – so might we!

Rehoboam		Jehoshaphat	Obadiah	Joel	
	900 BC	JUDAH			800 BC
Jeroboam I		Ahab	Elijah	Elisha	
		ISRAEL			
	Homer's epics written				

David
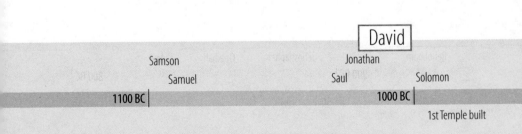

David: "Beloved"

DAY 105 — The sorrowful

2 Samuel 12:1–25; Psalm 51:1–19

David's conscience seems undisturbed by his great sin against Bathsheba and Uriah, and following Uriah's death in battle, he takes Bathsheba as his wife. God sends Nathan the prophet to David, who shares with him a barbed parable about a farmer whose sole possession was one ewe lamb. David, thinking it to be a true story, is deeply angered and says: "The man who did this deserves to die!" Nathan retorts: "You are the man!" David at last realises the enormity of his sin and confesses it to God. In spite of this, however, his family life is blighted and the death of his first child by Bathsheba is the first of many sorrows.

"Because of the Lord's great love we are not consumed, for his compassions never fail. They are new every morning; great is your faithfulness."
(Lam. 3:22–23)

FURTHER THOUGHT

Probably the only way God could save David from his self-deception was through Nathan's pointed parable. It took a parable to bring him face to face with himself. Read it once more and then ask yourself: Am I that man? Am I that woman? If so, then remember the forgiveness David found can be yours also.

	David	
	Jonathan	
Samson	Saul	Solomon
Samuel		
1100 BC	1000 BC	
		1st Temple built

2 Samuel 22:1–23:7

David contributed to the life of Israel, not only as its king, but as its foremost songwriter. He is described as "Israel's singer of songs" (2 Sam. 23:1). The psalms which David wrote, as well as others composed by different authors, make up the "heart" of the Bible. All human emotions are to be found in the Psalms – the welling fountain of feelings and imaginations, joys and griefs, cravings and aspirations, hope and despair, gloom and glory. More persistently than anywhere else in the Bible, the Psalms bring home to us the overwhelming sense of the reality and personality of God. The sight of His face is better to the psalmist than an abundance of corn and wine, and His presence by the side of the perplexed spirit soothes it into peace again.

"... give thanks in all circumstances, for this is God's will for you in Christ Jesus." (1 Thess. 5:18)

FURTHER THOUGHT

Why not make a commitment to meditate on and memorise a psalm that is short, yet full of joy and thanksgiving? We suggest Psalm 100. Memorise it and meditate upon it throughout today. Then, if you can, repeat it to someone before the day ends.

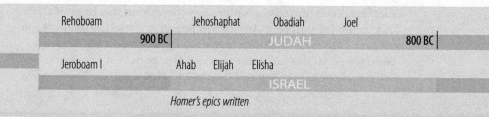

Rehoboam		Jehoshaphat		Obadiah	Joel		
	900 BC			JUDAH		800 BC	
Jeroboam I		Ahab	Elijah	Elisha			
				ISRAEL			
	Homer's epics written						

The Star of David

The Star of David is made up of two equilateral triangles forming a six-pointed star – a symbol which is used by Jews all over the world. There are many explanations of the symbolism of the Star of David. One is that in both Greek and Hebrew, the letter "D" is shaped as a triangle. Thus the star would represent two letter Ds – the first and last letters of David's name. The Star of David has been found in the ruins of a synagogue at Capernaum dating from the third century. But it is much older than that.
The Jews were forced to wear the Star of David in the Middle Ages, and again when they were persecuted in Germany by Hitler. To them it is a badge of honour, not of shame.

 Key Lesson – David

One commentator says of David: "It is rarely that a nation has associated all her attributes within the life of a single man. The David of Israel is not just the greatest of her kings, but the greatest shepherd, the greatest musician, the greatest soldier, and the greatest poet." Brave and chivalrous, energetic and prudent, a judge of men, a true lover of his country, just and wisely impartial – David had many excellent characteristics. His weaknesses, however, are undeniable – a fact the Bible does not attempt to disguise. The great sins of his life – his adultery with Bathsheba and the murder of Uriah – remind us that even "a man after God's own heart" is capable of the most revolting sins. The main lesson of David's life is this: no one can walk through life in moral uprightness without a close dependency on the Lord. David, despite his many fine qualities, was an utterly weak person without the help of God. That goes for you too. As someone put it: "The Christian life is not just your responsibility, but your response to His ability." Keep close to the Lord, for without His constant presence and companionship you will not be able to make it.

Solomon
Solomon: "Peace"

A triumph over enemies
1 Kings 1:1–2:46

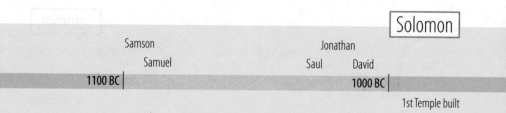

Solomon was born to David and Bathsheba after the death of their first child, and his name, which means "peace" or "peaceable", suggests that he was foreordained to do a special work for God. He comes into prominence when, towards the end of David's life, his eldest surviving son, Adonijah (the son by another wife – see 2 Samuel 3:2–5) makes a bid for the throne. Bathsheba tells David of this plot to overthrow him, and asks him not to delay in naming Solomon as his successor. David therefore orders Zadok the priest and Nathan the prophet to anoint Solomon as king, whereupon Adonijah, hearing of this, takes refuge in the sanctuary. Summoned before the new king, Adonijah bows in allegiance and is sent home unpunished. Later Solomon sees Adonijah as a threat to the throne, and orders his execution as well as that of Joab.

"And God raised us up with Christ and seated us with him in the heavenly realms in Christ Jesus ..." (Eph. 2:6)

FURTHER THOUGHT

Have you ever considered that Solomon's accession to the throne – bringing joy to every true Israelite and despair to Israel's enemies – is a beautiful picture of Jesus, the son of David, exalted to the throne of glory notwithstanding all who are in opposition? There are other parallels between these two events; see how many you can find.

Solomon

Samson
Samuel
Jonathan
Saul David

1100 BC
1000 BC

1st Temple built

Solomon

DAY 108 — A talent from God

1 Kings 3:4-28

Solomon begins his reign well, and follows in his father's footsteps by demonstrating a great love for the Lord and offering many sacrifices to Him at Gibeon. God appears to Solomon one night in a dream and says to him: "Ask for whatever you want me to give you" (v. 5). Solomon is deeply aware of his inadequacy as a ruler of Israel and asks the Lord for a wise and discerning heart. His principal concern is for the people over whom he is to rule and, because of this noble attitude, the Lord promises him wealth and honour as well as the wisdom which he requests. The wisdom which God gives to Solomon is clearly demonstrated in the way he handles the case of two prostitutes who come to him both claiming to be the mother of a certain child. Wisdom prevails and the problem is resolved.

"But the wisdom that comes from heaven is first of all pure; then peace-loving, considerate, submissive, full of mercy and good fruit, impartial and sincere. Peacemakers who sow in peace raise a harvest of righteousness." (James 3:17-18)

FURTHER THOUGHT

If God came to you today and said you could have one of the following, which would you choose? Friends – wealth – knowledge – honour – long life – power – prestige – fame – wisdom – security – happiness – popularity? If it was not wisdom – then your choice would be poor indeed.

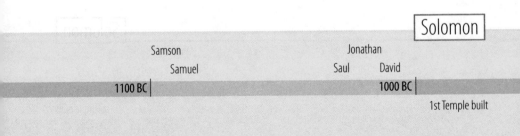

Solomon

Samson
Samuel
1100 BC

Jonathan
Saul   David
1000 BC

1st Temple built

A tranquil reign

1 Kings 4:1–34

Solomon demonstrates sound organisational ability – no doubt a by-product of the wisdom and discernment the Lord gave him – when he appoints a cabinet to help him govern. He also selects officials to govern twelve districts – to administer them and collect the taxes. During this period, rulers from all over the world bring Solomon gifts in exchange for the privilege of hearing the wisdom which God had given him. He shows expertise in many directions, ranging from human nature to natural science. He also undertakes the task of writing, and his contribution to the Old Testament is quite significant – Psalms 72 and 127, a large section of the book of Proverbs, the book of Ecclesiastes and the Song of Solomon. Altogether, he wrote 3,000 proverbs and 1,005 songs (1 Kings 4:29–34).

"Blessed the man who finds wisdom, the man who gains understanding, for she is more profitable than silver and yields better returns than gold." (Prov. 3:13)

FURTHER THOUGHT

Ever heard the saying: "Be careful what you want when you are twenty, because you will have its fruit by the time you are forty"? Those who make the right choices in early life reap the right rewards in later life. No wonder the Scripture says: "Wisdom is supreme; therefore get wisdom" (Prov. 4:7).

Rehoboam		Jehoshaphat	Obadiah	Joel	
900 BC		JUDAH		800 BC	
Jeroboam I	Ahab	Elijah	Elisha		
		ISRAEL			
	Homer's epics written				

Solomon

Solomon: "Peace"

DAY 110 — A Temple for worship

1 Kings 5:1–18; 8:1–66

It was King David's lifelong dream to build a Temple to the Lord in the city of Jerusalem, but it was left to his son, Solomon, to realise it. Solomon shares his plans for the building of the Temple with King Hiram of Tyre, a close friend of David's, and arranges for skilled Phoenician carpenters and stonemasons to prepare durable timber and dressed stonework. He conscripts thousands of Israelites to work alongside these craftsmen, and after seven years the Temple is completed. The ark of the covenant and the sacred furnishings are installed, and a dedication ceremony takes place in which the Almighty is joyously worshipped and adored. Solomon leads the worship with a powerful prayer and later exhorts the Israelites to be true to the Lord.

"One day Jesus was praying in a certain place. When he finished, one of his disciples said to him, 'Lord, teach us to pray ...'" (Luke 11:1)

FURTHER THOUGHT

Solomon's prayer at the dedication of the Temple is one of the longest prayers in the whole of Scripture. It is preserved, however, not just because of its length, but because of its breadth. Solomon's prayer is a prayer with wide horizons. Is your prayer life as broad as it is long?

Solomon

		Jonathan			Solomon
Samson		Saul	David	
Samuel				
1100 BC		1000 BC		1st Temple built

132

1 Kings 4:26; 9:17–28; 10:22–29

Earlier God had promised Solomon great riches – and how abundantly that promise is fulfilled. He acquires 1,400 chariots and 12,000 horses, not for warring purposes but because of the large international trade (10:28–29). Solomon also has huge fleets, operating in the Red Sea and the Mediterranean, trading goods in the countries they visit. His Phoenician-built ships return from the ports of the surrounding countries every three years, loaded with cargoes of ivory, gold and other riches. Affluence in Solomon's kingdom is such that silver is not considered to be a precious metal (10:21). Presents flow in from visitors who come from all parts of the world, increasing Solomon's personal wealth and the prosperity of his kingdom.

" 'I am the Alpha and the Omega,' says the Lord God, 'who is, and who was, and who is to come ...'" (Rev. 1:8)

FURTHER THOUGHT

Solomon seems to have had his priorities in the right order – he finished building God's house before he started work on his own. In other words – God first, himself last. Does that principle hold sway when you establish your priorities?

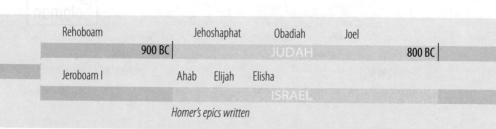

Rehoboam		Jehoshaphat	Obadiah	Joel	
	900 BC	JUDAH			800 BC
Jeroboam I		Ahab Elijah Elisha			
		ISRAEL			
Homer's epics written					

Solomon

Solomon: "Peace"

A testimony of grace

1 Kings 10:1-13

Solomon's expeditions to other countries in turn brought about closer relations with Sheba, in southern Arabia. The visit is returned by the queen of that region in person – doubtless for commercial reasons, hence the abundant interchange of "gifts". The Queen of Sheba plies Solomon with many difficult questions, but when he answers every one to her satisfaction and she views the magnificence of his court, she exclaims "not even half was told me". In answering the well-thought-out questions of the Queen of Sheba, Solomon becomes the embodiment of God's intention for Israel, and why He raised her up as a "special" person – namely, to take the hand of the pagan nations and lead them to the light and knowledge of the one and only true God.

"The Word became flesh and made his dwelling among us. We have seen his glory, the glory of the One and Only, who came from the Father, full of grace and truth." (John 1:14)

FURTHER THOUGHT

God's original intention of making Israel a "shop window" through which other nations could look and observe the benefits of serving the Lord was greatly hindered by the sin and wilfulness of the people. Today God's "shop window" is His Church – and the world is looking in. What, we wonder, do they see?

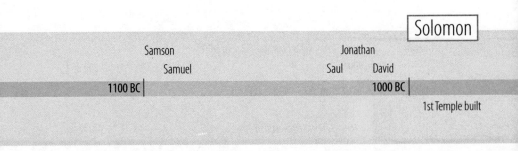

				Solomon
Samson		Jonathan		
Samuel		Saul	David	
1100 BC		1000 BC		
				1st Temple built

A transgression against God

1 Kings 11:1–43

When Solomon was young, he was so devoted to the Lord that he probably considered himself immune from the danger of marrying foreign women who worshipped idols (see Exodus 34:12–16). However, Solomon took wives from the Moabites, Ammonites, Edomites, Sidonians and Hittites, acquiring a harem of 700 wives and princesses, plus 300 concubines. Because he failed to maintain order in his home, his foreign wives practised idolatry and set up various shrines in and around Jerusalem. Solomon accomplished his goals of increasing foreign trade but overestimated his strength to resist the evil ways of his wives. The diligence with which he maintained orderliness changed from a positive force to a negative one, and marred his final years with disillusionment and despair.

"Your boasting is not good. Don't you know that a little yeast works through the whole batch of dough?" (1 Cor. 5:6)

FURTHER THOUGHT

How could one so wise turn away from following the Lord and become an idol worshipper? One thing is sure – it didn't happen overnight. All spiritual backsliding takes place by degrees. Be careful about the first step away from God – for one step soon leads to another.

Rehoboam		Jehoshaphat	Obadiah	Joel	
	900 BC	JUDAH			800 BC
Jeroboam I		Ahab	Elijah	Elisha	
		ISRAEL			
	Homer's epics written				

Solomon
– the man of wisdom and folly

	HIS WISDOM		HIS FOLLY
In his wise choice	**1 Kings 3:4-9**	In luxurious living	**1 Kings 4:22-23; 10:21**
In judicial insight	**1 Kings 3:16–28**	In marrying heathen women	
In surpassing other wise men			**1 Kings 11:1-2; Neh. 13:23-26**
	1 Kings 4:29-31		
In uttering proverbs and discourses		In excessive sensuality	**1 Kings 11:3**
	1 Kings 4:32-34		
In the building of the Temple		In oppressing the people	**1 Kings 12:4**
	1 Kings 5:1-6:38		
In his prayer of dedication		In sanctioning idolatry	**1 Kings 11:4-7**
	1 Kings 8:22-53		

Key Lesson
– Solomon

From a merely national and secular point of view, Solomon was without doubt one of the greatest kings of Israel. The impression he made on his contemporaries was quite astonishing, and the age in which he lived has been described as the Augustan age of the Jewish nation because of his attempts at getting the whole world to see the benefits of serving the true and living God. His prayer for wisdom was obviously abundantly answered, but although he began well, he allowed things to go on in his household which eventually brought about his downfall. The empire Solomon built crumbled soon after his death, because he had become preoccupied more with projects than with people. This, then, is the main lesson we learn from his life – we must be careful that we do not fasten upon things, and let them become more important than people. Solomon belongs to the peculiar class of those who begin well, and then have the brightness of their lives obscured toward the end. His morning sun rose beautifully, but it sank into a dark and depressing night.

Elijah

The prophet and the king

DAY **114**

1 Kings 17:1; 18:41-46; 21:17-24

All we know of Elijah before his dramatic appearance as the prophet of God is summed up in the words of 1 Kings 17:1: "Elijah the Tishbite, from Tishbe in Gilead." Elijah is first seen in a confrontation with King Ahab, who came to the throne about forty years after the death of Jeroboam, Israel's first king. Ahab was an ungodly king who encouraged the worship of false gods, and Elijah begins his ministry by prophesying that God is to pronounce judgement by bringing about a great drought. The drought lasts for more than three years, and results in the rejection of the idol god Baal and a return to the worship of the one true God. Because of the nation's repentance and Elijah's prayer of faith on Mount Carmel, the drought ends. Later Elijah and Ahab face each other again when the prophet predicts his doom and also that of his wife, Jezebel.

"... we ourselves, who have the first-fruits of the Spirit, groan inwardly as we wait eagerly for our adoption as sons, the redemption of our bodies." (Rom. 8:23)

FURTHER THOUGHT
A prophet has been defined as "someone in whom God groans". The definition is limited, of course, but it tends to show just what goes on in the heart of someone who shares God's concern for His world. In that sense, every one of us can be a prophet. Can God "groan" in you?

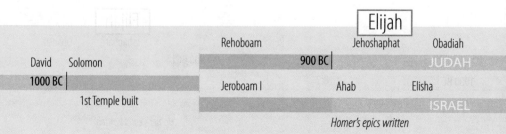

			Elijah	
	Rehoboam		Jehoshaphat	Obadiah
		900 BC		JUDAH
David Solomon				
1000 BC				
	Jeroboam I		Ahab	Elisha
1st Temple built				ISRAEL
		Homer's epics written		

Elijah
Elijah: "My God is Jehovah"

DAY 115   The prophet and the ravens
1 Kings 17:2-9

Elijah is told by the Lord to go into hiding by the brook Kerith, a tributary of the River Jordan. There he drinks from its waters and is miraculously fed each morning and evening by ravens. The silence of his surroundings, the long days and nights of solitude, the punctual arrival of his food, and the evident working of God's supernatural hand serve to develop within Elijah a deep sense of dependence upon God. As time goes on, the waters of the brook dwindle under the scorching heat of the sun until, at last, it becomes nothing but a dry channel. Then comes the word of the Lord to the prophet: "Go at once to Zarephath of Sidon and stay there. I have commanded a widow in that place to supply you with food" (v. 9)

"This is what the Sovereign Lord, the Holy One of Israel, says: 'In repentance and rest is your salvation, in quietness and trust is your strength ...'" (Isa. 30:15)

FURTHER THOUGHT

Elijah might not have realised it, but his experience at Kerith was part of the training for what happened on Carmel. It was there, in the quietness, that his ears were trained to hear the voice of God. Has God put you in a place of solitude at the moment? Then be encouraged – a Kerith is the prelude to a Carmel.

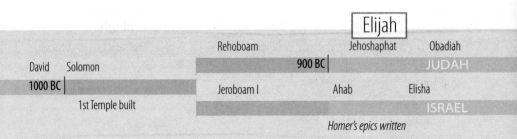

			Rehoboam		Jehoshaphat	Obadiah
David	Solomon			900 BC		JUDAH
1000 BC			Jeroboam I		Ahab	Elisha
	1st Temple built					ISRAEL

Elijah

Homer's epics written

The prophet and the widow

1 Kings 17:10-24

Elijah travels northward from the Jordan into Phoenicia, and ends up at Zarephath, a small port between Tyre and Sidon. Upon entering the town, he sees a widow gathering sticks and asks her for a drink of water. As she turns to bring him the water, he asks her also to bring him some food. At this point the woman tells him a sad tale: she has only enough food for one more meal, after which she and her son will starve to death. Elijah instructs her not to be afraid, but to go and bake a small cake for him first, and thereafter the God of Israel will provide for them all an unfailing supply of both oil and food. She obeys the prophet's command and discovers his words to be true. Not long after, the widow's son dies, but he is restored to life through the prophet's prayers.

"In everything I did, I showed you that by this kind of hard work we must help the weak, remembering the words the Lord Jesus himself said: 'It is more blessed to give than to receive.'"
(Acts 20:35)

FURTHER THOUGHT

In relation to the matter of giving to God, how often we say: "Lord, if You will give to me, then I will give You something in return." Yet sometimes God waits for us to make the first move. With that thought in mind, read Luke 6:38 again and see if it doesn't show up in a new light.

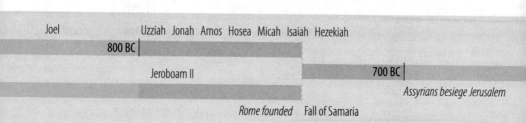

Joel   Uzziah   Jonah   Amos   Hosea   Micah   Isaiah   Hezekiah

800 BC

Jeroboam II   700 BC

Assyrians besiege Jerusalem

Rome founded   Fall of Samaria

DAY **117**

The prophet and Baal

1 Kings 18:1–46

After about three years of severe drought, the Lord speaks to Elijah and informs him that He will soon send rain. Elijah confronts Ahab once more, and tells him to gather the Israelites and all the prophets of Baal on Mount Carmel. There, two sacrifices are prepared and Elijah challenges the prophets of Baal to pray to their god to send fire from heaven to burn up their sacrifice – and he will do the same. The god who answers by fire is then to be acknowledged as the true God. The prophets of Baal pray earnestly hour after hour – but nothing happens. Elijah then orders the sacrifice he has prepared to be drenched with water. After praying a dramatically short prayer, fire falls from heaven and consumes the whole of the sacrifice as well as the stone altar. As a result of this supernatural happening, the people fall on their faces and cry out: "The Lord – he is God!"

"... he who doubts is like a wave of the sea, blown and tossed by the wind. That man should not think he will receive anything from the Lord; he is a double-minded man, unstable in all he does." (James 1:6–8)

FURTHER THOUGHT

"How long will you waver between two opinions?" Is Elijah's word to the people who had gathered on Mount Carmel the word of the Lord for you today? Are you hesitant about coming down firmly on God's side in some issue? Then today – right now – make up your mind to go God's way – whatever the consequences.

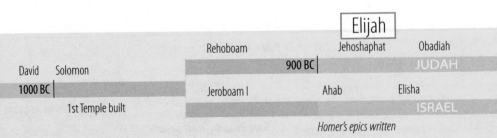

			Elijah	
	Rehoboam		Jehoshaphat	Obadiah
		900 BC		JUDAH
David Solomon				
1000 BC	Jeroboam I		Ahab	Elisha
1st Temple built				ISRAEL
		Homer's epics written		

1 Kings 19:1-18

Elijah completes the destruction of idol worship in Israel by executing all the prophets of Baal. As a result, Queen Jezebel, Ahab's wife, vows to kill Elijah. Hearing this threat, Elijah becomes extremely apprehensive and ends up in the desert fearing for his life. An angel is commissioned to support and strengthen Elijah in the midst of his depression, and after eating the food provided by God he gains sufficient strength to make the forty-day journey to Mount Horeb. There, as he sits in a cave, the Lord comes to him and speaks – but His message comes, not through the mighty wind, the earthquake or even the fire, but in a still small voice. God gives him three specific tasks, and assures him of the preservation of a faithful remnant in Israel.

"Why are you downcast, O my soul? Why so disturbed within me? Put your hope in God, for I will yet praise him, my Saviour and my God." (Psa. 42:5)

FURTHER THOUGHT

Like to see how an expert counsellor treats depression? Then look at God's prescription for Elijah's depression: sleep (v. 5); food (v. 6); conversation (v. 9); ventilation of feelings (v. 10); a change of perspective (vv. 11–12); and a new challenge (vv. 15–16). Ask the Lord to apply the same treatment to you the next time you feel depressed.

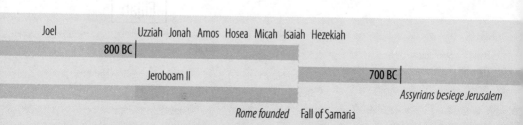

Joel   Uzziah Jonah Amos Hosea Micah Isaiah Hezekiah

800 BC

Jeroboam II   **700 BC**

Assyrians besiege Jerusalem

Rome founded   Fall of Samaria

DAY 119   The prophet and his successor

1 Kings 19:19–21

We have no record of Elijah following through on the commission which God gave him to anoint Hazael and Jehu (although we know they became kings in due course – see 2 Kings 8:15 and 9:13). However, we do have a vivid and detailed account of his meeting with Elisha. When Elijah meets his successor, he finds him ploughing in a field and, approaching him, casts over his shoulders the shaggy animal-skin cloak which he was accustomed to wear. This is a symbolic gesture to indicate that Elisha is to give up his work as a farmer and become a prophet. Elisha asks leave to say goodbye to his parents and, after permission is granted, he uses his wooden ox yokes – and probably his plough – as fuel to roast the oxen for a farewell feast.

"... Forgetting what is behind and straining towards what is ahead, I press on towards the goal to win the prize for which God has called me heavenwards in Christ Jesus." (Phil. 3:13–14)

FURTHER THOUGHT

The reason why some Christians get tangled up in the present is because they have never really broken with the past. Elisha knew the importance of breaking with the past in order to free himself for the future. Do you?

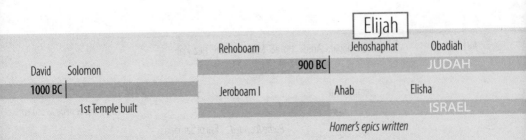

			Elijah	
		Rehoboam	Jehoshaphat	Obadiah
			900 BC	JUDAH
David	Solomon			
1000 BC		Jeroboam I	Ahab	Elisha
	1st Temple built			ISRAEL
			Homer's epics written	

2 Kings 2:1–25

The years between Elisha's call and Elijah's translation to heaven are not recorded in Scripture. Apart from delivering a message of judgement to King Ahab and another to Ahab's son Ahaziah, we know little of Elijah's activity. One of their joint responsibilities seems to have been the administration of various schools of prophets. The day arrives for Elijah to be taken up to heaven and, immediately prior to this event, he asks Elisha if he wants to make him a last request. Elisha asks that he might become a worthy successor, and he is told that his request will be granted if he sees Elijah go up into heaven. Elisha keeps his eyes on Elijah as he is caught up in a chariot and horses of fire, and receives the coveted cloak. His first miracle with the cloak is the opening up of the Jordan, and those looking on know that because of this miracle, he is truly Elijah's successor.

"Let us fix our eyes on Jesus, the author and perfecter of our faith, who for the joy set before him endured the cross, scorning its shame, and sat down at the right hand of the throne of God." (Heb. 12:2)

FURTHER THOUGHT
One thing, and one thing only, brought Elisha the coveted cloak of his master Elijah. He allowed nothing to deter or deflect him, but kept his eyes constantly on his master. And that, in a nutshell, is the secret of all spiritual blessing. So today and every day – keep your eyes upon Jesus.

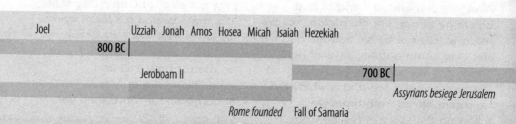

Joel — Uzziah Jonah Amos Hosea Micah Isaiah Hezekiah — 800 BC — Jeroboam II — 700 BC — *Assyrians besiege Jerusalem* — *Rome founded* — Fall of Samaria

Elijah the prophet

Elijah came from Gilead – rugged, highland country to the east of the River Jordan. His home was probably at Jabesh-Gilead, a town which was famous in Old Testament times. Grain could be grown in some places in Gilead, but the well-watered highlands were best for grazing sheep. Life here was simple and plain – very different from the luxury of Samaria. He was as stern and rugged as the country he came from. He blazed onto the scene of time, not only to confront Ahab, but also the prophets of Baal.

Key Lesson – Elijah

It is given to few to leave such a mark upon their own and succeeding generations as did God's servant Elijah. He is mentioned more times in the New Testament than any other Old Testament prophet. He did not introduce any new doctrine about Jehovah but, at a critical moment, saw what loyalty to the cause of the Almighty demanded – and of that cause he became a champion, not by mere words but by his actions and his life. One commentator says of him: "He came like a whirlwind, he burned like fire, and in a fire and a whirlwind he disappeared from time." In following the story of his life from Ahab's court, the climax on Mount Carmel, and on to Horeb, we watch a man very much like ourselves (James 5:17). He was subject to fluctuations in his spirit, at times gripped by depressive moods, prone to disillusionment and discouragement, beset by self-pity, but ever at God's disposal. The main lesson we learn from his life is this – whenever we place ourselves in God's hands, no matter how frail and insignificant we may feel, we accomplish far more than we can ever realise.

3

DAY **121**

Complete surrender

1 Kings 19:19–21

We have already looked at this passage when considering the ministry of Elijah, but it will do us no harm to consider it once more. There were four things which could have discouraged Elisha from following Elijah's call. First, he came from a prominent family and had the prospect of inheriting considerable material wealth. Second, he had a good relationship with his family, thus making it difficult for him to leave them. Third, he was leaving the position of foreman over at least eleven servants to assume a position of servitude. Fourth, he was breaking with a secure and peaceful life for one of danger and physical hardship. Yet he did not hesitate to do it.

"Trust in the Lord with all your heart and lean not on your own understanding; in all your ways acknowledge him, and he will make your paths straight."
(Prov. 3:5–6)

FURTHER THOUGHT

Someone has pointed out that whenever God called anyone to a special work in either the Old or New Testament, they were never idle but already engaged in a specific task. An honest calling in the world does not preclude us from receiving a higher and more heavenly call.

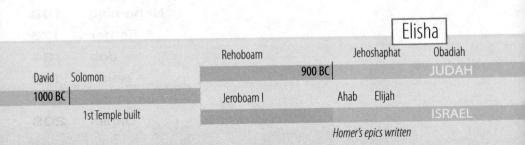

Elisha

		Rehoboam		Jehoshaphat	Obadiah
David	Solomon		900 BC		JUDAH
1000 BC		Jeroboam I		Ahab	Elijah
	1st Temple built				ISRAEL

Homer's epics written

The cloak received

2 Kings 2:1–25

Was Elisha disobedient in refusing to remain behind when his master asked him to (v. 2)? Some think so, but look again at the facts. Elisha was Elijah's companion for at least six years. During that time he had learned to discern the true wishes and desires that lay behind his master's words. He would have been able to distinguish between a test and a command by the very inflection of his master's voice. Elijah's words were a test, not a command. That Elijah was pleased by Elisha's refusal to remain behind is quite clear. He presses on, sees his master taken up to heaven, obtains the coveted cloak of power and goes out to accomplish twice as much as his master did.

"My son, give me your heart and let your eyes keep to my ways." (Prov. 23:26)

FURTHER THOUGHT

Elisha demonstrated that he had acquired a servant's heart by knowing and following the unspoken wishes of his master. Without that quality, no one can effectively serve as God's representative here on earth. Ask God to help you cultivate a "servant's heart".

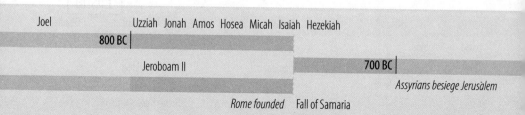

Joel

Uzziah Jonah Amos Hosea Micah Isaiah Hezekiah

800 BC

Jeroboam II

700 BC

Assyrians besiege Jerusàlem

Rome founded Fall of Samaria

Elisha

DAY 123 — Speaks with authority

2 Kings 3:1–27

The king of Judah, the king of Israel, and the king of Edom join together to make war on their common enemy, Moab, but on the journey south, disaster strikes because of lack of water. Faithful Jehoshaphat, king of Judah, suggests that they should seek the help of the Lord through one of His prophets. They go to Elisha, who condemns Joram, king of Israel, as being insincere, but for the sake of godly Jehoshaphat, he seeks the Lord on their behalf. A harpist is summoned and, as he plays, Elisha receives a prophetic word from God: "Make this valley full of ditches ... You will see neither wind nor rain, yet this valley will be filled with water, and you ... will drink" (vv. 16–17). The next morning the prophecy is fulfilled.

"The prayer of a righteous man is powerful and effective." (James 5:16b)

FURTHER THOUGHT

It is a blessing to be favoured with the company of those who have power with God and know how to engage in prevailing prayer. It is a pity that many of the governments and rulers of our day fail to understand this, for a nation may be greatly upheld by the fervent prayers of those who live under God's authority.

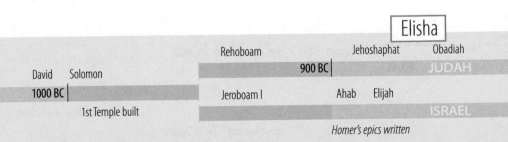

David	Solomon	Rehoboam	900 BC	Jehoshaphat	Obadiah
1000 BC					Elisha
	1st Temple built	Jeroboam I		Ahab	Elijah

JUDAH

ISRAEL

Homer's epics written

Miracles performed

2 Kings 4:1-44

Miracles flow fast and furious in Elisha's dynamic ministry. First, a widow who comes to Elisha saying that a creditor has come to take her two sons is saved through the miraculous supply of oil (vv. 1–7). Next, when Elisha stays in the home of a wealthy woman in Shunem, he predicts that she will have a son – a prophecy which is fulfilled. At a certain point in his life, the son is taken ill and dies, but is miraculously brought back to life through Elisha's prayers (vv. 8–37). Later, when some students at the school of the prophets are eating stew which has inadvertently been poisoned, Elisha again intervenes and produces a miracle. A further miracle is the feeding of 100 men with a small quantity of food.

"Jesus ... said, 'With man this is impossible, but with God all things are possible.'" (Matt. 19:26)

FURTHER THOUGHT

Does God work miracles today? Of course He does. Salvation is a miracle. Divine guidance is a miracle. Pause and give some thought today to the miracles which God has done for you. Begin with your conversion – then add others as they come to mind. And don't forget to say "thanks".

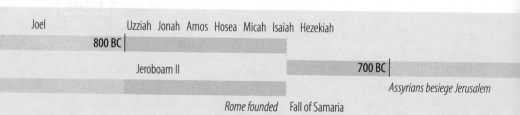

Joel

Uzziah Jonah Amos Hosea Micah Isaiah Hezekiah

800 BC

Jeroboam II

700 BC

Assyrians besiege Jerusalem

Rome founded Fall of Samaria

Elisha

Elisha: "God is my salvation"

DAY **125**

Temptation resisted

2 Kings 5:1-19

The healing of Naaman is, without doubt, one of the best known of Elisha's miracles. Naaman, a commander-in-chief of the Aramaean army, was a great and successful soldier – but he was a leper. His Israelite slave girl tells him there is a prophet in her home country who can cure him, and a letter is dispatched from the king of Aram to the king of Israel, asking for his help. The king of Israel regards this as an attempt to pick a quarrel, as he considers the request impossible to fulfil. When Elisha hears this, he sends for Naaman and tells him to go and wash in the River Jordan. Though resistant at first, he does as Elisha says and is healed. Elisha refuses the presents he is offered, and resists the temptation to take any credit to himself for the miracle.

"For my own sake ... I do this. How can I let myself by defamed? I will not yield my glory to another." (Isa. 48:11)

FURTHER THOUGHT

Although a Christian faces many temptations, one of the greatest is the temptation to take to oneself credit that is due only to God. Difficult though it may be for us to understand, it is a firm Scriptural principle that God will not share His glory with anyone else.

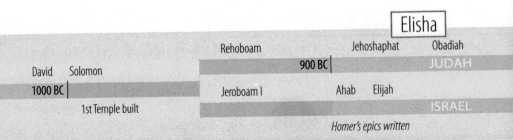

			Elisha	
	Rehoboam		Jehoshaphat	Obadiah
		900 BC		JUDAH
David Solomon				
1000 BC	Jeroboam I		Ahab Elijah	
1st Temple built				ISRAEL
		Homer's epics written		

Evidences of faith

2 Kings 6:1-7:20

During building operations, one of the company of prophets loses a borrowed axe-head in the River Jordan, and appeals to Elisha for help. Elisha miraculously causes the axe-head to float in the water so that it can be easily retrieved. Elisha's supernatural knowledge also enables him to keep the king of Israel informed of the Aramaean's every move in the war. Advised of this, the king of Aram attempts to capture Elisha, but he is foiled and frustrated by the miraculous acts of the prophet. Elisha's faith rises to every occasion, and nowhere is that more evident than in his prediction of relief in the great famine of Samaria. His prediction comes to pass the very next day.

"Now faith is being sure of what we hope for and certain of what we do not see." (Heb. 11:1)

FURTHER THOUGHT

Ever considered what faith really is? Take each letter of the word "faith" and see if you can think of various acrostics that spell out its meaning. Here's one to start with: Forsaking All I Trust Him. Now see how many you can come up with.

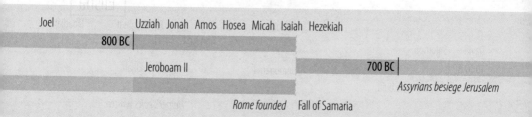

Joel

Uzziah Jonah Amos Hosea Micah Isaiah Hezekiah

800 BC

Jeroboam II

700 BC

Assyrians besiege Jerusalem

Rome founded   Fall of Samaria

Elisha

DAY 127

Victorious in death

2 Kings 13:1-21

Elisha died when he was about eighty years of age. During his long ministry he had been a prophet to whom rich and poor, great and small had turned for help. Toward the close of his life, he appears to be on good terms with King Jehoash, who visits him and shows deep concern over the prophet's approaching demise. On his deathbed, Elisha predicts the coming victory over Aram, instructing the king in a symbolic ritual with bow and arrows. The king, who is not a man of outstanding faith, limits the scope of the victory, thus making Elisha angry. One last miracle remains – after Elisha dies and is buried, his bones bring life to a dead man.

"... if the Spirit of him who raised Jesus from the dead is living in you, he who raised Christ from the dead will also give life to your mortal bodies through his Spirit ..." (Rom. 8:11)

FURTHER THOUGHT

Elisha asked Elijah for twice as much power as that which was shown by his master. Did he receive it? It is recorded that Elisha performed exactly twice as many miracles as did Elijah. He seemed to have more power in his dead bones than many of us have in our living bones!

					Elisha	
		Rehoboam			Jehoshaphat	Obadiah
			900 BC			JUDAH
David	Solomon					
1000 BC		Jeroboam I		Ahab	Elijah	
	1st Temple built					ISRAEL
			Homer's epics written			

152

Elijah and Elisha

The difference between Elijah and Elisha is much more striking than the resemblance. Elijah is the prophet of the wilderness, rugged and austere; Elisha is the prophet of civilised life, of the city and the court, with the dress, manners, and appearance of "other grave citizens". Elijah is the messenger of vengeance – sudden, fierce, and overwhelming; Elisha is the messenger of mercy and restoration. Elijah's miracles, with few exceptions, are works of wrath and destruction; Elisha's miracles, with but one notable exception, are works of beneficence and healing. Elijah is the "prophet of fire", an abnormal agent working for exceptional ends; Elisha is the "holy man of God" who "often comes our way", mixing in the common life of the people, and promoting the advancement of the kingdom of God in its ordinary channels of mercy, righteousness, and peace.

Key Lesson – Elisha

In the books of Kings, Elisha seems somewhat overshadowed by his powerful and illustrious master, Elijah, but there can be no doubt that he was a great and mighty prophet nevertheless. The outstanding lesson that we learn from Elisha's life is the importance of loyalty. But not just loyalty – a special kind of loyalty. Elisha learned how to know and follow the unspoken wishes of his master. Elisha was no doubt aware of the story of a previous servant of Elijah who, when instructed by Elijah to remain behind while he went into the wilderness to die, did exactly that. It is significant that, although the servant was not disobedient, this is the last mention of him in Scripture (1 Kings 19:2–3). Elisha demonstrated a sensitivity to Elijah's unspoken wishes, and was rewarded by God with a double portion of Elijah's spirit.

Hezekiah

Hezekiah: "Jehovah is my strength"

DAY 128 — A revival

2 Kings 18:1–12; 2 Chronicles 29:3–30:13

Hezekiah was the fourteenth king of Judah, and reigned in Jerusalem for some forty years. His first act in coming to the throne – at twenty-five years of age – was to reform the religious life of his people. True religion had been debased in Judah, and Hezekiah saw the need for immediate and sweeping changes. He destroyed idolatrous worship at various shrines, and even broke up the bronze serpent which had once been lifted up by Moses in the wilderness because the people of Judah had made it an object of worship. He restored worship in Solomon's Temple and invited people from around the nation to come to celebrate the Feast of the Passover, which had been neglected for many years.

"Love the Lord your God with all your heart and with all your soul and with all your mind and with all your strength." (Mark 12:30)

FURTHER THOUGHT

Is there anything in your life – material or spiritual – which you are cherishing and guarding, giving to it the worship and love due only to God Himself – anything you are making an idol of, burning incense to and thus obscuring the true vision of God? If so, get rid of it – today.

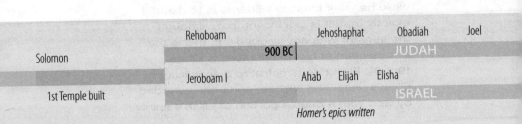

Solomon	Rehoboam		Jehoshaphat	Obadiah	Joel
		900 BC		JUDAH	
	Jeroboam I		Ahab Elijah Elisha		
1st Temple built				ISRAEL	
		Homer's epics written			

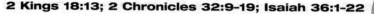

An attack

Hezekiah

Hezekiah: "Jehovah is my strength"

DAY 130 · A prayer

2 Kings 19:1–19; 2 Chronicles 32:20; Isaiah 37:14–20

When Hezekiah consulted Isaiah about the reviling words of the Assyrian field commander, he was told that his enemy, Sennacherib, would hear a rumour, return home and meet his death. Later, however, Hezekiah receives a threatening personal letter from Sennacherib demanding abject surrender. The king takes the letter into the Temple and spreads it out before the Lord. He prays that God will intervene to save His people and vindicate His Name before the heathen. Through the prophet Isaiah, God speaks to Hezekiah, assuring him that He will defend Jerusalem and that peace will once again come to Judah. The importance of this incident can be deduced from the fact that it is recorded more than once in Scripture.

"This is the confidence we have in approaching God: that if we ask anything according to his will, he hears us. And if we know that he hears us – whatever we ask – we know that we have what we asked of him."
(1 John 5:14–15)

FURTHER THOUGHT

Could it be that you, like Hezekiah, are confronted with a problem or situation which strikes fear and terror into your heart? Then do as Hezekiah did – and spread the matter out in believing prayer before the Lord. The God who answered Hezekiah will also answer you.

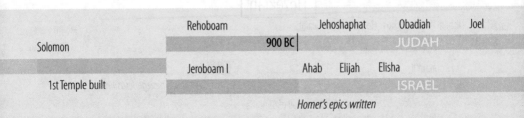

Solomon	Rehoboam		Jehoshaphat	Obadiah	Joel
		900 BC	JUDAH		
1st Temple built	Jeroboam I	Ahab	Elijah	Elisha	ISRAEL
	Homer's epics written				

2 Kings 19:20–37; 2 Chronicles 32:21–22; Isaiah 37:36

One night, as Jerusalem lies under siege by the Assyrian armies, God acts suddenly and brings about the death of 185,000 men by sending an avenging angel through the camp. Some commentators believe that the reference to a visiting angel is a picturesque way of saying that the army was overtaken by a powerful plague. The Scripture, however, is quite clear: "That night the angel of the Lord went out and put to death a hundred and eighty-five thousand men in the Assyrian camp" (2 Kings 19:35). Without doubt the deaths were due to God's supernatural intervention. Once Sennacherib realises that he is unable to fight against God, he returns home to meet his death at the hands of two of his sons – exactly as Isaiah predicted.

"... everyone born of God overcomes the world. This is the victory that has overcome the world, even our faith." (1 John 5:4)

FURTHER THOUGHT

Those who walk with God are not promised exemption from conflict, but they are promised victory in conflict. The victory may not materialise in the way we think or at the time we want – but in the end it comes. How can it not come? For "if God is for us, who can be against us?"

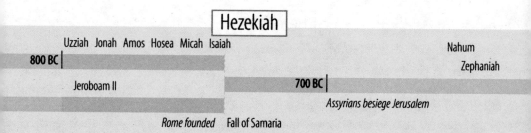

Hezekiah

Uzziah Jonah Amos Hosea Micah Isaiah

800 BC

Jeroboam II

700 BC

Assyrians besiege Jerusalem

Rome founded   Fall of Samaria

Nahum

Zephaniah

Hezekiah

DAY **132**

An extension

2 Kings 20:1-21

When Hezekiah fell ill, Isaiah visited him, telling him that he would not recover from his sickness and that he should prepare himself for death. Upon hearing this news, Hezekiah turns his face to the wall and cries out to God to heal him. God answers him by instructing Isaiah, who is just about to leave the palace, to return and inform the king that he will be healed from his sickness on the third day. God also indicated that Hezekiah would live another fifteen years. As a sign that this would truly happen, the sun's shadow was miraculously turned back in its natural decline. Under God's guidance, Isaiah prescribed a poultice of figs to draw out the infection in Hezekiah's boil, after which the king duly recovered.

"If you listen carefully to the voice of the Lord your God and do what is right in his eyes ... I will not bring on you any of the diseases I brought on the Egyptians, for I am the Lord, who heals you." (Ex. 15:26)

FURTHER THOUGHT

Most of us, when we fall sick, do everything we can to get well again. We visit the doctor, faithfully take the medicine he prescribes, and obediently follow his advice. Yet at such times, how many of us practise the principle contained in James 5:14? Worth thinking about?

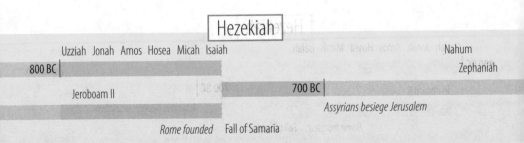

Uzziah Jonah Amos Hosea Micah Isaiah	Hezekiah	Nahum

800 BC

Zephaniah

Jeroboam II

700 BC

Assyrians besiege Jerusalem

Rome founded   Fall of Samaria

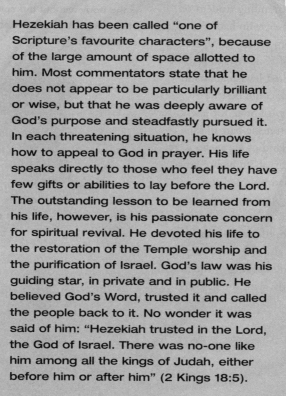

Hezekiah has been called "one of Scripture's favourite characters", because of the large amount of space allotted to him. Most commentators state that he does not appear to be particularly brilliant or wise, but that he was deeply aware of God's purpose and steadfastly pursued it. In each threatening situation, he knows how to appeal to God in prayer. His life speaks directly to those who feel they have few gifts or abilities to lay before the Lord. The outstanding lesson to be learned from his life, however, is his passionate concern for spiritual revival. He devoted his life to the restoration of the Temple worship and the purification of Israel. God's law was his guiding star, in private and in public. He believed God's Word, trusted it and called the people back to it. No wonder it was said of him: "Hezekiah trusted in the Lord, the God of Israel. There was no-one like him among all the kings of Judah, either before him or after him" (2 Kings 18:5).

DAY **133**

The scribe

Ezra 7:1-10

Ezra was an outstanding student of the law of Moses, who had descended from Aaron (v. 5), and a well-trusted official of King Artaxerxes I of Persia who administered Jewish affairs in his kingdom. His task could best be described as "Secretary of State for Jewish Affairs". He plays a strategic part in the return to their homeland of Jews who were still in exile in Babylon about eighty years after the first party had returned to Jerusalem. Ezra had diligently studied the Scriptures with a view to putting them into action in his own life and of teaching others to obey them also. He came to Jerusalem with the full backing of the king and, more importantly, with the blessing of God upon him.

"As the body without the spirit is dead, so faith without deeds is dead." (James 2:26)

FURTHER THOUGHT

Are you involved in teaching the truths of God's Word to others? Ezra's advice would be this: let your teaching be the overflow of a life that puts God's Word into practice day by day. Remember – you cannot make God's truth real to others until it is real to you.

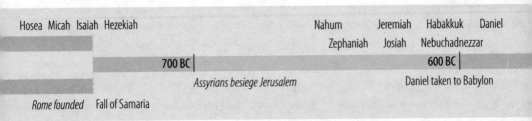

| Hosea | Micah | Isaiah | Hezekiah | | | Nahum | | Jeremiah | Habakkuk | Daniel |
| | | | | | | | Zephaniah | Josiah | Nebuchadnezzar | |

700 BC

Assyrians besiege Jerusalem

600 BC

Daniel taken to Babylon

Rome founded   Fall of Samaria

The leader

Ezra 7:11-28

Ezra receives great encouragement and support from King Artaxerxes in relation to the planned expedition to Jerusalem. The king makes a decree regarding financial provision for the task, and authorising Ezra to appoint suitable men as magistrates to administer the law and punish evildoers. All Jews who feel inclined to return to Jerusalem are free to depart, and Ezra is authorised to carry the offerings for the Temple, to purchase sacrificial animals and to use the rest of the money as he sees fit. A sizeable group decides to leave Babylon with Ezra, and they set out on the first day of the first month – Nisan – in 458 BC, the seventh year of King Artaxerxes' reign.

"For it is by grace you have been saved, through faith – and this not from yourselves, it is the gift of God – not by works, so that no-one can boast."
(Eph. 2:8–9)

FURTHER THOUGHT

History records that the group which left Babylon with Ezra amounted to less than 2,000 people – a small number for such an enormous task. But God always likes to engineer situations so that when the work is accomplished, He is seen to have had the biggest part in it!

			Ezra			
		Zechariah				
Ezekiel		Cyrus	Haggai	Esther	Nehemiah	Malachi
FALL OF JUDAH			500 BC			400 BC
	Exile in Babylon	2nd Temple built	Iron age begins in Britain		Nehemiah rebuilds walls of Jerusalem	
	Jerusalem destroyed	Zerubbabel and main party return		Ezra returns		

DAY 135

The administrator

Ezra 8:1–20

Ezra gathers those who have shown themselves eager and willing to return to Jerusalem at a camp by a canal, and conducts a roll-call. The list of families is similar to the earlier one recorded in chapter 2, and may indicate that some were now going to rejoin other members of the family who had returned earlier. Ezra's review shows up the fact that there are no Levites – ministers for the house of God – among the emigrants. Word is sent to a nearby Jewish community, and soon 38 Levites join the group along with 220 Temple servants. After a period of fasting and prayer for a safe journey, the company set out for the Holy City.

"Be very careful, then, how you live – not as unwise but as wise, making the most of every opportunity, because the days are evil. Therefore do not be foolish, but understand what the Lord's will is." (Eph. 5:15–17)

FURTHER THOUGHT

One dreads to think what might have happened if Ezra had taken things for granted and had not paused to make a careful check-up. Pause today in your busy life, and ask yourself: How am I doing as a Christian? Am I further forward in the Christian life now than I was this time last year?

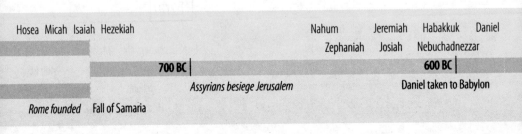

| Hosea | Micah | Isaiah | Hezekiah | | Nahum | Jeremiah | Habakkuk | Daniel |
| | | | | | Zephaniah | Josiah | Nebuchadnezzar | |

700 BC

Assyrians besiege Jerusalem

600 BC

Daniel taken to Babylon

Rome founded   Fall of Samaria

The example

Ezra 8:21–36

It is estimated by some commentators that the money and treasure which Ezra carried from Babylon to Jerusalem was worth, in present-day values, over a million pounds. Ezra decides, however, after fasting and prayer, to trust the Lord for protection on the 900-mile journey from Babylon to Jerusalem and not to ask the king for a military escort. Ezra wisely decides to have all the treasures in his possession weighed before and after the journey, thus lessening the possibility of any false accusations being made against him should he incur the wrath of those who might be against his spiritual reforms.

"... give thanks in all circumstances, for this is God's will for you in Christ Jesus." (1 Thess. 5:18)

FURTHER THOUGHT

Ezra's decision to trust in God rather than in military might was a daring step of faith. And when the exiles arrive safely, their gratitude knows no bounds. How grateful are you for God's leadings and deliverances in your life? Remember – gratitude is only as sincere as the effort you make to express it.

Ezra

		Zechariah				
Ezekiel	Cyrus	Haggai		Esther	Nehemiah	Malachi
FALL OF JUDAH		**500 BC**				**400 BC**
Exile in Babylon	2nd Temple built		Iron age begins in Britain	Nehemiah rebuilds walls of Jerusalem
Jerusalem destroyed	Zerubbabel and main party return			Ezra returns

DAY 137

The intercessor

Ezra 9:1-15

Upon his arrival in Jerusalem, Ezra learns that his fellow countrymen have become involved in mixed marriages with heathen women, and that this has been practised also by some of the priests and Levites. The news causes him considerable concern, and he shows his grief in the customary manner of those days – by tearing his garments and plucking out hair from his head and beard. Like-minded Jews gather around him until the time of the evening sacrifice, when Ezra pours out before God a prayer of confession and intercession. Although Ezra himself is not guilty of any offence, he identifies with the sin of his people – an act which can be observed in many Old Testament saints and prophets.

"... if my people, who are called by my name, will humble themselves and pray and seek my face and turn from their wicked ways, then will I hear from heaven and will forgive their sin and will heal their land." (2 Chron, 7:14)

FURTHER THOUGHT

Examine Ezra's prayer and you will find such words as "guilt", "sins", "ashamed" and "disgraced". How desperately we need intercessors like Ezra who will identify themselves with the sins of the nation, and cry to God in fervent, believing prayer for healing and restoration.

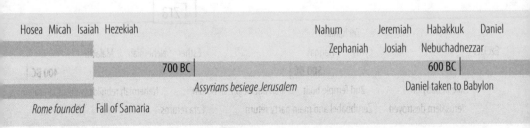

Hosea	Micah	Isaiah	Hezekiah			Nahum		Jeremiah	Habakkuk	Daniel
							Zephaniah	Josiah	Nebuchadnezzar	
			700 BC						600 BC	
			Assyrians besiege Jerusalem						Daniel taken to Babylon	
Rome founded	Fall of Samaria									

Ezra 10:1–44

A large crowd gathers around Ezra as he weeps and prays, and as they observe his grief they, too, weep bitterly. Shecaniah, one of the group, acts as spokesman and openly confesses their sin, expressing, at the same time, hope in God's mercy as they promise to put things right. Ezra calls upon the people to make a vow that they will rid themselves of their sin and bring their lives into line with God's law. After Ezra had fasted and prayed, a proclamation is made calling for a national assembly where a decision is made to let local officials handle the corrective details. Those with heathen partners are required to formally put away their spouses and children.

" Do whatever he tells you." (John 2:5)

FURTHER THOUGHT

Despite the driving rain, the issue was so important that it had to be dealt with immediately – an excellent example of how to tackle a spiritual problem. If a thing is worth doing, it is worth doing now. "Time will heal" may be true in relation to some things, but never in relation to sin.

Ezra

		Zechariah					
Ezekiel	Cyrus	Haggai		Esther	Nehemiah	Malachi	
FALL OF JUDAH		500 BC					400 BC
Exile in Babylon	2nd Temple built	*Iron age begins in Britain*		Nehemiah rebuilds walls of Jerusalem			
Jerusalem destroyed	Zerubbabel and main party return		Ezra returns				

DAY 139

The preacher

Nehemiah 8:1–18; Ezra 7:10–11

Soon after the rebuilding of Jerusalem's walls is completed, the people are gathered together to rededicate themselves to God. Ezra is the chief expositor of the law, and reads and preaches from a wooden platform, assisted by thirteen Levites (Neh. 8:1–8). The readings continue through the seven days of the feast (Neh. 8:18), punctuated by comments and explanations by Ezra. The effect of the reading of the law on the people is remarkable. They break out into weeping as they realise in how many ways they have transgressed God's commandments. The recognition of Ezra as chief expositor rested on the fact that he had put in many years of faithful and diligent study.

"Do your best to present yourself to God as one approved, a workman who does not need to be ashamed and who correctly handles the word of truth." (2 Tim. 2:15)

FURTHER THOUGHT

How much time do you give to diligent study and perusal of the Word of God? No one has ever entered into a great ministry of Bible exposition until he or she has spent time meditating on, analysing and memorising the Scriptures. There are no short cuts to effective Christian service.

	Zechariah			Ezra			
Ezekiel	Cyrus	Haggai			Esther	Nehemiah	Malachi
FALL OF JUDAH		500 BC					400 BC
Exile in Babylon	2nd Temple built		Iron age begins in Britain		Nehemiah rebuilds walls of Jerusalem		
Jerusalem destroyed	Zerubbabel and main party return			Ezra returns			

Ezra – *revivalist and reformer*

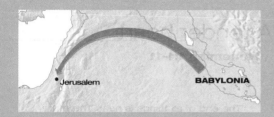

Jerusalem · BABYLONIA

Reconstruction. Restoration. Revival. After 70 years of captivity in Babylonia it is time for the Jews to return to their homeland. The first expedition, led by Zerubbabel, makes the 900-mile trek from Persia to Jerusalem to rebuild the temple. After a 58-year parenthesis, Ezra the priest sets out with his band of priests and Levites to rebuild the spiritual life of the returning exiles.

J Vernon McGee writes the following about Ezra:

"He is one of the characters who has not received proper recognition. Ezra was a descendant of Hilkiah, the high priest (Ezra 7:1), who found a copy of the law during the reign of Josiah (2 Chron. 34:14); Ezra, as a priest, was unable to serve during the captivity, but he gave his time to a study of the Word of God – he was a 'ready scribe in the law of Moses' (Ezra 7:6). Ezra was a revivalist and reformer. The revival began with the reading of the Word of God by Ezra (see Neh. 8). Also he probably was the writer of 1st and 2nd Chronicles and of Psalm 119, which exalts the Word of God. He organised the synagogue, and was the founder of the order of scribes, helped settle the canon of Scripture and arranged the Psalms."

Key Lesson – Ezra

The whole thrust of Ezra's life was to secure the worship of God, free from all contamination. In accomplishing this, he must have a devoted people also free from contamination, a priesthood still more separate, and a ritual carefully guarded and protected from defilement. There is something of the schoolmaster in Ezra, but like the law of God which he loved so devoutly, he is a schoolmaster who brings us to Christ. His contribution to the times in which he lived was outstanding, for he laid down a strong Biblical foundation upon which other reformers could build. The greatest characteristic of his life was his devotion and love for the Scriptures. He shows us that the more time we are prepared to spend in studying and perusing the Word of God, the more greatly and powerfully God is able to use us.

Nehemiah

DAY 140   A tender heart

Nehemiah 1:1–11

Nehemiah was a cupbearer – or, in modern language, a butler – at the court of King Artaxerxes I of Persia, a position of honour and influence. He hears from his brother that Jerusalem's walls are in ruins and the inhabitants greatly discouraged. Immediately Nehemiah enters upon a four-month period of prayer and fasting, during which time he identifies with the whole Jewish nation, and intercedes for them. Like Ezra, his contemporary, he confesses the sins of his people and takes their backsliding into his own heart. He particularly prays that God will give him favour with King Artaxerxes when he approaches him for permission to visit the ancient city in order to help restore it to its former glory.

"The end of all things is near. Therefore be clear minded and self-controlled so that you can pray." (1 Pet. 4:7)

FURTHER THOUGHT

Although other means are often necessary to bring about God's purposes, prayer must always be primary. Communion with God will best prepare us for our dealings with others. It is still true that "the prayer of a righteous man is powerful and effective" (James 5:16).

Hosea	Micah	Isaiah	Hezekiah		Nahum		Jeremiah	Habakkuk	Daniel
					Zephaniah	Josiah		Nebuchadnezzar	

700 BC   600 BC

Assyrians besiege Jerusalem   Daniel taken to Babylon

Rome founded   Fall of Samaria

A cupbearer in ancient times was expected to always be cheerful in a monarch's presence, and when the king notices Nehemiah's sadness, Nehemiah fears for the consequences. He explains to the king that his sadness arises from the news he has received concerning the city of Jerusalem, and the king graciously invites Nehemiah to make any request he wishes. After a quick prayer, Nehemiah ventures to ask the king's permission to go to Jerusalem and undertake the work of rebuilding the city's walls. The king grants his request, provides him with letters of authority and Nehemiah sets out with an armed escort on his long journey.

"Woe to you who are complacent in Zion, and to you who feel secure on Mount Samaria ..." (Amos 6:1)

FURTHER THOUGHT

Despite Nehemiah's comfortable position in Persia, he felt deep sadness over the broken-down walls of Jerusalem. In some places, the walls of God's Church need rebuilding, too. Does this cause you sorrow and pain? Or does business or pleasure so engage your attention that Zion's welfare means nothing to you?

			Nehemiah	
	Zechariah		Ezra	
Ezekiel	Cyrus	Haggai	Esther	Malachi
FALL OF JUDAH		500 BC		400 BC
Exile in Babylon	2nd Temple built	Iron age begins in Britain		Nehemiah rebuilds walls of Jerusalem
Jerusalem destroyed	Zerubbabel and main party return		Ezra returns	

Nehemiah

Nehemiah: "Jehovah comforts"

DAY 142 — A courageous spirit

Nehemiah 2:11–20

Upon his arrival at Jerusalem, one of the first things Nehemiah does is to survey the extent of the damage to the walls and gates of the city. Gathering together a small band of men, he instructs them to tell no one of his plans to rebuild the city walls until after he has completed his inspection – this being the reason why he conducts his survey under cover of darkness. When he later announces to the Jewish leaders that he has come to rebuild the ruined city walls and that he has God's blessing and King Artaxerxes' approval, everyone is keen to proceed with the work. Sanballat and Tobiah are highly displeased, and do everything they can to hinder the project.

"Consider it pure joy, my brothers, whenever you face trials of many kinds, because you know that the testing of your faith develops perseverance. Perseverance must finish its work so that you may be mature and complete ..." (James 1:2–4)

FURTHER THOUGHT

If God has called you to do a special work for Him, then you must come to terms right away with the fact that at some time you will face opposition. Don't be discouraged by this, for the stronger the opposition the bigger the opportunity. Satan never opposes anything that is insignificant.

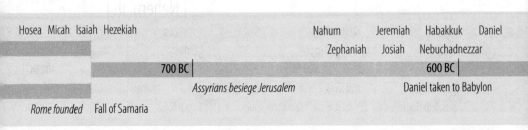

| Hosea | Micah | Isaiah | Hezekiah | | Nahum | Jeremiah | Habakkuk | Daniel |
| | | | | | Zephaniah | Josiah | Nebuchadnezzar | |

700 BC

Assyrians besiege Jerusalem

600 BC

Daniel taken to Babylon

Rome founded   Fall of Samaria

An undaunted will

Nehemiah 3:1–32; 4:1–11

As the Jews worked steadily under Nehemiah's inspiring leadership, the walls of the city soon begin to rise once more. Sanballat and Tobiah continue their opposition by pouring scorn on the builders and criticising every move that is made. The propaganda war waged by Sanballat and Tobiah is unsuccessful, however, and Nehemiah and the workmen give themselves even more wholeheartedly to the task in hand. A further attempt is made to halt the work of rebuilding when some of Jerusalem's neighbours plot a concerted attack. The Jews pray to God for protection and mount a guard to keep the enemy under constant observation. Despite all obstacles, the walls continue to rise.

"I have told you these things, so that in me you may have peace. In this world you will have trouble. But take heart! I have overcome the world." (John 16:33)

FURTHER THOUGHT

Some Christians think that God should preserve His people from difficulties when they are doing His will, but the genius of Christianity is that God enables us to overcome all difficulties while accomplishing the work which He has set us to do.

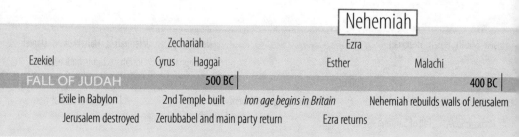

Nehemiah

		Zechariah			Ezra		
Ezekiel		Cyrus	Haggai		Esther	Malachi	
FALL OF JUDAH			**500 BC**				**400 BC**
	Exile in Babylon	2nd Temple built		*Iron age begins in Britain*		Nehemiah rebuilds walls of Jerusalem	
	Jerusalem destroyed	Zerubbabel and main party return			Ezra returns		

Nehemiah

DAY 144   A diligent plan

Nehemiah 4:12–23

Some of Israel's enemies make their way into the city of Jerusalem with a view to damaging the morale of the workmen, and spread a rumour that there is to be a surprise attack. Although Nehemiah has letters of approval for what he is doing, he realises that these do not preclude such an attack in this remote part of the Persian empire. He decides to keep half the men on armed guard while the other half work, and for all to carry arms. He works alongside his workmen, staying in the same clothes for twenty-four hours a day, with a trumpeter beside him to sound the alarm in case of attack. His carefully laid plans are diligently followed, and day by day the work progresses.

"As God's fellow-workers we urge you not to receive God's grace in vain ... I tell you, now is the time of God's favour, now is the day of salvation."
(2 Cor. 6:1–2)

FURTHER THOUGHT

Someone said that the Christian life is "a sword and trowel exercise". Like Nehemiah's workers, we must go about our task with a tool in one hand and a weapon in the other. And why? Look up 1 Peter 5:8 and you'll see!

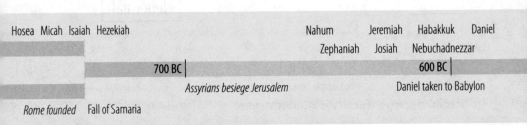

| Hosea | Micah | Isaiah | Hezekiah | | Nahum | Jeremiah | Habakkuk | Daniel |
| | | | | | Zephaniah | Josiah | Nebuchadnezzar | |

700 BC | 600 BC |

Assyrians besiege Jerusalem   Daniel taken to Babylon

Rome founded   Fall of Samaria

Having failed to stop the building of the walls by ridicule, rumours and threats, an attempt is made by Israel's enemies to get rid of Nehemiah himself. He receives an invitation to a conference, but refuses to attend, saying: "I am carrying on a great project and cannot go down" (v. 3). After this has happened several times, an open letter is sent to him accusing him of planning to revolt and set himself up as king, but Nehemiah boldly refutes their lies. Their plans once again having failed, Sanballat and Tobiah hire Shemaiah to lure Nehemiah into a compromising situation in which he could be discredited as a coward – but he wisely avoids the trap (vv. 10–13).

"... for Satan himself masquerades as an angel of light. It is not surprising, then, if his servants masquerade as servants of righteousness. Their end will be what their actions deserve."
(2 Cor 11:14–15)

FURTHER THOUGHT

Ever heard Satan saying to you: "Come down from those high standards ... Be a Christian if you like, but don't be so fanatical ... Take things a little easier ..."? Then give him this answer: "I am doing a great work and I cannot come down."

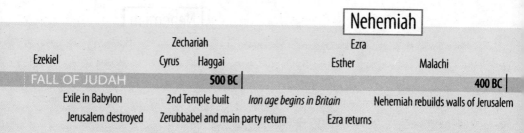

				Nehemiah	
	Zechariah			Ezra	
Ezekiel	Cyrus	Haggai		Esther	Malachi
FALL OF JUDAH		**500 BC**			**400 BC**
Exile in Babylon	2nd Temple built		*Iron age begins in Britain*		Nehemiah rebuilds walls of Jerusalem
Jerusalem destroyed	Zerubbabel and main party return			Ezra returns	

Nehemiah

DAY 146   A completed task

Nehemiah 7:1-73

It takes just fifty-two days for Nehemiah to complete the tremendous task of rebuilding the ruined walls of Jerusalem. Of course, the walls did not have to be built from ground level throughout, but it was a gigantic task nevertheless – especially when you consider the opposition and problems that beset the project. What a prayerful and inspiring leader Nehemiah proved to be. Having completed the task, however, Nehemiah does not rest on his laurels, but appoints godly men to supervise the guarding of the newly fortified city and its inhabitants. He then organises a census of all the families of Israel, so that he can better administer the life and development of the community.

"I urge, then, first of all, that requests, prayers, intercession and thanksgiving be made for everyone – for kings and all those in authority, that we may live peaceful and quiet lives in all godliness and holiness." (1 Tim. 2:1–2)

FURTHER THOUGHT

Did you notice that the priests who could not prove their ancestry were dismissed from the priesthood (Neh 7:64)? Nehemiah knew that unless the priesthood was pure, it would soon destroy the moral and spiritual fibre of the people. Pray for your pastor or spiritual leader right now.

		Nehemiah		
	Zechariah		Ezra	
Ezekiel	Cyrus	Haggai	Esther	Malachi
FALL OF JUDAH		500 BC		400 BC
Exile in Babylon	2nd Temple built	Iron age begins in Britain	Nehemiah rebuilds walls of Jerusalem	
Jerusalem destroyed	Zerubbabel and main party return		Ezra returns	

The gates of Nehemiah

	Picture of the Christian life
The Sheep Gate (3:1)	This speaks of the cross **(John 10:11)**
The Fish Gate (3:3)	This speaks of soul-winning **(Matt 4:19)**
The Jeshanah or Old Gate (3:6)	This speaks of our old nature **(Rom 6:1–23)**
The Valley Gate (3:13)	This speaks of suffering and testing **(2 Cor. 1:3–5)**
The Dung Gate (3:14)	This speaks of the works of the flesh **(Gal. 5:16–21)**
The Fountain Gate (3:15)	This speaks of the Holy Spirit **(John 7:37–39)**
The Water Gate (3:26)	This speaks of the Word of God **(John 4:10–14)**
The Horse Gate (3:28)	This speaks of believers' warfare **(Eph 6:10–17)**
The Inspection Gate (3:31)	This was thought to be the judgement gate and therefore speaks of the judgement seat of Christ **(1 Cor. 3:9–15; 2 Cor. 5:10)**

Key Lesson – Nehemiah

Without doubt, Nehemiah was one of the most energetic, shrewd and resourceful of all the Old Testament characters. Despite fierce opposition, he succeeded in rebuilding the walls of Jerusalem in only fifty-two days. This was his greatest contribution to the reconstruction of Jewish faith and worship and the inauguration of the post-exilic Jewish state. Nehemiah was a deeply devout man, and the retention of his faith and patriotism amid the pressures of a heathen environment show that he possessed "the inner walls that protect the soul's secret shrine". His confidence that he was doing God's work shone through in everything he did. The main lesson to be learned from his life, however, is the importance of speedily referring each decision and crisis to God in simple, forthright prayer. And anyone who hasn't yet learned that lesson will be prone to fear, anxiety and despair.

Esther
Esther: "Star"

DAY **147**

A beautiful maiden

Esther 2:1–7

The story of Esther begins in the palace of King Xerxes who, after giving a six-month display of his imperial wealth, brings things to an end with a great feast. After seven days of feasting and revelry the king summons his wife, Queen Vashti, to appear before the assembled company and show off her beauty. This she refuses to do and is promptly deposed by the angry despot. When Xerxes' anger cools, he begins to have second thoughts about his rash decision (v. 1), but his courtiers urge him to choose a successor to Vashti. Many beautiful maidens are brought to the palace for him to select his new queen, one of them being the orphan Jewess, Hadassah – or, as she later came to be known – Esther.

"If I rise on the wings of the dawn, if I settle on the far side of the sea, even there your hand will guide me, your right hand will hold me fast."
(Psa. 139:9–10)

FURTHER THOUGHT

Did you know that the book of Esther is the only book in the Bible in which the Name of God is not mentioned? But though His Name is not to be seen anywhere in its pages, His guiding hand is evident in every chapter. A little bit like life – don't you think?

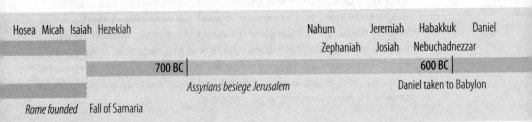

| Hosea | Micah | Isaiah | Hezekiah | | Nahum | Jeremiah | Habakkuk | Daniel |
| | | | | | Zephaniah | Josiah | Nebuchadnezzar | |

| 700 BC | | 600 BC |

Assyrians besiege Jerusalem — Daniel taken to Babylon

Rome founded   Fall of Samaria

Esther 2:8-16

Mordecai, the cousin of Esther, had been brought to Babylon as a captive by Nebuchadnezzar (v. 6) and had adopted the orphaned Esther as his daughter. Esther was extremely beautiful and caught the attention of the keeper of the king's harem, who arranged for her to have an early meeting with the king. During the year-long period of preparation which was required before being presented to the king, Esther acted with grace and discretion, followed the advice that was given to her and was greatly admired by all who saw her. King Xerxes was captivated by Esther's beauty, and loved her more than all the other women he had seen.

"'For my thoughts are not your thoughts, neither are your ways my ways,' declares the Lord." (Isa. 55:8)

FURTHER THOUGHT

Do you begin to see why Mordecai and Esther did not return to Jerusalem with the other expatriates? God wanted to use them in His plan to save the Jews in Persia from extinction. He often allows our personal plans to fail so that we might contribute to His bigger and better ones. Learned that yet?

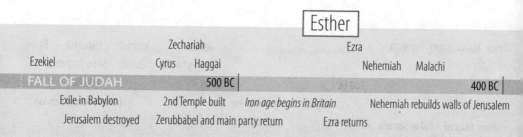

	Zechariah				Ezra		
Ezekiel	Cyrus	Haggai				Nehemiah	Malachi

FALL OF JUDAH   500 BC   Esther   400 BC

Exile in Babylon   2nd Temple built   *Iron age begins in Britain*   Nehemiah rebuilds walls of Jerusalem

Jerusalem destroyed   Zerubbabel and main party return   Ezra returns

Esther

Esther: "Star"

DAY 149

Crowned as queen

Esther 2:17-23

Hebrew tradition places Esther among the three most beautiful women who have ever lived, and the king, having made his choice, sets the royal crown upon her head. He organises a great banquet in Esther's honour, and issues a decree that everyone in his kingdom is to benefit from a reduction in tax! Esther now occupies the highest position in the Persian empire open to a woman – and one which is soon to prove crucial to the survival of all the Jews living there. Mordecai overhears a plot against the king's life and informs Esther who, in turn, conveys the information to the king. After investigation, the two conspirators are convicted and hanged – the whole affair being recorded in the official archives.

"Are not two sparrows sold for a penny? Yet not one of them will fall to the ground apart from the will of your Father. And even the very hairs of your head are all numbered. So don't be afraid; you are worth more than many sparrows." (Matt. 10:29–31)

FURTHER THOUGHT

It might seem irrelevant that after the hanging of the two conspirators, all the details of the event are written down, including Mordecai's name. But God's sovereignty works through seeming irrelevancies. Have you discovered that yet?

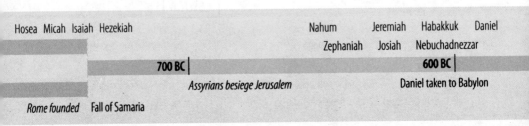

| Hosea | Micah | Isaiah | Hezekiah | | Nahum | Jeremiah | Habakkuk | Daniel |
| | | | | | Zephaniah | Josiah | Nebuchadnezzar | |

700 BC

Assyrians besiege Jerusalem

600 BC

Daniel taken to Babylon

Rome founded   Fall of Samaria

Willing to perish

Esther 3:1–4:17

King Xerxes promotes an Agagite by the name of Haman to be his prime minister, decreeing that everyone should acknowledge his prominent position by bowing down before him. This Mordecai refuses to do, and when challenged, explains that because he is a Jew he cannot agree to bow down before anyone but God. Upon hearing his, Haman becomes extremely angry and determines to destroy, not only Mordecai, but every Jew in the Persian empire. Cunningly, he persuades the king to issue a royal decree calling for the massacre of all the Jews. Mordecai, hearing of this decree, pleads with Esther to intercede with the king, affirming that this could well be the reason why she finds herself in the royal palace.

"Therefore, I urge you, brothers, in view of God's mercy, to offer your bodies as living sacrifices, holy and pleasing to God – this is your spiritual act of worship." (Rom. 12:1)

FURTHER THOUGHT

The strength and power of Esther's magnificent decision has been summed up most powerfully by J. Drinkwater. Ponder the prayer and make it your very own: "Knowledge we ask – knowledge Thou hast lent But, Lord, the will – there lies our bitter need, Give us to build above the deep intent The deed ... the deed."

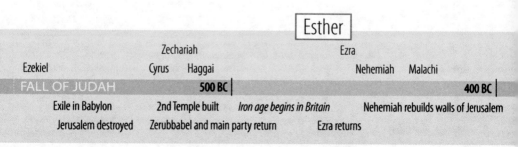

		Zechariah		Ezra		
Ezekiel		Cyrus	Haggai		Nehemiah	Malachi
FALL OF JUDAH			500 BC			400 BC
	Exile in Babylon		2nd Temple built	*Iron age begins in Britain*		Nehemiah rebuilds walls of Jerusalem
	Jerusalem destroyed		Zerubbabel and main party return		Ezra returns	

Esther

Esther

Esther: "Star"

DAY 151   A tactful approach

Esther 5:1–14

After considering Mordecai's request to intercede with Xerxes for the life of her people, Esther puts on her royal robes, enters the inner court and seeks an audience with the king. When Esther is given permission to approach the king, she invites him and Haman to join her in a meal later that day. At the meal the king asks Esther to make her request, but she declines and invites them to another meal the next day. Haman tells his wife and friends about the growing anger he feels against Mordecai, and they suggest that he build a gallows and arrange the next day for Mordecai to be hanged. That night the king is unable to sleep, and asks that the archives be read to him. He hears during the reading of Mordecai's part in foiling the plot against him.

"But when the time had fully come, God sent his Son, born of a woman, born under law, to redeem those under law, that we might receive the full rights of sons." (Gal. 4:4–5)

FURTHER THOUGHT

What is the explanation for Esther's delaying tactics? Had she lost her nerve? Some commentators think so. Perhaps a more correct interpretation is that her prayer and fasting had sensitised her to the proper timing for her request. After all, doesn't time spent with God enable us to detect His perfect timing in everything?

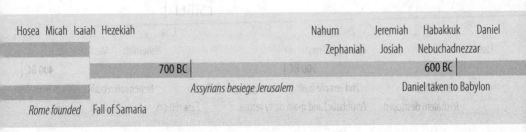

Hosea	Micah	Isaiah	Hezekiah				Nahum		Jeremiah	Habakkuk	Daniel
							Zephaniah		Josiah	Nebuchadnezzar	
				700 BC						600 BC	
					Assyrians besiege Jerusalem					*Daniel taken to Babylon*	
Rome founded		Fall of Samaria									

180

A courageous request

Esther 6:1–7:10

Once the king has been made aware of Mordecai's part in saving his life, he gives orders that Mordecai is to be publicly honoured – and Haman, much to his dismay, is obliged to enter into the celebrations. At dinner Esther boldly denounces Haman, and courageously identifies with her doomed people, pleading with the king to save them from destruction. The king, in great anger, orders Haman to be executed on the very gallows which he had built for Mordecai. Now that Mordecai's relationship to Esther is out in the open, the king summons Mordecai and appoints him as Haman's successor, giving him the same power that Haman had possessed (Esth. 8:2).

"The wicked man flees though no-one pursues, but the righteous are as bold as a lion." (Prov. 28:1)

FURTHER THOUGHT

Esther's intercession is a model on which we, as Christians, can safely build. She is bold, simple, plain and direct. "All intercession," it has been said, "starts with identification." It begins when we allow the groan of God to enter our own souls.

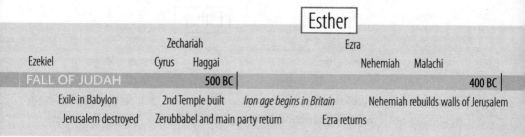

			Esther		
	Zechariah			Ezra	
Ezekiel	Cyrus	Haggai		Nehemiah	Malachi
FALL OF JUDAH		500 BC			400 BC
Exile in Babylon	2nd Temple built	*Iron age begins in Britain*		Nehemiah rebuilds walls of Jerusalem	
Jerusalem destroyed	Zerubbabel and main party return		Ezra returns		

Esther

DAY **153**

A mighty deliverance

Esther 8:1-9:17

H aman, the arch-enemy of the Jews, is now dead, but the decree he inspired ordering the massacre of the Jews still stands. Queen Esther tearfully and eloquently pleads with the king for her people to be spared. Xerxes then issues another decree, devised by Mordecai, which authorises the Jews to defend themselves against any attacks which may be made on them arising from the first edict. As a result, more than 75,000 of their enemies perish, and the Jews celebrate their mighty deliverance, calling the celebration "Purim". To this day the book of Esther is read by the Jews every year at the Feast of Purim (see Esther 9:32).

"And we know that in all things God works for the good of those who love him, who have been called according to his purpose." (Rom. 8:28)

FURTHER THOUGHT

Cast your mind back over the story of Esther and Mordecai right now, and does not the sovereignty of God appear in a more awesome light than ever before? Let this truth entwine itself around your heart – nothing can frustrate the purpose of our great and wonderful God. Nothing!

	Zechariah			Ezra		
Ezekiel	Cyrus	Haggai			Nehemiah	Malachi
FALL OF JUDAH		**500 BC**				**400 BC**
Exile in Babylon	2nd Temple built		*Iron age begins in Britain*		Nehemiah rebuilds walls of Jerusalem	
Jerusalem destroyed	Zerubbabel and main party return			Ezra returns		

Esther

God's providence in Esther

The name of God never appears in the book of Esther. For this reason, the early Church was somewhat reluctant at first to accept this book as part of the inspired canon, but it was soon regarded as such. In spite of the omission of any name for deity, there is no other book in all the Bible where God is more evidently at work behind the scenes, than in this book. The key in understanding the book of Esther is the word "providence" – literally meaning, "to provide in advance". Providence has been defined by the great theologian, Strong, as follows: "Providence is that continuous agency of God by which He makes all events of the physical and moral world fulfil the original design with which He created it." Providence has also been defined as "the hand of God in the glove of history." Thus we can, with full justification, pen the words of Romans 8:28 across the book of Esther: "We know that in all things God works for the good of those who love him, who have been called according to his purpose."

Key Lesson – Esther

Queen Esther is one of the greatest heroines of Jewish history, whose story is read every year at the Feast of Purim. Election to the high office of queen had no effect on Esther's love and loyalty toward her people. She remained unspoilt amid the pomp and splendour of her surroundings. She was capable, energetic, brave and patriotic – a strong, unselfish woman conquering almost insuperable opposition and choosing a course of terrible danger to herself for the sake of her beloved people. Esther had a deep sense of destiny in her life – a feeling that she had "come to royal position for such a time as this" (Esth. 4:14). This is undoubtedly the main lesson we learn from her life – the fact that God's timing is punctual and perfect. We must learn to trust that timing, and recognise that our presence in God's kingdom is not by chance, but by choice. Each one of us has come to the kingdom "for such a time as this".

DAY 154

His terrible trials

Job 1:1-22

Job is one of the most outstanding characters in the whole of Scripture. In Ezekiel 14:14, God declares that his righteousness is on a par with that of Daniel and Noah. At the beginning of his career, Job appears to be a very rich man, with much livestock and a large household. Satan sees Job's spiritual and material prosperity and slanders him before God, affirming that Job's spirituality will crumble if his material assets are removed. God allows Satan to put Job through a period of testing and soon, through a series of catastrophes, the good man loses his children, his servants and his livestock. Job's faith withstands these trials, and he refuses to blame God or fall into sin.

"These have come so that your faith – of greater worth than gold, which perishes even though refined by fire – may be proved genuine and may result in praise, glory and honour when Jesus Christ is revealed." (1 Pet. 1:7)

FURTHER THOUGHT

See how Satan slanders Job. This is a common device of slanderers – to suggest that which they have no reason to think is true. But as there is nothing we should dread more than being hypocrites, so there is nothing we need to dread less than being called and counted so without cause.

Job

Noah

Abraham

3000 BC

2000 BC

Flood

Great Pyramid Age in Egypt begins

Job 2:1–10

Satan once again presents himself in the heavenly court, and when God reminds him that Job still retains his faith and integrity, Satan argues that if Job suffers physically, his faith will fail. God therefore permits Satan to afflict Job with ill health, but will not permit his life to be endangered. Job contracts a loathsome skin disease which causes him to be expelled from society. He sits in the town refuse dump, where he is advised by his wife to curse God and die. Despite his personal suffering, however, Job stubbornly refuses to say anything against God, thus making Satan's second test ineffective.

"What, then, shall we say in response to this? If God is for us, who can be against us?" (Rom. 8:31)

FURTHER THOUGHT

We ought never to forget that however formidable an enemy Satan appears, he is an enemy on a leash. He can only work within certain limits – limits that are set by the grace and wisdom of God. If God did not put a leash on that "roaring lion", how easily he would overcome us.

Isaac

| 1900 BC |

Bronze Age begins in Britain

Abraham leaves Ur

Jacob

| 1800 BC |

Job

DAY 156 — His misguided friends

Job 2:11-13; 4:1-21; 8:1-22; 11:1-20; 32:1-22; 16:2

Three of Job's friends come to visit him and sit with him for seven days in silent sympathy. They believe that Job's loss of health, family and possessions is due to the fact that God is punishing him for some secret sin, and attempt to convince Job that this is the cause of his problems. Job stoutly denies this, and hours of disputing follow in which a fourth and younger man joins in. The arguments move backwards and forwards and no one is convinced. After a while Job is almost driven to distraction by the attempts of his friends to counsel him, and their lack of real empathy and understanding drive him to look for true comfort in God.

"Therefore let us stop passing judgment on one another. Instead, make up your mind not to put any stumbling-block or obstacle in your brother's way." (Rom. 14:13)

FURTHER THOUGHT

Job's friends started their ministry of counselling well – by sitting with him in silent sympathy. How sad that they allowed themselves to become judgmental, thus undoing the work they had begun. When next you sit down with someone in trouble, remember that it's better to say nothing than to say the wrong thing.

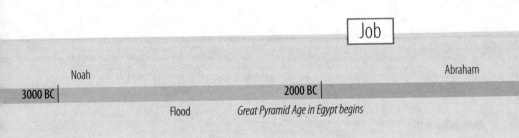

Job

Noah   Abraham

3000 BC   2000 BC

Flood   *Great Pyramid Age in Egypt begins*

His honest response

Job 6:1-7:21

In chapter 6 we see how Job responds to the remarks made by one of his friends, Eliphaz the Temanite. The seven-day silence had been broken by an outburst from Job in which he curses the day he was born (Job 3:1–19). He now justifies himself for that cry of anguish (6:1–7), and asks that God will terminate his life and thus bring his pain and suffering to an end (vv. 8–9). He goes on to rebuke his friends for not trying to understand his predicament (vv. 14–21) and asks for honest words that will show him where he is wrong (vv. 24–27), promising that their honesty will be matched by his (v. 28). Job then speaks directly to God, and honestly shares his thoughts and feelings with the Almighty.

"Why are you downcast, O my soul? Why so disturbed within me? Put your hope in God, for I will yet praise him, my Saviour and my God." (Psa. 42:5)

FURTHER THOUGHT

One of the most damaging things we can do to our personality is to fail to honestly acknowledge our personal feelings – whatever they may be. Repressed or suppressed feelings contribute to inner conflict. So the next time you feel down, don't hide those feelings. Do as Job did, and talk to God about them.

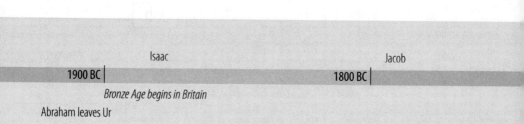

Isaac

1900 BC

Bronze Age begins in Britain

Abraham leaves Ur

Jacob

1800 BC

DAY **158**

His glorious God
Job 38:1–41:34

The speeches of the four wise men and of Job being ended – God now speaks. First He describes His creative works in the inanimate world (ch. 38), and then goes on to the animate creation (ch. 39–41). The Almighty unfolds the intricacies of the natural order which He has created and over which He has control. Examples are given of the different types of creatures, and their strengths and weaknesses. Job is encouraged with His ways – however strange and inscrutable (40:1–2). He begins to sense his own insignificance in the midst of a great creation and wishes to remain silent (40:3–5). Job is reminded that he is just a creature and cannot truly challenge his Creator.

"Do you not know? Have you not heard? The Lord is the everlasting God, the Creator of the ends of the earth. He will not grow tired or weary, and his understanding no-one can fathom." (Isa. 40:28)

FURTHER THOUGHT

Ever thought that the main reason why people get downcast and discouraged is because of a loss of perspective? They fail to see things from God's point of view. Have you lost your spiritual perspective? Then read through these chapters once more. We'll be surprised if you don't feel a whole lot different.

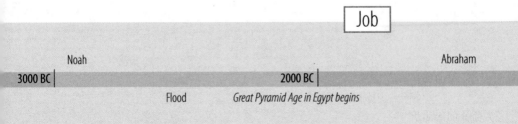

Job

Noah   Abraham

3000 BC | 2000 BC |

Flood   *Great Pyramid Age in Egypt begins*

Job 42:1-6

Job had demanded to meet God face to face so that he could argue his case (Job 23:3–7) – but now that he meets Him, he humbly repents and acknowledges that had he known what he was talking about, he would never have presumed to question the ways of the Almighty. His conclusion is that if God does not work in the way that Job thinks He ought to, then there is a good and just reason for it – even though it may be hidden from Job's understanding. The God who was such a delightful reality to Job in the days of his prosperity had not ceased to be. Job realises that the Almighty, through unseen, unfelt and unrecognised, and veiled by tragedy, still cared for him. This conviction brings him through the fog of confusion to renewed confidence.

"'For my thoughts are not your thoughts, neither are your ways my ways,' declares the Lord. 'As the heavens are higher than the earth, so are my ways higher than your ways and my thoughts than your thoughts.'"
(Isa. 55:8–9)

FURTHER THOUGHT

Job's counselling session with God brings him to the awareness that the ways of the Almighty are always for the best. If only we could acknowledge this at the beginning of our troubles, then we would come out with less spiritual wear and tear at the end!

Isaac

1900 BC

Bronze Age begins in Britain

Abraham leaves Ur

Jacob

1800 BC

DAY 160

His bountiful blessings

Job 42:7-17

Job's trials are now over and Satan has lost a battle (later, through Christ, he was to lose the war!). Job's full restoration begins when he turns from focusing on his own troubles and problems to intercede for his friends. His acquaintances, friends and relatives gather around and give him comfort and consolation, but the greatest blessings come directly from God. The Lord's blessing upon Job is even greater than he knew in the earlier part of his life, and he is blessed with ten children (seven sons and three daughters), a tremendous amount of livestock, and lives for another 140 years. Job died in a ripe old age full of joy and honour.

"Now instead, you ought to forgive and comfort him, so that he will not be overwhelmed by excessive sorrow." (2 Cor. 2:7)

FURTHER THOUGHT

Why was it that when Job prayed for his friends, God suddenly turned the spiritual tide in his favour? Some think Job was angry with his friends, and the moment he gave up his anger, God was able to move mightily in his life. Are you angry with anyone today? Then pray for that person – now.

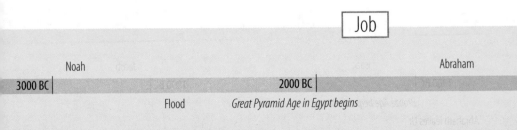

Job

Noah

Abraham

3000 BC | 　　　　　　　　　　　　2000 BC |

Flood　　　　Great Pyramid Age in Egypt begins

Some reasons for **Job's suffering**

To silence Satan **1:9-11; 2:4-5**

To face himself **42:3-4**

To reveal God **42:5**

To refine his character **42:6**

To help his friends **42:7**

To pray for his critics **42:10**

To demonstrate God's goodness **42:13-15**

Key Lesson – Job

The name of Job has been a household word in every generation since the days in which he first made his appearance. Proverb after proverb has grown out of the story. In almost every language on the face of the earth, men use such phrases as "the patience of Job", "the poverty of Job" or "Job's comforters". The image of Job, seated amid the ashes with a saintly halo around his head, has adorned the walls of cottages as well as cathedrals. The great characteristic of Job is not, as might first appear, his patience – but rather, his righteousness. He had lived a righteous life, yet he is treated by God as if he were unrighteous. His friends regard him as a sinner and his wife encourages him to curse God and die. Despite, at times, his desolating doubts, he remains righteous in it all, and stands for all time as evidence of the fact that no matter what happens, or how many doubts may fill our hearts, it is possible to live righteously for God in the midst of a seemingly cruel world.

Isaiah

Isaiah: "Salvation of Jehovah"

DAY 161

A definite call

Isaiah 6:1-13

While still a young man, Isaiah received a vision in the Temple which was to change the entire course of his life. First, he is given a vision of the Almighty God who is truly holy, surrounded with majesty, and worshipped by adoring angels. Next he is given a vision of himself, and is overwhelmed by a sense of his own sinfulness and the sinfulness of his nation. He sees himself as a "man of unclean lips" (v. 5). He is forgiven and cleansed, and hearing God's call, "Who will go for us?" he responds and receives a vision of the people to whom he must carry the Lord's message. He is to go to these people even though they will prove deaf to his message and blind to the truth (vv. 9–10).

"Where there is no vision, the people perish ..." (Prov. 29:18, AV)

FURTHER THOUGHT

"No one", said a famous preacher, "can do a truly effective work for God until, like Isaiah, he has caught a true vision of the holiness of God, the sinfulness of his own heart, and the deepest needs of those to whom he is called." Have you had such a vision? If not, pray that God will reveal Himself to you afresh today.

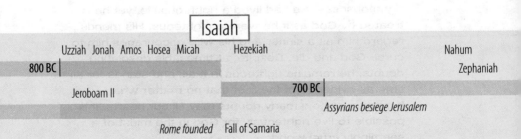

Isaiah

| Uzziah | Jonah | Amos | Hosea | Micah | Hezekiah | | Nahum |
| | | | | | | | Zephaniah |

800 BC

Jeroboam II

700 BC

Assyrians besiege Jerusalem

Rome founded   Fall of Samaria

Isaiah – *the Bible in miniature*

The book of Isaiah may be compared to the Bible

THE BIBLE	ISAIAH
Sixty-six books	Sixty-six chapters
• The Old Testament has thirty-nine books	• The first section of Isaiah has thirty-nine chapters
• The New Testament has twenty-seven books	• The last section of Isaiah has twenty-seven chapters
• The Old Testament covers the history and sin of God's people	• Isaiah chapters 1–39 do the same
• The New Testament describes the person and ministry of Christ	• Isaiah chapters 40–66 do the same
• The New Testament begins with the ministry of John the Baptist	• The second section (ch. 40) begins by predicting this ministry
• The New Testament ends by referring to the new heavens and new earth	• Isaiah ends his book by describing the same thing (compare Isa. 66:22 with Rev. 21:1–3)

THE MESSIAH IN ISAIAH

His conception	**7:14–15**
His name	**9:6; 42:1**
His commission	**11:1-2; 53:2**
His message	**50:4-5**
His ministry	**35:5-6; 9:1-2; 42:2-7**
His suffering	**50:6; 52:14**
His death	**53:1-12**
His resurrection	**52:13**
His rule	**9:7; 32:1**

DAY **162**

A praising heart

Isaiah 12:1-6

As Isaiah looks forward to the coming of the kingdom of God on earth (described in chapter 11) he breaks out into a song of thanksgiving and praise. The words of this song were later sung by those who had been exiled from Judah and were returning after long captivity. The words are especially suitable for those who have come to Christ for the first time, or for a believer, when peace has been renewed after a period of backsliding. Through Jesus Christ, the branch from Jesse, the divine anger is turned away from mankind and we can experience peace. Those whom God reconciles He also comforts. They are taught to triumph in God and rejoice in Him.

"How good it is to sing praises to our God, how pleasant and fitting to praise him!" (Psa. 147:1)

FURTHER THOUGHT

Has God delivered you from a sickness, a habit, a bondage – or a recent bout of backsliding? Then use this opportunity to praise Him by singing these words of God back to Him. Don't just read them – sing them! Make up your own tune and sing it out – as loudly as you can. Then note the difference this makes to your whole day.

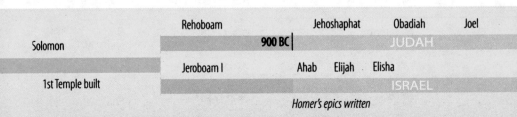

Solomon		Rehoboam		Jehoshaphat	Obadiah	Joel
			900 BC		JUDAH	
		Jeroboam I		Ahab Elijah Elisha		
1st Temple built					ISRAEL	
		Homer's epics written				

An unshakable confidence

Isaiah 25:1-12

Again Isaiah bursts into song. This time God is worshipped as the One who does wonderful things and remains forever exalted. He puts down the strong and cares for the weak. As God weakens the strong who are proud and secure, so He strengthens the weak who know how to depend completely upon Him (vv. 1–5). The reception of repentant sinners is likened to a feast. There is a veil spread over the nations, but this veil will be destroyed by the light of Christ's gospel shining in the world (vv. 6–9). God shall bring down the pride of His enemies by one humbling judgment after another. The destruction of Moab is typical of Christ's victory on the cross and the pulling down of Satan's strongholds.

"Sing for joy to God our strength; shout aloud to the God of Jacob!" (Psa. 81:1)

FURTHER THOUGHT

Here's your assignment for today – take the first verse of this great song of rejoicing and memorise every word. Bring them to mind at least once every hour. Then, as you go to sleep tonight, let these words be the last thought in your mind.

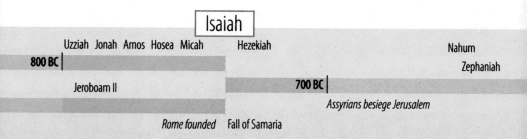

Isaiah

Uzziah Jonah Amos Hosea Micah   Hezekiah   Nahum

800 BC | Zephaniah

Jeroboam II   700 BC |

Assyrians besiege Jerusalem

Rome founded   Fall of Samaria

Isaiah

Isaiah: "Salvation of Jehovah"

DAY **164**

A great God

Isaiah 40:1–31

Isaiah speaks a comforting word to the people of his day – words that come directly from God to His people. This is called "prophecy" – a word which contains the thought, not only of foretelling, but forthtelling. As Isaiah speaks forth the word of the Lord, take heed to what is being said, for this could be as truly God's word to your heart as it was to the people of Isaiah's day. Life is a warfare, but the struggle will not last for ever. Troubles are removed in love when sin is pardoned. All created beings sink to nothing in comparison with the Creator, who has the command of all creatures and of all created beings. Go forth in God's strength, not in your own, and like the eagle you will soar over all difficulties and problems.

"The wind blows wherever it pleases. You hear its sound, but you cannot tell where it comes from or where it is going. So it is with everyone born of the Spirit." (John 3:8)

FURTHER THOUGHT

Isaiah does in this chapter what a physician would do as he walks into a sick person's room which is filled with stale air – he throws open the windows and lets in the fresh breeze. Are you feeling spiritually jaded at the moment? Then look out and look up: "God's in His heaven – all's right with the world."

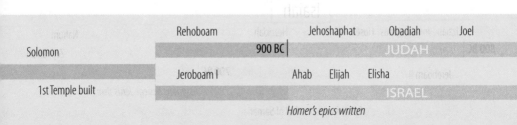

	Rehoboam		Jehoshaphat	Obadiah	Joel
Solomon		900 BC	JUDAH		
	Jeroboam I		Ahab Elijah Elisha		
1st Temple built			ISRAEL		
		Homer's epics written			

Isaiah 53:1-12

Nowhere in all the Old Testament is it so plainly and fully prophesied that Christ should suffer and then enter into His glory, as in this chapter. It is, without doubt, one of the most moving and solemn passages to be found anywhere in the Word of God. When placed alongside Psalm 22, which also relates to the crucifixion, there emerges a picture of Christ's suffering on the cross which is utterly amazing – especially when you consider that it was written hundreds of years before the event. Isaiah foresees the Messiah giving His life for mankind (vv. 4–8), His burial in a rich man's tomb (v.9), His resurrection (v. 10) and His return to heaven to rule and reign (vv. 11–12).

"In bringing many sons to glory, it was fitting that God, for whom and through whom everything exists, should make the author of their salvation perfect through suffering." (Heb. 2:10)

FURTHER THOUGHT

"Were the whole realm of nature mine, That were an offering far too small, Love so amazing, so divine, Demands my soul, my life, my all."

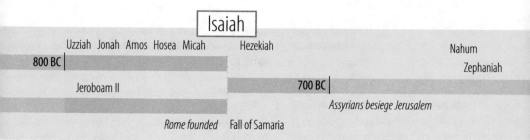

Isaiah

Uzziah   Jonah   Amos   Hosea   Micah   Hezekiah   Nahum

800 BC   Zephaniah

Jeroboam II   700 BC

                                                     Assyrians besiege Jerusalem

Rome founded   Fall of Samaria

Isaiah

DAY 166   A heart for the lost

Isaiah 55:1–13

Isaiah was pre-eminently an evangelist, and this is one of his greatest evangelistic sermons. The first two verses describe life apart from God with its hunger and false values, and he gives an eloquent appeal for all to accept the salvation which the Messiah will bring. The exciting note he introduces – something that had never been seen quite so clearly before – is that when the Messiah comes, the gospel will be for everyone, not just for Jews (v. 5). Salvation, however, is not automatic; repentance and conversion are necessary if a person is truly to rejoice in God (vv. 6–7). There will be great peace and permanent joy when God's salvation is complete (vv. 12–13).

"Do you not say, 'Four months more and then the harvest'? I tell you, open your eyes, and look at the fields! They are ripe for harvest." (John 4:35)

FURTHER THOUGHT

How do you feel about the subject of evangelism? If you believe that men and women are lost without Christ, then evangelism becomes an urgent necessity. And, as someone said: "Evangelism is not complete until the evangelised become evangelists."

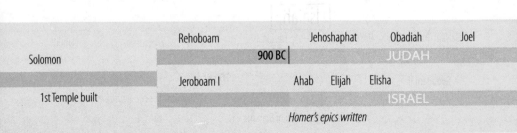

		Rehoboam		Jehoshaphat		Obadiah	Joel
Solomon			**900 BC**			JUDAH	
		Jeroboam I		Ahab	Elijah	Elisha	
1st Temple built						ISRAEL	
			Homer's epics written				

A fervent zeal

Isaiah 62:1-12

The prophet foresees the day when God will be able to rejoice over His people and delight in them. Jehovah is the builder of the new Jerusalem and all its inhabitants will be holy (v. 12). The coming of this day should preoccupy all God's children, and we should make it a matter of earnest and constant prayer (vv. 6–7). The art of prayer is reminding God of what He has promised to do. This is what the Old Testament characters did over and over again – they put their finger on God's promises and held Him to them! God is zealous in His desire to bring all these things to pass, and this zeal should be shared by all of His redeemed people.

"This is the covenant I will make with them after that time, says the Lord. I will put my laws in their hearts, and I will write them on their minds." (Heb. 10:16)

FURTHER THOUGHT

When next you pray, consider adopting this policy of the Old Testament saints – reminding God of His gracious and unimpeachable promises. Find a promise or a covenant and hold it up before the Lord. Don't be afraid – God delights to be reminded of His Word.

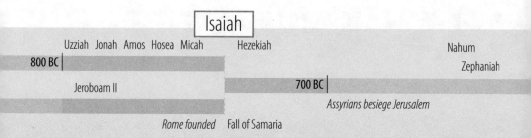

Isaiah

Uzziah Jonah Amos Hosea Micah   Hezekiah   Nahum

800 BC   Zephaniah

Jeroboam II   700 BC

Assyrians besiege Jerusalem

Rome founded   Fall of Samaria

Key Lesson – Isaiah

Isaiah is regarded by Bible commentators as "the greatest evangelist of the Old Testament". Both the tone and subject of his writings justify that description. The spirit of concern and compassion for those who reject the offer of God's mercy pulsates through the whole of his prophecy, and it is this which makes him, more than all other Old Testament writers, the preacher of good tidings. The summons to declare those good tidings to the nations has been, and is still being obeyed by the many who have preached – and are still preaching – the gospel in a pagan world. The main lesson, therefore, that we learn from Isaiah is the importance and relevance of sharing the good news of our God with the world. Evangelism has been described as "one beggar telling another where to find bread". You don't have to stand in a pulpit to do that – you can do it right there in the locality where you live.

An immediate protest

Jeremiah 1:1–19

DAY **168**

Jeremiah was the son of a priest and doubtless received a strong spiritual upbringing. While still a young man, God spoke to him and told him that he had been appointed as a prophet even before he was born (v. 5). Jeremiah protests that he is too young to start speaking out as a prophet to his nation, but God rebukes him for this and gives him a clear and definite commission. He is also assured that he need never be afraid because he will enjoy divine protection throughout his entire life. The Lord touches his mouth, telling him that He has put His word on Jeremiah's lips and that his ministry will be one of both pulling down and building up.

"Don't let anyone look down on you because you are young, but set an example for the believers in speech, in life, in love, in faith and in purity." (1 Tim. 4:12)

FURTHER THOUGHT

Those who have a message to deliver from God should not fear because of their youthfulness or inexperience. When God calls a person to share His truth with others, He also clothes that person with supernatural might and power. Has God called you to a specific work? Then go about the task – "nothing doubting" (Acts 11:12 AV).

Jeremiah						
Nahum		Habakkuk	Daniel			Zechariah
Zephaniah	Josiah	Nebuchadnezzar		Ezekiel	Cyrus	Haggai
		600 BC		FALL OF JUDAH		500 BC
		Daniel taken to Babylon		Exile in Babylon	2nd Temple built	
				Jerusalem destroyed		

Jeremiah

Jeremiah: "Jehovah exalts"

A proclaimed judgment

Jeremiah 2:1–37

Jeremiah is given a strong and powerful word from the Lord, charging Judah with a catalogue of serious sins. First, they are accused of a degree of unfaithfulness that is not to be found even among the heathen nations (vv. 10–11). Next they are accused of rejecting God's endless supply of fresh water – His divine life and power – in favour of the stagnant water of self-centredness and self-interest which they have collected in their own leaky cisterns – an action which God sees as appallingly evil. They are charged further with turning to Assyria and Egypt for help, instead of trusting the God of their salvation. Having forsaken the Lord for the worship of idols, judgement is then pronounced.

"Now is the time for judgment on this world; now the prince of this world will be driven out. But I, when I am lifted up from the earth, will draw all men to myself." (John 12:31–32)

FURTHER THOUGHT

How sad that the message of coming judgment seems to have been greatly watered down in some sections of today's Church. It may be missing from many modern pulpits, but it is not missing from the Bible. Just look up Acts 17:30–31 and see!

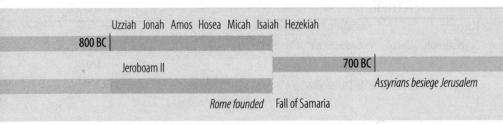

Uzziah Jonah Amos Hosea Micah Isaiah Hezekiah

800 BC

Jeroboam II

700 BC

Assyrians besiege Jerusalem

Rome founded   Fall of Samaria

A weeping heart

Jeremiah 4:19–21; 8:18–9:11

Once Jeremiah is made aware of the approaching judgment which is to fall upon Judah, he experiences a great concern for the plight of his people. His concern deepens into anguish as the people fail to heed his warnings and continue in their sinful and rebellious ways. It is clear that God's people are spiritually sick and wounded because of their sins, and their unwillingness to repent causes the prophet's heart to break. He weeps and weeps as he feels within his own spirit the grief that God feels in heaven. Such is the stupidity, the ignorance and the evil of the people that Jeremiah wishes he could weep day and night for the eventual repentance and contrition of his fellow countrymen.

"As he approached Jerusalem and saw the city, he wept over it ..."
(Luke 19:41)

FURTHER THOUGHT

What kind of concern do you have for those who break God's commandments and overturn His laws? Do you simply condemn them – or do you cry to God for their rebirth? Many are willing to criticise sinners, but few are prepared to weep for them.

Jeremiah

Nahum			Habakkuk	Daniel				Zechariah	
Zephaniah	Josiah	Nebuchadnezzar		Ezekiel			Cyrus	Haggai
		600 BC		FALL OF JUDAH			**500 BC**	
		Daniel taken to Babylon		Exile in Babylon		2nd Temple built	
				Jerusalem destroyed			

Jeremiah

Jeremiah: "Jehovah exalts"

DAY 171

A persecuting family

Jeremiah 12:1–17

J eremiah, it seems, was a lonely man who, because of the special work God had called him to do, was forbidden to marry (Jer. 16:1–2). It seems also that his family are not terribly supportive of him and he becomes the victim of treachery by his brothers (v. 6). His problems deepen when his life is threatened by the inhabitants of Anathoth, his home town, who set out to silence him and stop him uttering the words which have been given him by God. When he becomes concerned about the prosperity of the people around him and enquires of the Lord what is to be done about it, he is not given a direct answer but told that there are difficult and testing times to come.

"Blessed are you when people insult you, persecute you and falsely say all kinds of evil against you because of me. Rejoice and be glad, because great is your reward in heaven ..."
(Matt. 5:11–12)

FURTHER THOUGHT

It's hard to be rejected but it's especially hard when those who reject you are members of your own family. Has this happened to you? Then be careful that the poison of self-pity does not creep in and corrode your soul. Self-pity has shipwrecked thousands of Christians. Don't let it ruin you.

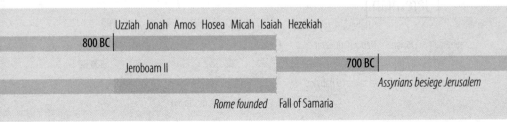

Uzziah Jonah Amos Hosea Micah Isaiah Hezekiah

800 BC

Jeroboam II

700 BC

Assyrians besiege Jerusalem

Rome founded   Fall of Samaria

A single purpose

Jeremiah 16:1-21

It is obvious that God requires absolute singleness of heart from His servant Jeremiah. He is forbidden to take upon himself the responsibilities of caring for a wife and family, and is thus spared the distress of losing his loved ones in the widespread plagues and judgement that God is going to send upon the people of Judah. A picture is painted for him of the awful calamities that are to fall upon the land because of Judah's unfaithfulness, which will result in many not only dying, but remaining unburied. Laughter and gladness are to cease and wedding feasts will be no more. Jeremiah is commissioned to fearlessly pronounce that all this is due to Judah's sin – their own and also that of their forefathers.

"... be obedient to those who are your earthly masters, with fear and trembling, in singleness of heart ... rendering service with a good will as to the Lord and not to men ..."
(Eph. 6:5, 7 RSV)

FURTHER THOUGHT

Recent research conducted among professional men and women who had made a success of their lives showed that one of the key factors in their success was singleness of purpose. More than at any other time in history, God needs His servants to be single-minded. Are you like this?

Jeremiah						
Nahum		Habakkuk	Daniel			Zechariah
Zephaniah	Josiah	Nebuchadnezzar		Ezekiel	Cyrus	Haggai
		600 BC		FALL OF JUDAH		500 BC
		Daniel taken to Babylon		Exile in Babylon	2nd Temple built	
				Jerusalem destroyed		

Jeremiah

Jeremiah: "Jehovah exalts"

DAY **173**   A comforting word

Jeremiah 29:1–32

Jeremiah sits down to write a letter to the Jews who had been carried away captive into Babylon, among whom were Johoiachin the king, and a number of priests and prophets. Ezekiel, too, was to be found among these captives. Jeremiah has heard that some false prophets are raising vain hopes among the exiles by predicting an early return to Jerusalem, but Jeremiah tells them that they are to carry on their normal activities as their captivity will last seventy years. In the meantime, they are to pray for those with whom they live and seek their welfare. Then, when the allotted time of captivity has expired, God will bring them home.

"So then, let us not be like others, who are asleep, but let us be alert and self-controlled." (1 Thess. 5:6)

FURTHER THOUGHT

Just as there was a time scheduled on God's calendar for the return of the Jews to Jerusalem, so there is a time appointed when Christ will come again. And how are we to live in the meantime? Carefully, prayerfully and with concern for those around us.

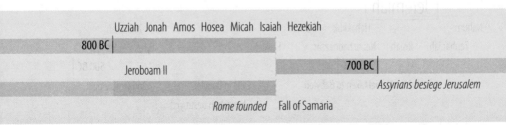

Uzziah Jonah Amos Hosea Micah Isaiah Hezekiah

800 BC

Jeroboam II

700 BC

Assyrians besiege Jerusalem

Rome founded   Fall of Samaria

A human response

Jeremiah 19:14–20:18

After Jeremiah had stood in the Temple and prophesied the imminent fulfilment of the evils that the Lord had spoken concerning Judah and Jerusalem, the unbelieving people of his day mercilessly beat him and put him in the stocks. His feelings are most powerfully recorded in this passage, and reveal the deep humanity and sensitivity of this dedicated servant of the Lord. Obviously it hurt him greatly to be hated and ridiculed, but yet he had to be faithful in speaking out the words which God had told him to say. He vacillates between confident faith (vv. 11, 13) and abject misery (vv. 14–18), cursing the day that he was born (compare Job 3:2–26).

"Now it is required that those who have been given a trust must prove faithful." (1 Cor. 4:2)

FURTHER THOUGHT

It is one of the highest tests of character to faithfully do what God has asked you to do, even when your own heart is hurting. Many Christians fail at this point and say such a state of existence is impossible. But is it? Turn to 2 Corinthians 12:9 and see!

Jeremiah					
Nahum		Habakkuk	Daniel		Zechariah
Zephaniah	Josiah	Nebuchadnezzar	Ezekiel	Cyrus	Haggai
		600 BC	FALL OF JUDAH	500 BC	
	Daniel taken to Babylon		Exile in Babylon	2nd Temple built	
			Jerusalem destroyed		

Imagery in Jeremiah

"So I went down to the potter's house, and I saw him working at the wheel. But the pot he was shaping from the clay was marred in his hands; so the potter formed it into another pot, shaping it as seemed best to him. Then the word of the Lord came to me: 'O house of Israel, can I not do with you as this potter does?' declares the Lord. 'Like clay in the hand of the potter, so are you in my hand, O house of Israel.'" (Jeremiah 18:3–6)

Key Lesson – Jeremiah

No Old Testament character is so intimately known to us as Jeremiah. It is not simply that we are informed concerning the many events of his life, but we are shown something of the way he feels. It has been said that "we can never know anyone until we know how that person really feels". In this respect, Jeremiah marks an epoch in the history of prophecy. Some of the other prophets – for example, Isaiah – are so absorbed in their message that they exhibit little or no personal feeling. Not so Jeremiah. He was a loving, priestly character who felt the unbelief and sin of his nation as a heavy, almost overwhelming burden. Who does not remember the words: "Let my eyes overflow with tears night and day, without ceasing ..." (Jer. 14:17)? The main lesson of his life is brought out in Jeremiah 8:21: "Since my people are crushed, I am crushed ...". He was willing to be hurt, and then use those hurts to deepen his sensitivity to the needs of his people and to the will and purposes of God.

Compromise spurned

Daniel 1:1–21

Daniel, along with other young men from the nobility of Judah, who had been taken as captives to Babylon, was chosen for his good looks and talents to serve in King Nebuchadnezzar's court. The Babylonians did not observe the Jewish food laws nor prepare "kosher" meat (Lev. chs. 11, 17). Daniel and three of his companions decide not to compromise their religious beliefs by eating the food provided by the king, and request a vegetarian diet. The courtier in charge of them becomes alarmed at their request until Daniel suggests a ten-day trial in which he and his companions eat vegetables, and the others eat meat. At the end of this period of trial, Daniel and his companions appear wiser and healthier than the others.

"...the wisdom that comes from heaven is first of all pure; then peace-loving, considerate, submissive, full of mercy and good fruit, impartial and sincere." (James 3:17)

FURTHER THOUGHT

How easy it would have been for Daniel to have stubbornly refused to eat the king's meat, and forced an unnecessary confrontation. Wisdom dictated a better approach – that of designing a creative alternative. Do you feel you lack wisdom? Then turn to James 1:5 to see how to obtain it.

Daniel					
Nahum	Jeremiah	Habakkuk			Zechariah
Zephaniah	Josiah	Nebuchadnezzar	Ezekiel	Cyrus	Haggai
		600 BC	FALL OF JUDAH		500 BC
		Daniel taken to Babylon	Exile in Babylon	2nd Temple built	
			Jerusalem destroyed		

Daniel

Daniel: "God is my Judge"

Wisdom displayed

Daniel 2:1-49

Not long after Daniel and his companions take up their court duties, they are faced with a severe test. King Nebuchadnezzar has a dream which greatly troubles him – a dream which no one can interpret. Angry at their inability to explain his dream, the king pronounces the death penalty to all his wise men, including Daniel and his friends. Daniel acts with prudence and discretion toward the commander of the king's guard, who is sent to carry out the death sentence, and is permitted to see the king. As Daniel talks with the king, he is given supernatural understanding of the dream, and interprets it to the king's satisfaction. Daniel is then appointed as the chief over all the wise men of Babylon.

"... God has revealed it to us by his Spirit. The Spirit searches all things, even the deep things of God."
(1 Cor. 2:10)

FURTHER THOUGHT

Daniel was deeply thankful to God for imparting to him the wisdom by which he could interpret Nebuchadnezzar's dream. How much more should we be thankful to God for making known to us His plan of salvation – a plan which no amount of earthly wisdom could ever have conceived!

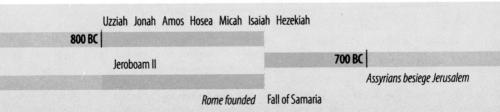

Uzziah Jonah Amos Hosea Micah Isaiah Hezekiah

800 BC

Jeroboam II

700 BC

Assyrians besiege Jerusalem

Rome founded   Fall of Samaria

Daniel 4:1–37

King Nebuchadnezzar has another dream, and when his Chaldean interpreters fail to interpret it, he sends for Daniel and acknowledges that the Spirit of God rests upon him. On hearing the dream and simultaneously receiving the interpretation from God, Daniel is alarmed because the dream predicts the king's temporary madness. Daniel breaks the news as sensitively and as tactfully as he can, and advises the king to repent and live righteously so that God's judgement upon him might be suspended. The king ignores Daniel's advice, and a year later judgement falls when he is dethroned and expelled from his palace to live in the fields and eat grass like cattle. When later, his reason returns, he is greatly humbled, acknowledging that Daniel's God is the true God.

"He chose the lowly things of this world and the despised things ... to nullify the things that are, so that no-one may boast before him." (1 Cor. 1:28-29)

FURTHER THOUGHT

Pride and conceit are sins that beset great men. They are apt to take the glory to themselves rather than give it to God. It is helpful to remember that while the proud word was in the king's mouth, the powerful word came from God. It always does!

Daniel					
Nahum	Jeremiah	Habakkuk			Zechariah
Zephaniah	Josiah	Nebuchadnezzar	Ezekiel	Cyrus	Haggai
	600 BC		FALL OF JUDAH		**500 BC**
	Daniel taken to Babylon		Exile in Babylon	2nd Temple built	
			Jerusalem destroyed		

Daniel

Daniel: "God is my Judge"

DAY 178 — Truth disclosed

Daniel 5:1-31

Belshazzar, the son of Nabonidus, decides to hold a great feast in the city of Babylon, and does something which greatly displeases the Lord. He calls for the sacred vessels which Nebuchadnezzar had brought from the Temple in Jerusalem to be set on his table so that his lords and ladies might drink from them. This sacrilegious act brings about a supernatural intervention. During the course of the feast, a hand appears which writes a message upon the wall of the banqueting chamber. When the terrified king calls for Daniel to interpret the writing, he is told that God's judgment is about to fall upon him. Sentence is carried out the same night, when Darius invades the city and Belshazzar is put to death.

"It is because of him that you are in Christ Jesus, who has become for us wisdom from God – that is, our righteousness, holiness and redemption." (1 Cor. 1:30)

FURTHER THOUGHT

Ponder for a moment what might happen if you were picked up and weighed in the scales of God's justice. How would you fare? If Christ is resident in your life then you need fear nothing, for the weight of His righteousness more than outweighs the demands of the law. Hallelujah!

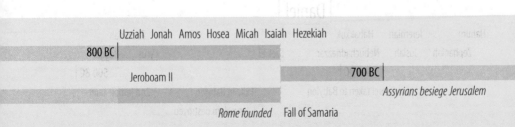

Uzziah Jonah Amos Hosea Micah Isaiah Hezekiah

800 BC

Jeroboam II

700 BC

Assyrians besiege Jerusalem

Rome founded   Fall of Samaria

212

Faith demonstrated

Daniel 6:1-28

Darius is now king of Babylon, and Daniel is in his eighties. The king thinks so highly of Daniel that he plans to appoint him to a position of high authority, second only to himself. Those answerable to Daniel become extremely jealous of him, and attempt to find some fault in him that they can report to the king. Unable to do so, they work on the king's vanity and get him to make a decree which forbids the worship of any god or man except Darius. Naturally Daniel refuses to accept the decree and openly prays to God, whereupon he is thrown into a lions' den. The whole situation causes the king great distress, but he is consoled when, after a sleepless night, he visits the lions' den and finds Daniel alive and unharmed.

"Peter and the other apostles replied: 'We must obey God rather than men!'" (Acts 5:29)

FURTHER THOUGHT

Remember what we said earlier about Daniel's wisdom in avoiding an unnecessary confrontation? In relation to the matter of prayer, however, there can be no creative alternative - confrontation is unavoidable. But knowing when to confront, and when to design a creative alternative, is what wisdom is all about.

Nahum					Zechariah	
	Jeremiah	Habakkuk				
Zephaniah	Josiah	Nebuchadnezzar	Ezekiel		Cyrus	Haggai
		600 BC	FALL OF JUDAH			500 BC
		Daniel taken to Babylon	Exile in Babylon		2nd Temple built	
			Jerusalem destroyed			

Daniel

213

Daniel

DAY 180 — A vision received

Daniel 7:1-8:27

Daniel is given several visions which relate to the events which will happen in the future, including the setting up of God's kingdom on the earth. The archangel Gabriel is sent to assist Daniel – a man "highly esteemed" (Dan. 9:23) – to explain and interpret the visions. The visions which Daniel received have one main purpose – to impress upon men's minds the fact that all power belongs to the Most High, who permits empires to rise only as they contribute to His overall purposes. Gabriel names the world powers from Babylon up until the coming of God's kingdom on earth – pictured in an earlier vision as "a rock ... cut out, but not by human hands" (Dan. 2:34). Many believe this refers to the coming of Christ, who will arrive in the days of the ten kings (Dan. 2:44–45).

"He who testifies to these things says, 'Yes, I am coming soon.' Amen. Come, Lord Jesus." (Rev. 22:20)

FURTHER THOUGHT

What do you believe about the second coming of Jesus Christ? Do you believe it is near? Many do. Remember, however, that the whole point and purpose of prophecy is not to alight on a date, but to encourage us ever to be ready for that wonderful event. Would you be ready to meet Him if Christ came today?

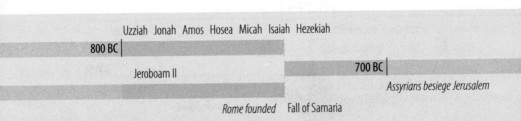

Uzziah Jonah Amos Hosea Micah Isaiah Hezekiah

800 BC

Jeroboam II

700 BC

Assyrians besiege Jerusalem

Rome founded   Fall of Samaria

Daniel 9:1-10:21

Daniel was, above all things, a man of prayer. He turns to the Lord and applies himself to prayer and supplication with fasting, putting on sackcloth and ashes. In his prayer he confesses the transgression of his nation, acknowledges the justice of divine punishment, and seeks God for mercy and restoration. The prayer is composed largely of reminiscences from Deuteronomy, the prayer of Solomon and the prayers of Jeremiah. As he mourns and fasts, Gabriel once again appears to him to comfort him and reveal further details of the future which awaits God's people and the world. Many of Daniel's prophecies reappear in the book of Revelation, where similar imagery is employed.

"Then Jesus told his disciples a parable to show them that they should always pray and not give up." (Luke 18:1)

FURTHER THOUGHT

This great prayer of Daniel's was prompted by his diligent reading of the Scriptures. And what a prayer it is! You just can't tell what depth of prayer you might reach after meditating on the Word of God. If you can – after your reading today – spend some time in prayer. Maybe you will reach greater depths than ever before.

Daniel

Nahum	Jeremiah	Habakkuk				Zechariah	
Zephaniah	Josiah	Nebuchadnezzar	Ezekiel		Cyrus	Haggai
		600 BC	FALL OF JUDAH			500 BC
	Daniel taken to Babylon		Exile in Babylon	2nd Temple built
			Jerusalem destroyed

Daniel – *The man of prayer*

When:	First year of Persian rule 539 BC (9:2)
Reason:	Daniel's understanding of Jeremiah's prophecy (9:2)
Basis:	The promise of God (9:4)
	The mercy of God (9:9, 18)
Confession:	"We have sinned!" (9:5, 8, 9, 11, 15, 16)
Content:	That God would bring them out of Babylon as He once did out of Egypt (9:15)
	That God would forgive (9:19)
	That God would allow the Temple to be rebuilt in Jerusalem (9:16, 17)
	"While I was ... in prayer ... Gabriel ... came to me ..." (9:21).

An upright man 6:3
An evil clan 6:4–5
A devious plan 6:6–16
A praying man 6:10
A divine ban 6:17–22

Key Lesson – Daniel

The key to Daniel's truly successful and prosperous life can be traced to an important decision he made as a young man: "Daniel resolved not to defile himself" (Dan. 1:8). His faithfulness to that early decision can be seen on at least four important occasions. His record is without blame. Just as Pilate had to proclaim concerning Jesus, "I find in him no fault" (John 18:38, AV), so Daniel's accusers could find no blame in him (Dan. 6:4). The main lesson we learn from Daniel's life is the importance of being aware that God is watching and evaluating every one of our words, thoughts, actions and attitudes. This awareness enables us to always keep our spiritual standards high.

4

Amos

Amos: "Strong" or "A bearer of burdens"

DAY 182   A herdsman and fruit gatherer

Amos 7:14-17; 1:1

A mos was a native of Tekoa, a small town south of Jerusalem, and by occupation a herdsman and fig farmer. He lived during the reign of Uzziah and was a contemporary of Isaiah and Hosea. Although he had not received any training in the schools of the prophets that existed at that time, he exercised a very powerful and important ministry. Doubtless, as he went about his work in the fields and in the vineyards, he took advantage of his rural surroundings to quietly meditate and pray. The Bible often draws a veil over the years of preparation in the lives of God's servants, as if this period is too personal and sacred for inspection. This is the way it was with many Old Testament characters, such as Moses and Elijah, and the best example in the New Testament is that of our Lord Himself.

"For the revelation awaits an appointed time; it speaks of the end and will not prove false. Though it linger, wait for it; it will certainly come and will not delay." (Hab. 2:3)

FURTHER THOUGHT

Every Christian has to pass through what is known as the "silent years" before God can entrust him with a work to do for Him. Perhaps you are there right now. If so, make good use of these weeks and months, for the more you learn in the "silent years", the more effective you will be in the serving years.

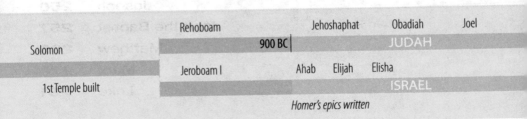

1st Temple built	Solomon		Rehoboam		900 BC	Jehoshaphat		Obadiah	Joel
			Jeroboam I			Ahab	Elijah	Elisha	
						JUDAH			
						ISRAEL			
					Homer's epics written				

A prophet

Amos 7:10–13, 15

The Scripture does not give us any information about Amos' ancestors or whether he had a wife or family, but the call of God to become a prophet must have caused a great upheaval in his life. He rose to the challenge, however, and became a strong prophet who carried out the task of proclaiming a message of judgment to the unresponsive king and nation with great courage. When Amos travels north to Bethel, the centre of King Jeroboam II of Israel, a priest who hears his prophecies accuses him of sedition, and instructs him to return to Judah from whence he has come. Amos stoutly maintains that despite his lack of prophetic ancestry and training, he has received a call from God to convey the prophetic word to the people.

"Do your best to present yourself to God as one approved, a workman who does not need to be ashamed and who correctly handles the word of truth." (2 Tim. 2:15)

FURTHER THOUGHT

How do you feel about the issue of "training" in Christian things? Some overvalue it, while others undervalue it. The important thing is first to be sure of God's call to the ministry He has for you, and then to be open to ways in which you can make your personal ministry more effective for Him.

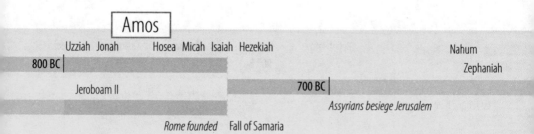

	Amos						
	Uzziah	Jonah	Hosea	Micah	Isaiah	Hezekiah	Nahum
800 BC							Zephaniah
	Jeroboam II				700 BC		
					Assyrians besiege Jerusalem		
		Rome founded	Fall of Samaria				

Amos

Amos: "Strong" or "A bearer of burdens"

DAY 184   Israel's neighbours denounced

Amos 1:3–15; 2:1–3

Amos' ministry consists of a number of denunciations. First, he denounces Israel's neighbours, Syria (vv. 3–5), Philistia (vv. 6–8), Tyre (vv. 9–10), Edom (vv. 11–12), Ammon (vv. 13–15), and Moab (2:1–3). Not one nation escapes the fierce denunciation of the prophet as he condemns the heathen nations for their crimes against humanity. Some commentators feel that Amos should not have denounced them as they were not judged by the same standards as Israel, but they were still guilty of transgressing the law of right and wrong which God has written into the human conscience. This point is emphasised by the apostle Paul in his letter to the Romans: "All who sin apart from the law will also perish apart from the law, and all who sin under the law will be judged by the law" (Rom. 2:12).

> "For the message of the cross is foolishness to those who are perishing, but to us who are being saved it is the power of God." (1 Cor. 1:18)

FURTHER THOUGHT

Is it not true that the note of denunciation is missing from many of today's pulpits? Some say it is better to present the "good news" that Christ has come to save us from sin, and leave the work of denunciation to the Holy Spirit. What do you think?

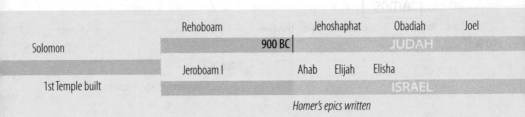

	Rehoboam		Jehoshaphat		Obadiah	Joel
Solomon		**900 BC**			JUDAH	
	Jeroboam I		Ahab	Elijah	Elisha	
1st Temple built					ISRAEL	
		Homer's epics written				

Israel reproved

Amos 2:4-12; 3:1-8

Having poured out strong and fierce denunciation against the surrounding nations, Amos now concentrates on the nation of Israel and accuses them of a long catalogue of sins. The evils that are rife among God's people are dragged into the light and unsparingly denounced. They are accused of selling the righteous into slavery (2:6), greed, injustice and cult prostitution (2:7), harsh treatment of debtors and intemperance (2:8, 12a), and ingratitude towards God (2:9–11). It was to Israel that Amos was specially sent, and it is against her that the full force of his moral indignation is hurled. Israel is God's family (3:1), and because of this, "it is time for judgment to begin with the family of God" (1 Pet. 4:17b). The prophet announces God's imminent punishment of all Israel's sins, and proclaims his own authority as God's appointed prophet to convey God's reproofs and judgments.

"For it is time for judgment to begin with the family of God; and if it begins with us, what will the outcome be for those who do not obey the gospel of God?" (1 Pet. 4:17)

FURTHER THOUGHT

As it is a Scriptural principle that judgment begins with the family of God, take a moment before you go any further to reflect on the things you may be permitting in your own life that are displeasing to Him. Then make a positive decision to turn from them – every one.

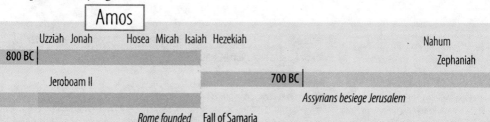

Amos

Uzziah Jonah	Hosea Micah Isaiah Hezekiah	Nahum
800 BC		Zephaniah
Jeroboam II	700 BC	
	Assyrians besiege Jerusalem	
Rome founded	Fall of Samaria	

Amos

DAY 186　　Judgment pronounced

Amos 2:13; 3:9–15; 4:1–6:14

There can be little doubt that Amos's message, consisting as it did of reproof and judgement, was a difficult one to speak out – yet he does not hesitate to do so. The people, however, unlike the Ninevites who repented as soon as they heard the word of the Lord, are hostile to both Amos's words and his person. It is interesting to note that Amos directed his condemnation, not only to the men of Israel, but also to the women (4:1–3) – indicating that the whole society was morally sick and infirm. The keynote of Amos's prophecies is the necessity of righteousness. He has nothing to say against religion as such, except where it is useless and ritualistic. The people's worship at Bethel and Gilgal is condemned as abhorrent (4:4–5; 5:5), and is about to be brought to an end.

"... having a form of godliness but denying its power. Have nothing to do with them." (2 Tim. 3:5)

FURTHER THOUGHT

Someone has said: "Whenever religion goes wrong, it goes very, very wrong." How hurtful it must be to God, who so much desires His people's worship, to see them approaching Him through a ritual that is devoid of all meaning. Perhaps this is a good moment to check on your own approach to the worship of God.

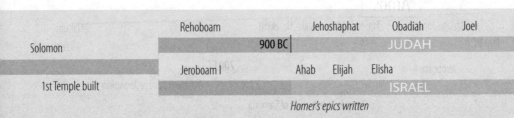

	Rehoboam		Jehoshaphat	Obadiah	Joel
Solomon		900 BC	JUDAH		
	Jeroboam I		Ahab　Elijah　Elisha		
1st Temple built			ISRAEL		
		Homer's epics written			

Amos 7:1–9; 8:1–14; 9:1–10

Amos receives five visions, each containing a symbol: (1) locusts (7:1–3) – signifying an invasion which is averted by Amos's intercession; (2) fire (7:4–6) – utter destruction again averted in answer to prayer; (3) a plumbline (7:7–9) – showing the judgment of the religious and political structures of Israel; (4) a basket of summer fruit (ch. 8) – signifying imminent and inevitable judgment; (5) A shaken sanctuary (9:1–10) – showing that God Himself will judge His people for their debased forms of worship. Each vision is followed by a longer or shorter explanation, and their aim is to reinforce in symbolic language the fact that although Jehovah had previously relented, He could do so no more, for the time of mercy had now passed by.

"Now is the time for judgment on this world; now the prince of this world will be driven out." (John 12:31)

FURTHER THOUGHT

In these days when God's mercy seems to be so stretched out, how important it is to keep in mind that one day – perhaps very soon – judgment will surely come. Ponder this thought and allow it to stir you to greater prayer and service for your Lord.

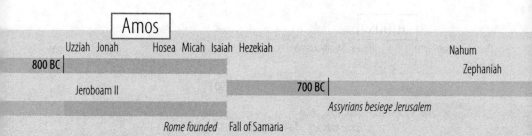

Amos

Uzziah Jonah Hosea Micah Isaiah Hezekiah Nahum

800 BC Zephaniah

Jeroboam II 700 BC

Assyrians besiege Jerusalem

Rome founded Fall of Samaria

DAY 188 — Restoration promised

Amos 9:11–15

After so many predictions of gloom and doom, the prophet gives a prophecy concerning ultimate restoration for a remnant of Israel – a restoration that will be lasting and permanent (v. 15). The Temple will be rebuilt, the kingdom will assume its ancient boundaries, nature will be transfigured and the people shall dwell for ever in the land given them by God. This restoration, says Amos, will come through the house of David (v. 11), and refers, of course, to the coming Messiah. It might sound somewhat fanciful, but when Jesus travelled along the Emmaus Road with the two disconsolate disciples and expounded from the Scriptures "what was said ... concerning himself" (Luke 24:27), He may well have referred to this prophecy of Amos given some 700 years earlier. Whether He did or not, it is a precious and important part of God's eternal truth.

"Jesus answered them, 'Destroy this temple, and I will raise it again in three days.'" (John 2:19)

FURTHER THOUGHT

Imagine you do not have a New Testament and you are asked by a friend your reasons for believing in the birth, death and resurrection of Jesus. Make an outline of what you would say, drawing only on the Old Testament. You'll be surprised at the things you will learn.

Amos				
Uzziah Jonah	Hosea Micah Isaiah Hezekiah			Nahum
800 BC				Zephaniah
Jeroboam II		700 BC		
			Assyrians besiege Jerusalem	
	Rome founded	Fall of Samaria		

Amos denounces the nations

Nation	Crime	Punishment
Syria (Amos 1:3–5)	• Had often harassed Israel	• The capital at Damascus to be burned • Their strongholds to be broken • Their citizens to be enslaved
Phoenicia (1:9,10)	• Had broken their peace covenant with Israel	• The burning down of the forts and palaces in Tyre, their chief city
Israel (2:6–16)	• Had accepted bribes • Had enslaved the poor • Had committed adultery • Had stolen • Were totally unthankful • Had caused the innocent to sin	• Their punishment would make them groan as a loaded-down wagon • Their armies would stumble in battle
Ammon (1:13–15)	• Had murdered Jewish women	• Their cities to be burned • Their citizens to be enslaved
Philistia (1:6–8)	• Had sold Israelites into slavery to Edom	• The burning of their four main cities: Gaza, Ashdod, Ashkelon and Ekron
Judah (2:4,5)	• Had rejected the Word of God • Had disobeyed the God of the Word	• Their Temple in Jerusalem to be destroyed
Moab (2:1–3)	• Had desecrated the tombs of the dead	• They would be defeated in battle
Edom (1:11,12)	• Had murdered many Jews	• The destruction of their cities

Key Lesson – Amos

Amos has been described by a commentator as "one of the most wonderful appearances in the history of the human spirit". The way he observes the sights and sounds of the natural world is quite amazing. "Vultures wheel and swoop, lions cry out of the wilderness, the snake lies curled in the stonework, the bear growls, the earth quakes. His conception of God's great law is equally inspiring. He affirms that from the far-reaching justice of Jehovah no nation is exempt, not even Israel, and from His all-seeing eye there can be no escape." The most important lesson one gathers from the life of Amos is the fact that God not only uses those with great education and training such as Isaiah or Jeremiah, but He also takes up people like Amos, a simple herdsman whom God called to speak His word. Amos was one of God's great "laymen" – you can be another!

Jonah

Jonah: "Dove"

DAY 189 — An unwelcome charge

Jonah 1:1-3

Jonah, a Hebrew prophet, exercised his prophetic ministry in the eighth century BC. His father's name was Amittai, and he came from Gath Hepher, a little town near Nazareth. Jonah is mostly known for his mission to the Gentiles, but his prophecy that Jeroboam would restore Israel's border (2 Kings 14:25) shows that he had a prophetic ministry to his own people, too. When Jonah was told to go to the heathen city of Nineveh and pronounce the destruction awaiting the inhabitants if they did not repent of their wickedness, so unwelcome to the Hebrew prophet was this charge that he set out, at his own expense (v. 3), toward Tarshish (probably a town in Spain). If going to Nineveh is what God wants for Jonah, it is certainly not what Jonah wants for himself, so he sets out in the opposite direction.

"Whatever your hand finds to do, do it with all your might ..." (Eccl. 9:10)

FURTHER THOUGHT

Jonah was charged with a task that he didn't want. He didn't mind preaching, but he liked to choose his congregation. Are you running away from a task which God has given you to perform? Then you had better reconsider – God will have His way in the end.

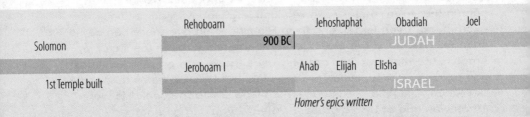

		Rehoboam		Jehoshaphat		Obadiah	Joel
Solomon			900 BC			JUDAH	
		Jeroboam I		Ahab	Elijah	Elisha	
1st Temple built					ISRAEL		
			Homer's epics written				

An unworthy witness

Jonah 1:4–16

Not long after the ship which is carrying Jonah leaves the port of Joppa, it heads into a great storm – one which had been whipped up by the Almighty Himself. The heathen sailors pray fervently to their gods for protection, and proceed to throw the cargo overboard. The captain wakes up the sleeping prophet and rebukes him for his seeming indifference, urging him to pray to his God, too. As the storm continues, the sailors begin to suspect that it has a supernatural source, and is due to the behaviour of someone on board. Lots are cast to find the culprit and "the lot fell on Jonah" (v. 7). Jonah is then closely questioned, whereupon he tells everything and asks the sailors to throw him overboard. This they do, with a prayer that the act will not be held against them.

"But you will receive power when the Holy Spirit comes on you; and you will be my witnesses in Jerusalem, and in all Judea and Samaria, and to the ends of the earth." (Acts 1:8)

FURTHER THOUGHT

Whenever we take a way that is other than God's way, we not only throw our own lives out of balance, but we affect those who are around us too. Being an unworthy witness means that we won't be able to live with ourselves – or with others.

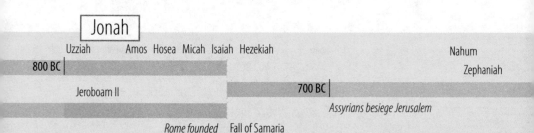

Jonah		
Uzziah	Amos Hosea Micah Isaiah Hezekiah	Nahum
800 BC		Zephaniah
Jeroboam II	700 BC	
	Assyrians besiege Jerusalem	
Rome founded	Fall of Samaria	

Jonah

Jonah: "Dove"

DAY 191 — An unusual event

Jonah 1:17–2:10

Thrown overboard by the frightened yet reluctant sailors, who showed a compassion towards him that he was not prepared to demonstrate toward the Ninevites, Jonah faces what seems to be certain death. But the Lord has not abandoned the disobedient prophet, and initiates an unusual plan for his rescue and recovery. At the Lord's command, a large fish swallows Jonah, inside which the prophet is entombed for three days and nights. From deep inside the fish, Jonah prays to the Lord, and shares his experiences and thoughts with God. He realises that for a man who has treated God the way he has, God has indeed been good to him. From now on things are going to be different: "I, with a song of thanksgiving, will sacrifice to you," says Jonah. And so, once again, God acts, by causing the fish to eject Jonah on to the shore of his home country.

"You will seek me and find me when you seek me with all your heart." (Jer. 29:13)

FURTHER THOUGHT

There are really no limits to the times or places when we can pray. Jonah proves this. He prayed on the deck of the ship, in the sea itself and later in the stomach of a large fish. Remember, it's not where you pray, but how you pray that is important.

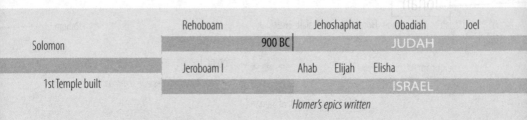

	Rehoboam			Jehoshaphat		Obadiah	Joel
Solomon			900 BC			JUDAH	
	Jeroboam I			Ahab	Elijah	Elisha	
1st Temple built						ISRAEL	
	Homer's epics written						

Jonah 3:1–10; 4:1; Luke 11:30–32

Back on dry land, the chastened prophet is recommissioned by God to carry out the task which he earlier refused. This time Jonah obeys implicitly, and makes his way to Nineveh to proclaim God's word. On his first day in the great city of Nineveh, Jonah finds a suitable spot and announces the message which God has given him: "Forty more days and Nineveh will be overturned." His message produces an immediate response, and the people proclaim a fast and put on sackcloth to demonstrate the depth of their repentance. But it isn't only the people who react in repentance; so, too, does the king of Nineveh. He descends from his throne, takes off his robe, puts on sackcloth and sits in the dust. And just to make sure the people are behind him, he issues a royal proclamation that the whole of Nineveh must repent.

" ... if my people, who are called by my name, will humble themselves and pray and seek my face and turn from their wicked ways, then will I hear from heaven and will forgive their sin and will heal their land." (2 Chron. 7:14)

FURTHER THOUGHT

Jonah's call to Nineveh to repent found an immediate and wholehearted response. How wonderful it would be if our own nation responded so quickly to God's word of truth. But it would be even more wonderful if we Christians responded just as quickly!

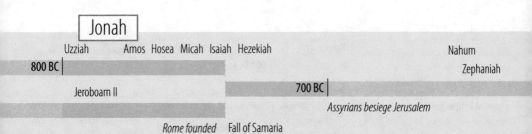

Jonah

Uzziah   Amos Hosea Micah Isaiah Hezekiah   Nahum

800 BC   Zephaniah

Jeroboam II   700 BC

Assyrians besiege Jerusalem

Rome founded   Fall of Samaria

Jonah
Jonah: "Dove"

DAY 193 — An unwise prayer

Jonah 4:1-3

Although Jonah's will has been subdued by the events and experiences through which he has passed, his deep inner feelings concerning his mission seem not to have changed. The success of his mission, instead of bringing him joy and delight, produces in him great anger and bitterness. He seems to have no desire to remain in a world in which Gentiles as well as Jews are able to experience the mercy and compassion of the Lord. God's heart is bigger than Jonah wants it to be, and it is all too much for him. He looks defiantly into the face of God and prays. Prays? Hardly! What comes out of his mouth is more like a catalogue of complaints. Examine his prayer carefully and we will be surprised if you don't agree that his words are shot through with self-pity and self-concern.

"When you ask, you do not receive, because you ask with wrong motives, that you may spend what you get on your pleasures." (James 4:3)

FURTHER THOUGHT

How glad we ought to be that God is a "listening God", who listens intently to our prayers even when they are shot through with self-centredness and personal pique. How glad we ought to be, too, that some of our prayers are not answered!

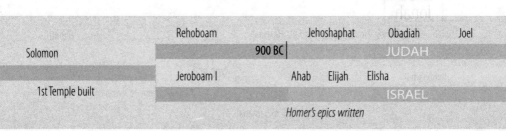

Solomon	Rehoboam		Jehoshaphat	Obadiah	Joel
		900 BC	JUDAH		
1st Temple built	Jeroboam I	Ahab	Elijah	Elisha	
			ISRAEL		
	Homer's epics written				

230

An ungrateful response

Jonah 4:4–6

God challenges Jonah to investigate his emotions to see whether or not they are justified, but Jonah seems deaf to God's voice. In fact, it seems Jonah has the sulks, and is in no mood for a question and answer session with the Almighty. Jonah leaves the repentant and mourning city, erects a shelter for himself and sits down to await the end of the forty-day period. Did he hope, deep in his heart, that the repentance of the Ninevites would still not avert God's wrath? It seems so. God, however, who has shown great love and tenderness to the city of Nineveh, demonstrates that same degree of love for Jonah by providing a sheltering vine to protect him from the burning rays of the sun. Jonah appears to feel a degree of gratitude for the shade which God has provided, but there are still deep roots of ingratitude within his heart.

"... give thanks in all circumstances, for this is God's will for you in Christ Jesus." (1 Thess. 5:18)

FURTHER THOUGHT

How sad that our minds can become so warped that we fail to see the goodness of God even in the midst of our rebellion. George Herbert put it well when he said: "Thou hast given so much to me ... Give me one thing more – a grateful heart." Make this your own prayer – today.

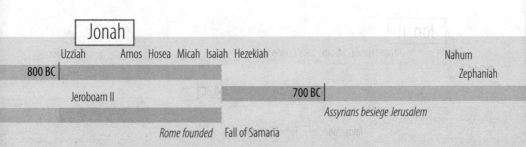

Jonah

Uzziah   Amos Hosea Micah Isaiah Hezekiah   Nahum

800 BC | Zephaniah

Jeroboam II   700 BC |

Assyrians besiege Jerusalem

Rome founded   Fall of Samaria

Jonah

Jonah: "Dove"

An unrepentant reply

Jonah 4:7-11

At dawn the next day, the vine which God had provided to shelter Jonah from the burning rays of the sun is attacked by a worm and thus dies. As the sun climbs high in the sky, God sends a hot east wind which makes Jonah furious, and once again he wishes he was dead. How sad that the prophet seems more angry over the collapse of the sheltering vine than over the possible destruction of a whole city. The Lord's object lesson, designed to show Jonah the inconsistency of his heart, and His further challenge concerning his unrighteous anger, meets with little response from Jonah. Jonah is upset about a plant, but seems to care little about the people. He remains completely unrepentant and unwilling to show mercy and compassion to the Ninevites. How true it is that there are none so deaf as those who do not wish to hear.

"Finally, all of you, live in harmony with one another; be sympathetic, love as brothers, be compassionate and humble." (1 Pet. 3:8)

FURTHER THOUGHT

Life is certainly mixed up when a man's values are such that he can have more pity for a plant than for the vast population of a great city like Nineveh.
How about you? Do you value things more than people? If so, then make sure you don't go into the rest of the day with an unrepentant spirit.

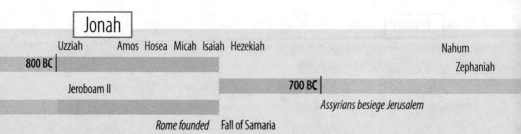

Jonah							
Uzziah	Amos	Hosea	Micah	Isaiah	Hezekiah	Nahum	
800 BC						Zephaniah	
Jeroboam II				700 BC			
				Assyrians besiege Jerusalem			
	Rome founded	Fall of Samaria					

Numerous cases have been reported of men who have survived the ordeal of being swallowed by a whale. *The Princeton Theological Review* (Oct. 1927) tells of two incidents, one in 1758 and the other in 1771, in which a man was swallowed by a whale and vomited up shortly afterwards with only minor injuries. One of the most striking instances comes from Francis Fox, in *Sixty-Three Years of Engineering*, who reports that this incident was carefully investigated by two scientists. In 1891, the whaling ship, *Star of the East*, was near the Falkland Islands. The lookout sighted a large sperm whale. Two boats were lowered, one of which was upset by a lash of the whale's tail, so that its crew fell into the sea. One of them was drowned, but James Bartley simply disappeared. After the whale was killed, the crew set to work removing the blubber. The sailors were startled by something in the stomach which gave spasmodic signs of life, and inside was found the missing sailor, doubled up and unconscious. Within three weeks he recovered from the shock and resumed his duties.

Key Lesson – Jonah

Jonah was one of the most mixed up of all the Old Testament prophets. His failure was not that he was a false prophet, but a disobedient one – and also one who thought more of his own reputation than he did of the people's good and the glory of God. Jonah would probably have enjoyed seeing Jehovah avenging Himself on His adversaries, and when the Lord deprives him of his fierce and patriotic satisfaction, he becomes vexed and angry. There are many lessons we can learn from Jonah's life – the fact, for example, that God will pursue His purposes in our lives despite our inner or outer rebellion. The greatest lesson we learn from Jonah, however, is the need to surrender our right to our reputation, for if we become preoccupied with how people think about us, it can soon affect and interfere with the individual life-message which God has given each one of us to share with the world.

Zechariah

Zechariah: "Jehovah is renowned" or "Jehovah has remembered"

DAY 196 — A warning prophet

Zechariah 1:1–6

Zechariah was the son of Berekiah and the grandson of Iddo, both of whom were priests in Israel. Iddo was one of the priests who returned with Zerubbabel from the captivity in Babylon when they were charged by Cyrus, king of Persia, to rebuild the Temple in Jerusalem (Neh. 12:4). Zechariah's earlier prophecies and visions relate to the need for a proper approach to worship in the Temple, the first step being that of true repentance and confession. Zechariah warns of the results that will follow if the people, like their forefathers, do not heed God's commandments.

"In the past God overlooked such ignorance, but now he commands all people everywhere to repent." **(Acts 17:30)**

FURTHER THOUGHT

How essential it is to be continually open to the warnings and entreaties of God! The key to a good relationship with the Lord is summed up in Zechariah 1:3 – write out the words so that they are locked into your soul.

Hosea	Micah	Isaiah	Hezekiah				Nahum		Jeremiah	Habakkuk	Daniel
							Zephaniah		Josiah	Nebuchadnezzar	
				700 BC						600 BC	
				Assyrians besiege Jerusalem						Daniel taken to Babylon	
Rome founded		Fall of Samaria									

I n this long section of reading, there are eight visions, all revealing God's concern for the Jewish people – those whom He has chosen to worship Him. First he hears of God's compassion for Jerusalem (1:7–17). Then he sees four craftsmen coming to break the power of the hostile nations (1:18–21). Next he sees a new Jerusalem that becomes a home for both Jew and Gentile (2:1–13). Then he is given a vision of Joshua, the high priest, clothed in clean garments (3:1–10). He sees next a seven-branched candlestick of solid gold being replenished by two olive trees (4:1–14). Then he sees a very large scroll flying through the air bearing God's curse on sin (5:1–4), and a woman sitting in a basket who personifies wickedness (5:5–11). Finally he sees four chariots driven by angelic beings, symbolising God's active control of the world (6:1–8).

"As Moses went into the tent, the pillar of cloud would come down and stay at the entrance, while the Lord spoke with Moses." (Ex. 33:9)

FURTHER THOUGHT

In all of Zechariah's night visions there is one unifying thought which expresses a central message and consists of three phrases: "I am very jealous for Jerusalem ... I am very angry with the nations ... I will return to Jerusalem with mercy." Can you spot them?

Zechariah						
				Ezra		
Ezekiel	Cyrus	Haggai		Esther	Nehemiah	Malachi
FALL OF JUDAH		500 BC				400 BC
Exile in Babylon	2nd Temple built		*Iron age begins in Britain*		Nehemiah rebuilds walls of Jerusalem	
Jerusalem destroyed	Zerubbabel and main party return			Ezra returns		

Zechariah

Zechariah: "Jehovah is renowned" or "Jehovah has remembered"

DAY 198 — A challenging prophet

Zechariah 7:1-10

Since Zechariah came from a family of priests, he would doubtless have taken part in the fasting and mourning which took place annually in the fifth month, the month in which Jerusalem had been burnt by the Babylonians and the Temple destroyed. A deputation comes to enquire whether this fast should continue now that the rebuilding of the Temple is nearing completion, and they are challenged by the prophet to examine the motives which have prompted them to keep this fast over so many years. His implication is that their participation lacks spiritual reality (v. 5). The prophet follows his challenge, however, with a word that one day in the future God will turn the situation to such good account that their fast days will become feast days (8:19).

"Since you died with Christ to the basic principles of this world, why, as though you still belonged to it, do you submit to its rules: 'Do not handle! Do not taste! Do not touch!'?" (Col. 2:20-21)

FURTHER THOUGHT

What if a well-respected preacher stepped into your church pulpit this coming Sunday, and challenged you and the rest of the congregation by saying that your worship consisted of nothing more than form or ceremony? Would it offend you? But what is more - would it be true?

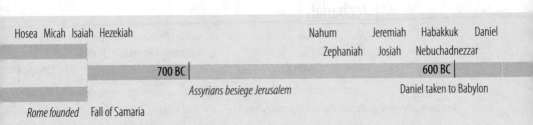

Hosea	Micah	Isaiah	Hezekiah			Nahum		Jeremiah	Habakkuk	Daniel
						Zephaniah	Josiah		Nebuchadnezzar	
				700 BC					600 BC	
				Assyrians besiege Jerusalem				Daniel taken to Babylon		
	Rome founded	Fall of Samaria								

A consoling prophet

Zechariah 8:1–9:17

Zechariah was a prophet who not only gave warnings of God's judgments and challenged the people to live at a higher spiritual level, he also gave a number of prophecies of hope and consolation for the future of Israel (8:1–23). The judgment of Israel's enemies is predicted, and the coming of the Prince of Peace, first in humility (9:9), and then in triumph to rule over all nations (9:10). There can be little doubt that Christ's entry into Jerusalem on Palm Sunday was a partial fulfilment of this prophecy, and all Bible students draw hope and inspiration from the fact that the day will come when He will come again in power and glory to complete Zechariah's great prophetic word. In that day, we are told, His people will shine like jewels in His crown (9:16).

"Look, he is coming with the clouds, and every eye will see him, even those who pierced him; and all the peoples of the earth will mourn because of him. So shall it be! Amen." (Rev. 1:7)

FURTHER THOUGHT

Although sin has played havoc with God's creation – and to a certain extent still does – the day will come when sin will be banished for ever. What is your response to this great and wonderful truth? May it be the last four words of Revelation 22:20.

		Zechariah			Ezra			
Ezekiel		Cyrus	Haggai			Esther	Nehemiah	Malachi
FALL OF JUDAH			500 BC					400 BC
Exile in Babylon		2nd Temple built	*Iron age begins in Britain*			Nehemiah rebuilds walls of Jerusalem		
Jerusalem destroyed		Zerubbabel and main party return			Ezra returns			

DAY 200 — A doomsday prophet
Zechariah 10:1–11:17

Zechariah contrasts the good things God gives to His people with the false consolation received by the followers of other gods. A true prophetic ministry not only conveys the message of God, but also the **feelings** of God, and here Zechariah imparts to the people something of the Lord's anger against the leaders and priests of Judah, who are careless and insensitive to the well-being of the people (10:3). The only hope, it seems, is to look beyond human frailty and draw inspiration and courage from the fact that one day a Leader will come – the Messiah by name – who will gather His people from all over the world to form one nation under His guidance and rule. Many believe that this prophecy has a direct reference to the return of the Jews to Israel in our own generation.

"Oh Jerusalem, Jerusalem ... how often I have longed to gather your children together, as a hen gathers her chicks under her wings, but you were not willing!" (Luke 13:34)

FURTHER THOUGHT
One great preacher said: "I have been kept from sin, not so much by the fact that my transgression breaks God's law, but that it breaks God's heart." Can you see what he meant? Sin is something that hurts God. Never forget – God has feelings too!

Hosea	Micah	Isaiah	Hezekiah			Nahum		Jeremiah	Habakkuk	Daniel
						Zephaniah		Josiah	Nebuchadnezzar	
				700 BC					600 BC	
			Assyrians besiege Jerusalem						Daniel taken to Babylon	
Rome founded		Fall of Samaria								

A Messianic prophet

Zechariah 12:1–14:21

Zechariah has already prophesied concerning Christ's entry into Jerusalem, and now he changes the figure to that of the Good Shepherd who comes to rescue His flock which was doomed to slaughter (11:7). Students of Scripture cannot help noticing in chapters 11 and 13 a picture of Christ's earthly life and ministry. Was He not the Good Shepherd who gave His life for His sheep? Was He not ultimately rejected and slain? Did not His shed blood provide cleansing for sin (13:1)? The prophetic vision that follows covers the activities that surround the second coming of Christ, and the establishing of His kingdom on the earth.

"This same Jesus, who has been taken from you into heaven, will come back in the same way you have seen him go into heaven." (Acts 1:11)

FURTHER THOUGHT

If there is one verse in Zechariah that is worth underlining, it is 14:4. This verse tells us that when Christ returns, His feet will touch down on the Mount of Olives. How close are we to that great event, we wonder?

Zechariah

				Ezra		
Ezekiel	Cyrus	Haggai		Esther	Nehemiah	Malachi

FALL OF JUDAH — 500 BC — 400 BC

Exile in Babylon — 2nd Temple built — *Iron age begins in Britain* — Nehemiah rebuilds walls of Jerusalem

Jerusalem destroyed — Zerubbabel and main party return — Ezra returns

Zechariah and the Prince

His First Coming	His Second Coming
He comes to pasture the flock of God **(Zech. 11:7)**	The cruel reign of the antichrist **(11:16)**
He is rejected by Israel's leaders **(11:8)**	Jerusalem to be surrounded and taken **(14:2)**
	Two-thirds of the Jews to perish **(13:8)**
He thus set aside Israel **(11:10)** (Possible meaning of His breaking the staff called Favour)	One-third of the Jews to be saved **(13:9)**
	Christ to appear upon the Mount of Olives **(14:4, 8)**
He makes His triumphal entry into Jerusalem **(9:9)**	Armageddon to be fought **(12:3; 14:2, 3)**
He is sold for thirty pieces of silver **(11:12)**	God's enemies to be destroyed **(12:4, 9; 14:12-15)**
He predicts the destruction of Jerusalem **(11:14)** (Possible meaning of His breaking the staff called Union)	Israel to recognise Christ **(12:10-14)**
	Israel to be cleansed **(13:1)**
He is crucified **(12:10)**	Israel to be settled in the land **(10:6-12; 8:8)**
	Gentiles to worship the Lord **(14:16-19)**
	Jerusalem to be filled with happy boys and girls **(8:5)**
	Christ to build the Temple **(6:13)**
	Christ to rule as the Priest-King over all the world **(6:13; 9:10)**

Key Lesson - Zechariah

Zechariah is regarded by many Bible commentators as one of the most endearing of all the prophets, for despite his strong denunciation of sin and hypocrisy he manifests a tender and sympathetic heart. It is not easy to draw the line sharply between the two camps of light and darkness, and at the same time to seek out and applaud the latent good – yet, nevertheless, Zechariah seems to accomplish this. This great-hearted prophet has a clear sense of the redeeming process in history, and holds tenaciously to the truth that no matter what the present may be, God will ultimately work out all things for good. The lesson we learn, therefore, from Zechariah is that no matter what are the causes for our present despondency, they are far outweighed by the future prospects. The apostle Paul puts it like this: "For our light and momentary troubles are achieving for us an eternal glory that far outweighs them all." (2 Cor. 4:17)

Hebrews 11:1–12:1

A s we are about to pass from studying Old Testament characters and move into the New, it seems appropriate to pause and consider what it was that inspired these great heroes of the past in their witness and testimony for God. The writer to the Hebrews gives us the answer in a single word – **faith**. Although some of the personalities we have looked at in the Old Testament section of our studies are not mentioned in Hebrews 11 – the "Westminster Abbey of the Bible" – there can be little doubt that each one of them lived and worked by faith. They accomplished great exploits for God because they lived in the sure and certain hope that what they were doing had an eternal meaning and purpose.

"... everyone born of God overcomes the world. This is the victory that has overcome the world, even our faith." (1 John 5:4)

FURTHER THOUGHT

Faith believes that God has revealed something about the future – not everything, but something. And what He has revealed is quite enough for us to know. If you can live like that, then your name, too, will be found among the great parade of history's heroes and heroines of faith.

200 BC

100 BC

DAY 203

A chosen handmaid

Luke 1:26–38

Mary is without doubt one of the loveliest characters in the whole of Scripture. Like her husband-to-be, Joseph, she appears to have been of lowly station, and was in the line of descent from King David. The fact that she was chosen by God to be the mother of Jesus implies that she was one of the most devout and favoured of all women. The sudden appearance of the angel Gabriel greatly troubles Mary, but he soon calms her fears and makes the announcement that she shall have great honour – and also great sorrow – in being the mother of the incarnate Son of God. After enquiring as to how this prophecy will be fulfilled, as she is unmarried and a virgin, Mary humbly accepts her high calling despite the problems it will cause both to her and to her espoused husband, Joseph.

"For he chose us in him before the creation of the world to be holy and blameless in his sight ..." (Eph. 1:4)

FURTHER THOUGHT

Mary has been called "the first lady of Christendom". Some tend to make too much of her, others too little. Take a moment today to ponder on the hallmarks of this fine and devout woman, and give thanks to God for the part she played in being the mother of our Lord.

| Mary |

Joseph

100 BC | 5 BC | AD 1 |

BIRTH OF CHRIST

A praising response

Luke 1:46-56

Having been told that her elderly relative Elizabeth is also miraculously expecting a baby, Mary leaves Nazareth in a hurry to visit Elizabeth at her home in the hill country of Judea. As soon as Elizabeth greets Mary, the baby in Elizabeth's womb leaps at the sound of Mary's voice, which occasions Elizabeth to break forth in the inspired words: "Blessed are you among women, and blessed is the child you will bear!" Mary responds with a hymn of praise to God – now often referred to as "The Magnificat" – which Luke records in full. Mary stays with Elizabeth for three months before returning to Nazareth, and finds that in the meantime Joseph, too, has been visited by an angel, who assures him that God is at work and that he should not continue with his plan to divorce Mary for unchastity. Can you imagine what relief this information would have brought to her?

"'I will declare your name to my brothers; in the presence of the congregation I will sing your praises.'" (Heb. 2:12)

FURTHER THOUGHT

Mary's inner feelings are impossible to fully understand or analyse, because they were unique. She responds to the situation, however, with gratitude and praise. It demands great spiritual maturity and love for God to turn every occasion into praise. Have you arrived at that stage in your spiritual life yet?

AD 10

AD 20

Death of Augustus

DAY 205   A servant's heart

Luke 2:40-52

Here Luke gives a brief account of the early life of Jesus, and shows how God's hand was upon Him in those important years of development. As He grew in physical size and stature, however, it must have been obvious to Mary and Joseph that He had a spiritual perception that was much greater than they could ever have imagined. Their awareness of this quality comes to a head when He is twelve years old. After reprimanding Him for not keeping up with them when they left Jerusalem to return to Nazareth, He says: "Didn't you know I had to be in my Father's house?" Mary recognises that something unique and divine is happening in Jesus' life, and although she cannot understand it (v. 51), she meditates much on it in her heart.

"For who is greater, the one who is at the table or the one who serves? Is it not the one who is at the table? But I am among you as one who serves." (Luke 22:27)

FURTHER THOUGHT

Those who are greatly used by God are those who possess a "servant's heart". But how can you tell whether you have such a heart? It's simple: the heart of a servant is preoccupied with ministry – the heart of a non-servant is preoccupied with manipulation.

Mary

Joseph

100 BC   5 BC   AD 1

BIRTH OF CHRIST

A godly mother

John 2:1-12; Matthew 13:55-56; Mark 6:3

Tradition states that Mary was widowed before Jesus and her other sons and daughters by Joseph grew to adulthood, and that Jesus became the head of the household, supporting them by working as the village carpenter in succession to Joseph (Mark 6:3). Perhaps this is why Mary instinctively turns to Jesus for help when, at the wedding feast in Cana, the wine runs out. Jesus appears to rebuff His mother's concerned approach, but there is much more to it than that; Jesus is simply showing her that this is the time when their relationship must change, for He must now focus on developing His ministry. Mary, godly woman that she was, must have sensed this too. Her godliness would have carried her through. It is important to realise that the use of the term "woman", as to the woman of Samaria and again from the cross, in no way implies disrespect.

"Your beauty should not come from outward adornment ... Instead, it should be ... the unfading beauty of a gentle and quiet spirit, which is of great worth in God's sight. For this is the way the holy women of the past who put their hope in God used to make themselves beautiful ..." (1 Pet.3:3–5)

FURTHER THOUGHT

"Godliness," says a Christian commentator, "is acting as God would do if He were in your shoes." How difficult it is to see everything that happens to us from God's perspective – but how marvellous it is when we overcome that difficulty and learn to see life from His point of view.

AD 10

AD 20

Death of Augustus

DAY **207**

A follower of Jesus

John 2:1–10; Mark 3:31–35

Mary, despite the unusual and unexpected things that are taking place in the life of her firstborn Son, Jesus, continues to have deep faith in Him nevertheless. We see a glimpse of this in the words she speaks to the servants during the crisis that developed at the wedding feast in Cana: "Do whatever he tells you" (John 2:5). Mary continued to be a follower of Jesus throughout His entire ministry, even though at times she was greatly tested. On one occasion His friends and family tried to restrain Him over what they saw as a developing religious frenzy or madness (Mark 3:21). Mary sensed, however, that her Son was about the work of His heavenly Father, and was loyal to Him to the day that He died upon the cross – and beyond.

"Then he went down to Nazareth with them and was obedient to them. But his mother treasured all these things in her heart." (Luke 2:51)

FURTHER THOUGHT

At Calvary Mary experienced the fulfilment of the startling prophecy that was given to her prior to Jesus' birth – "A sword will pierce your own soul too" (Luke 2:35) – but she stayed to watch and weep. What a comfort her presence must have been to our Lord in those last hours on the cross. Give thanks for that.

Mary

Joseph

100 BC | | 5 BC | AD 1 |

BIRTH OF CHRIST

Maternal love

John 19:1-27

Imagine the pain that Mary must have felt as she saw Jesus pinned to a Roman cross. Imagine, also, the agony she must have endured as she saw the fire of life fade from her Son's eyes, and heard His great cry of dereliction: "My God, my God, why have you forsaken me?" (Matthew 27:46). Traditional paintings show Mary receiving Jesus' torn and bleeding body from the cross. We have no Biblical evidence for this, of course, but it is reasonable to assume that Mary, loving Him as she did, would have stayed as close to Him as possible, not only in the hours prior to death but also in the hours after death. It is little wonder that history is so full of respect and adulation for a mother whose love for her Son reached one of the highest peaks humanity has ever known.

"May the Lord make your love increase and overflow for each other and for everyone else, just as ours does for you." (1 Thess. 3:12)

FURTHER THOUGHT

It is not every woman who could have borne the ordeal of seeing her son nailed to a cross! How revealing this is of her true character and worth. When we are willing to bear hurt rather than run away from it, it implies we are in charge of our emotions, and not that our emotions are in charge of us.

AD 10 |

AD 20 |

Death of Augustus

DAY 209   In the Upper Room

Acts 1:1-14

There is one more scene in the life of Mary – her presence in the Upper Room. About 120 people are gathered together for prayer, and among them is "Mary the mother of Jesus". Although tradition has a lot to say about her following the events which took place at Pentecost, this is in fact where the Bible takes its leave of her. It is interesting to note that despite her devout character, her sacrificial spirit and the quality of her life, she is still in as much need of receiving the gift of the Holy Spirit as any of the others. Had we been able to kneel alongside Mary in that Upper Room and ask her why, being the mother of the Lord, she thought it necessary to wait for the promised Holy Spirit, she would probably have said: "Bringing Him into the world was what I did for Him; the gift of the Holy Spirit is what He does for me."

"Do not get drunk on wine, which leads to debauchery. Instead, be filled with the Spirit." (Eph. 5:18)

FURTHER THOUGHT

Have you received your own personal Pentecost? Are you a truly Spirit-filled person? If not, then kneel today in God's presence and invite Him to fill you, just as He did the early disciples, until you are full to overflowing.

Mary

Joseph

100 BC | 5 BC | AD 1 |
BIRTH OF CHRIST

Mary's role

Mary's role as the mother of Jesus ordains motherhood, whether actual or spiritual, to be the true calling of woman and shows its great and sacred nature. In her entire acceptance she manifested the initial strength of her character. She beheld from the beginning the greatness of a divine purpose being fulfilled, and remained faithful in response as it gradually developed before her. Again, in social life, Mary took the part of service, by active kindness, and by bringing others into obedience to Christ. Thus, strong and brave under the inspiration of love, she followed to the foot of the cross, thereby suffering to learn something of the mystery of the sacrifice which was being offered by her Son, and to offer her best also.

Key Lesson – Mary

What a model of true womanhood was Mary of Nazareth. Her simple faith in the power and goodness of God; her willing acceptance of the path that destiny had marked out for her; her belief that God would, in time, fulfil His promises and bring to pass what He purposed – these, combined with the simple and humble duties of home, motherhood and family mark her out as one of the greatest women – if not the greatest – who has ever lived. There are many lessons one can learn from her life, but perhaps the most important is the fact that the sadness and sorrow she suffered because of all that happened to her Son did not produce in her any sense of estrangement or alienation. The meaning of her name. as we saw, is "bitterness", and all that her name meant truly came to pass. What a victory we achieve, however, when, like Mary, we use the sorrows and hurts of life to keep us close to our Lord, rather than letting them drive us from Him.

DAY **210**

An ordinary man

Matthew 1:18–19

Joseph was an inhabitant of Nazareth. A humble carpenter by trade, he was, like Mary, a descendant of King David (Matt. 1:20). He had a high reputation and was considered to be a good and honourable man (v. 19). Joseph has been described as "the forgotten man" in the story of the birth of Jesus Christ, but he was, of course, as the foster-father of our Lord, an important personality. Most men would have resented the title which he receives in the New Testament – "the husband of Mary" (v.16). Not Joseph, however. He knew his place and was content to remain where God had put him.

"He chose the lowly things of this world and the despised things – and the things that are not – to nullify the things that are, so that no-one may boast before him." (1 Cor. 1:28–29)

FURTHER THOUGHT

How sad that we often equate ordinariness with ineffectiveness. By far the majority of those whom God has used down the ages have been ordinary men and women who have become extra-ordinary because of their trust and faith in a great God. Has this something to say to you?

Joseph

Mary

100 BC

5 BC | AD 1 |
BIRTH OF CHRIST

Matthew 13:55; Mark 6:3

Carpentry, although an honourable profession, rarely brought riches. Doubtless Joseph's skills would have brought him into contact with most of the villagers of Nazareth, as well as the surrounding towns, as he laboured in such tasks as building furniture, repairing buildings and making agricultural implements. Why God should choose such an ordinary man to be the foster-father of His incarnate Son is a mystery that we will never fully understand. It highlights once again, however, the fact that ordinariness is no bar to usefulness, and that even a common carpenter can, in God's hands, become a man of great spiritual importance.

"Accept one another, then, just as Christ accepted you, in order to bring praise to God." (Rom. 15:7)

FURTHER THOUGHT

Isn't it encouraging to realise that God is more interested in what we are than who we are, and that character is much more important to Him than our profession or academic brilliance?

DAY 212   A spiritual dreamer

Matthew 1:20-23

Mary, though engaged to Joseph, was carrying in her womb the baby Jesus. This was extremely difficult to comprehend and, as Joseph was a just and reasonable man, he considered how he might avoid making Mary a public example by divorcing her quietly. While Mary is visiting her cousin Elizabeth, Joseph is visited by an angel who tells him in a dream that he must not be afraid to take Mary as his wife. The miraculous nature of the event begins to impress itself on Joseph's heart, as he now realises that Mary is carrying in her womb the promised Messiah, Jesus, the Son of the living God.

" ... no prophecy of Scripture came about by the prophet's own interpretation. For prophecy never had its origin in the will of man, but men spoke from God as they were carried along by the Holy Spirit."
(2 Pet. 1:20–21)

FURTHER THOUGHT

Question: How and why did Joseph understand the words of the angel? Answer: Because he knew the Old Testament prophecy concerning the promise of Christ's coming! If God spoke to you today about a Biblical promise, would you know where to find it in Scripture?

Joseph

Mary

100 BC		5 BC	AD 1
			BIRTH OF CHRIST

Matthew 1:24–25

Now that Joseph's problem concerning Mary's pregnancy is resolved, he shows no hesitation in proceeding with the marriage ceremony. Thus Mary and her unborn child are brought under Joseph's protection and care. Joseph, however, refrains from physically consummating the marriage until after the birth of Jesus. Here one can see again Joseph's deep devotion to God. He laid aside his own physical desires in the interests of Mary's condition, and followed to the letter the commands of the archangel Gabriel. What a glimpse this gives us into the reason why God selected Joseph to be the foster-father of His Son.

"'Does the Lord delight in burnt offerings and sacrifices as much as in obeying the voice of the Lord? To obey is better than sacrifice, and to heed is better than the fat of rams.'"
(1 Sam. 15:22)

FURTHER THOUGHT

F.W. Robertson has pointed out: "It is not said, after keeping God's commandments, but in keeping them there is great reward. God has linked these two things together, and no man can separate them – obedience and power."

AD 10 |

AD 20 |

Death of Augustus

DAY **214**

A protective parent
Matthew 2:13–15

Joseph's life as a humble carpenter was disrupted by the evil designs of King Herod, who was bent on killing the infant King of the Jews (see Matthew 2:1–12). At this time, Joseph receives another supernatural dream in which he is told to escape to Egypt with Mary and her child, and to remain there until it is safe to return. Although he was made aware of God's continual care by receiving His guidance through this dream, Joseph must have possessed great faith and resourcefulness to go and live in a foreign land with a young wife and a small child. This, too, lets in another ray of light on the character of Joseph, who protected Jesus as if He had been his very own son.

"Fathers, do not exasperate your children; instead, bring them up in the training and instruction of the Lord." (Eph. 6:4)

FURTHER THOUGHT

Take a blank piece of paper and make an outline of the ways in which Joseph was obedient to God's commands. You might like to use this outline as the basis of a talk in the future. First, however, let it speak to you. Only then will it speak to others.

Joseph

Mary

100 BC | 5 BC | AD 1 |

BIRTH OF CHRIST

A considerate father

Luke 2:41–52

Having been told in another dream to return home, Joseph arrived in Nazareth and settled back into his normal routine. This included an annual visit to Jerusalem for the Passover Feast (v. 41). When Jesus was twelve years of age, He was taken to the city by Mary and Joseph. On the return journey Jesus was discovered to be missing, but after three days was found listening and talking to the religious teachers in the Temple. When Mary reprimands Jesus for staying behind, He replies in words that somewhat mystify them. Nevertheless, though not quite comprehending the meaning of His words, Joseph and Mary showed a consideration that suggests they sensed God was at work in the heart and life of their beloved son.

"My son, keep your father's commands and do not forsake your mother's teaching ... For these commands are a lamp, this teaching is a light, and the corrections of discipline are the way to life." (Prov. 6:20, 23)

FURTHER THOUGHT

Question: What is the greatest attitude a parent can show to their offspring? Answer: Consideration. Children need to know you are on their side, not just on their back.

Death of Augustus

There can be little doubt that Joseph of Nazareth contributed to Jesus' early life in a most wonderful way. Joseph's life is highlighted by the fact that he was willing to take on a role for God that brought him misunderstanding and suspicion – but he stayed with it in the knowledge that as long as God had spoken, the opinions of others mattered little. Is that a characteristic which God might perhaps be wanting to build into you at this moment? If so, then ask the Holy Spirit to inculcate in your life the same character qualities which were in his.

John the Baptist

John: "God is gracious"

Chosen in birth

Luke 1:1-80

Zechariah, an elderly priest, is chosen by lot to enter the inner sanctuary of the Temple and minister at the altar of incense when he is confronted by the archangel Gabriel. The angel announces that, despite her advanced age, Zechariah's wife Elizabeth is to bear him a son whose name will be John. A promise is also given that John will be filled with the Holy Spirit from his birth, and that his mission is to prepare Israel for the coming of the Messiah. Zechariah, despite his deep spirituality (v. 6), finds this difficult to believe and expresses his doubt to the angel. As a result of his unbelief, he is struck dumb and remains like this until after John is born.

"... your eyes saw my unformed body. All the days ordained for me were written in your book before one of them came to be." (Psa. 139:16)

FURTHER THOUGHT

Although the circumstances surrounding John's birth were somewhat unusual, every human birth is of immense importance to God. God has no favourites. He was as interested in your birth as He was in John's. Do you doubt that? Then read the text for today.

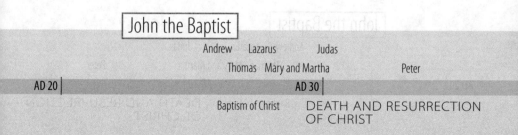

John the Baptist

| Andrew | Lazarus | Judas |
| Thomas | Mary and Martha | Peter |

AD 20 | AD 30 |

Baptism of Christ | DEATH AND RESURRECTION OF CHRIST

DAY 217

Obedient in heart

Matthew 3:1–12

John was the last of the Old Testament prophets, and his name, "God is gracious", had special significance, indicating that a new age was dawning in Israel – the age of grace. The archangel Gabriel promised Zechariah that John would be filled with the Holy Spirit from his birth, and that he would turn many to God. John's ministry and conduct show quite clearly that this promise was abundantly fulfilled, as under the Spirit's direction he calls huge numbers of Israel's population to repentance and baptism in water. John prefers the life of an ascetic and makes his abode in the desert, drawing his congregations from Jerusalem and the area around the lower Jordan.

"Although he was a son, he learned obedience from what he suffered ..." (Heb. 5:8)

FURTHER THOUGHT

"Every great person," said William Ward, "has first learned how to obey, whom to obey and when to obey." There can be little doubt that obedience was the key to John's spiritual greatness. It is the key to your spiritual success also. Is there an area in your Christian life where you have not obeyed? Then put things right today.

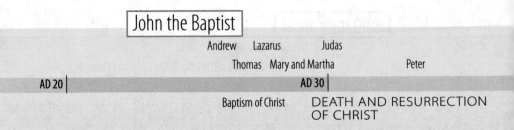

	John the Baptist				
		Andrew	Lazarus	Judas	
		Thomas	Mary and Martha		Peter
AD 20				AD 30	
		Baptism of Christ		DEATH AND RESURRECTION OF CHRIST	

Powerful in preaching

Mark 1:1–8; John 5:33–35

John's extremely large congregations included such people as tax collectors and soldiers, as well as members of the two main religious groups, the Pharisees and Sadducees. He addresses his hearers in strong and forthright language and insists on them showing the evidence for their repentance by being baptised in the Jordan and in their changed lives. His main message to Israel is that they must not trust in their nation's relationship with God for salvation, but that they must personally take their place before Him in genuine humility and repentance. He promises them that when the Messiah comes, He will baptise with heavenly fire!

"Let the word of Christ dwell in you richly as you teach and admonish one another with all wisdom, and as you sing psalms, hymns and spiritual songs with gratitude in your hearts to God." (Col. 3:16)

FURTHER THOUGHT

Preaching has been defined as "a manifestation of the living Word, by the written Word and through the spoken word". John the Baptist most certainly achieved that. Pray right now for your own minister and his pulpit ministry. Ask God to help him draw people closer to Christ.

Cornelius		Paul		Aquila and Priscilla		
Stephen	Philip the Evangelist	Barnabas		Lydia	Timothy	Silas
AD 40				**AD 50**		
Paul's conversion	1st missionary journey			2nd missionary journey		

DAY **219**   Humble in spirit

John 1:15–36

The forthright ministry of John succeeds in drawing large crowds of people to the banks of the lower Jordan and this, in turn, causes the Jewish authorities to send men to examine his credentials. When asked to give an account of himself, John describes himself merely as a "voice". "My task," he says in effect, "is to call attention to the One who is to come ... whose sandals I am not worthy to untie." John denies any suggestion that he is a reincarnation of Elijah or that he is the prophet they are expecting (Deut. 18:18). One theme dominates the heart and mind of John – how to make himself appear smaller and the Messiah appear bigger.

"... whoever humbles himself like this child is the greatest in the kingdom of heaven." (Matt. 18:4)

FURTHER THOUGHT

"Humility," said a woman to a preacher after he had expounded the subject in a sermon, "is one of my greatest assets." Sounds like she had missed the point! "Really great men," said John Ruskin, "have the feeling that greatness is not in them, but through them." Do you agree?

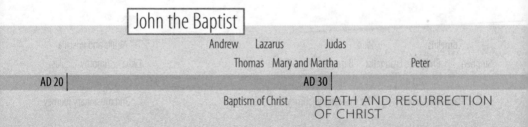

John the Baptist

	Andrew	Lazarus		Judas		
	Thomas	Mary and Martha			Peter	
AD 20				AD 30		
	Baptism of Christ			DEATH AND RESURRECTION OF CHRIST		

Matthew 14:1–12; Mark 6:14–20

John not only preached to the multitudes, but he appears to have had access to the court of Herod Antipas, who recognises him as a righteous and holy man (Mark 6:20). Herod seems to find John's words fascinating and yet perplexing. When John fearlessly denounces Herod for marrying his brother's wife, he is thrust into prison in the hope that he will be silenced. John's denunciation of Herod's marriage causes his wife, Herodias, to become angry and she decides to bring about his death. This desire, however, is thwarted by Herod until she traps him into ordering John's execution by way of a rash oath Herod makes to her daughter after she has danced for him.

"Consecrate yourselves and be holy, because I am the Lord your God." (Lev. 20:7)

FURTHER THOUGHT

"Holy in character" – what a testimony. Holiness really means "healthiness". And character? Someone said: "Character is what a man is in the dark." Ask yourself right now: Am I a "healthy" person? And what am I like in the dark?

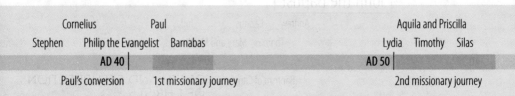

Cornelius		Paul			Aquila and Priscilla		
Stephen	Philip the Evangelist	Barnabas			Lydia	Timothy	Silas
	AD 40				AD 50		
Paul's conversion		1st missionary journey			2nd missionary journey		

John the Baptist
John: "God is gracious"

Clear in testimony
John 3:22–36; 10:40–41

John, having made clear in his message that he is neither Elijah returned to earth, nor the Messiah, now proceeds to identify Jesus of Nazareth as the true Messiah and begins to proclaim this truth in the most decisive terms. He rejoices in the fact that Jesus' public ministry begins to flourish, and affirms in even clearer language than before that he is only the forerunner of the Son of God and is totally reconciled to the idea of Christ's ministry eclipsing his own. He makes clear also a fact that must have staggered some of the Jews of his day – that Christ's ministry was not to take away merely the sins of the nation, but the sins of the world.

"He came as a witness to testify concerning that light, so that through him all men might believe." (John 1:7)

FURTHER THOUGHT

If you were arrested on the charge of being a Christian and given three minutes to give your testimony, what would you say? Would it be as clear as John's testimony to Christ? If you can, sit down today and write out your Christian testimony in about 500 words. Then read it to a friend or family member for comment!

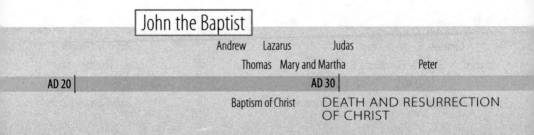

John the Baptist

Andrew   Lazarus   Judas

Thomas   Mary and Martha   Peter

AD 20

AD 30

Baptism of Christ   DEATH AND RESURRECTION OF CHRIST

Human in adversity

Matthew 4:12; 11:1-15; Luke 7:24-29

John's ministry is spoken highly of by Jesus, who gives eloquent testimony to his greatness as a prophet (Matt.11:7–15). Imprisonment, however, shows up a little doubt in the heart of John, who sends a message to Jesus asking: "Are you the one who was to come, or should we expect someone else?" Jesus encourages John's disciples to carry back to John the news that they have themselves seen the evidence for Christ's deity in the miracles which He is performing. He also gives them a Scripture passage to convey to John – Isaiah 35:5–6 – verses that John would doubtless recognise as confirmation that Jesus was truly who John first thought Him to be – Messiah, the Son of God.

"Thomas said to him, 'My Lord and my God!' Then Jesus told him, 'Because you have seen me, you have believed; blessed are those who have not seen and yet have believed."
(John 20:28–29)

FURTHER THOUGHT

Do you ever find yourself doubting your Christian experience? Then don't worry. "Doubt," as Os Guinness puts it, "is faith in two minds." Do as John did with his doubts - bring them to Jesus. Lay them at His feet and ask Him for an encouraging and reassuring word.

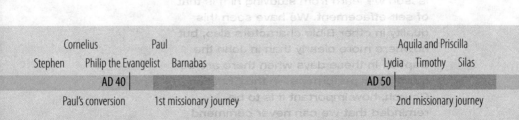

Cornelius		Paul			Aquila and Priscilla		
Stephen	Philip the Evangelist	Barnabas			Lydia	Timothy	Silas
AD 40					**AD 50**		
Paul's conversion		1st missionary journey				2nd missionary journey	

The man from the desert

John the Baptist wore "clothing made of camel's hair". Still today Bedouin wanderers and shepherds wear an "abayeh" – an outer cloak or mantle made of hair from a goat or camel. The hair is clipped from the neck, back and hump of the camel and woven into cloth. The cloak lasts a lifetime. It protects the wearer against heat by day and cold by night, as well as rain and dust. It could be used as a carpet or as a tent. John lived on wild honey and locusts. An invasion of locusts can be disastrous, for they settle on crops and trees and devour everything, but locusts can also be eaten for food. They are caught in the morning when they are numb with cold or their wings are wet from dew. Although usually boiled in salt water or roasted, they are sometimes dried in the sun, ground into powder, mixed with honey and made into cakes.

Key Lesson – John the Baptist

Jesus paid tribute to many people in His ministry, but no honours were greater than those which He conferred on John the Baptist. Listen to some of the statements Christ made concerning him: "A lamp that burned and gave light" ... "more than a prophet" ... "the greatest born of women". John's spiritual stature and character are obvious to anyone who reads the account of his life but the main lesson we learn from studying him is that of self-effacement. We have seen this quality in other Bible characters also, but nowhere more clearly than in John the Baptist. In these days when there are so many "star performers" in the Christian Church, how important it is to be reminded that we can never commend Jesus and ourselves at the same time.

His call

Matthew 9:1–13; Mark 2:14

Matthew was the son of Alphaeus, and was also known as Levi. He was a tax collector by profession – one of the ostracised group of Jews (and other nationalities) who made their living by collecting taxes on behalf of the Romans. His work involved applying pressure on unwilling people to pay their taxes, and thus he would be accustomed to seeing many unfriendly faces come to his booth. Jesus approaches him with great friendliness and respect, however, and bids him leave his work and become His disciple. Matthew immediately responds to Jesus' invitation and enters into a life of new service, this time not of getting, but of giving. Later he became the author of one of the "Synoptic" Gospels. Matthew wrote his Gospel to emphasise the fact that Jesus was the Messiah, the Son of the living God.

"Whoever serves me must follow me; and where I am, my servant also will be. My Father will honour the one who serves me." (John 12:26)

FURTHER THOUGHT

Can you remember the day when Christ called you to be His disciple? What were you doing? What did He say to you? How did the call come? Pause for a moment now and reflect on your own personal call to commitment. Then thank Him for making you one of His present-day disciples.

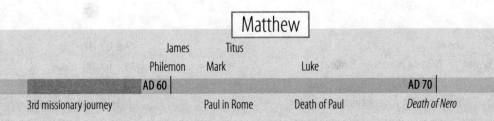

	Matthew		
	James	Titus	
	Philemon	Mark	Luke
	AD 60		AD 70
3rd missionary journey		Paul in Rome	Death of Paul	Death of Nero

DAY 224 His profession
Matthew 10:1-15; 9:9

The profession to which Matthew had committed himself prior to being called to be Jesus' disciple was one which would have brought him few friends. The system of tax collecting in those days was open to great abuse, the collectors making themselves rich at their neighbours' expense. It was no wonder that tax collectors became known as "the hated breed". No Jewish rabbi, for example, would consider eating with a tax collector, as they were considered ceremonially unclean, due to working on the Sabbath and from their constant contact with the Gentiles. How incredible it must have been, both to Matthew and to those who knew him, when Jesus invited him to give up his work as a tax collector and join Him as one of His disciples.

"Brothers, think of what you were when you were called. Not many of you were wise by human standards; not many were influential; not many were of noble birth. But God chose the foolish things of the world to shame the wise; God chose the weak things of the world to shame the strong." (1 Cor. 1:26–27)

FURTHER THOUGHT
Neither Matthew's position as a tax collector, nor his gains by it, could detain him when he heard Christ's call. He left his job without a moment's hesitation, and although we read that some of the disciples who were fishermen occasionally returned to fishing, we never again find Matthew plying his old trade.

Cornelius	Paul		Aquila and Priscilla	
Stephen	Philip the Evangelist	Barnabas	Lydia	Timothy	Silas
AD 40			AD 50		
Paul's conversion	1st missionary journey		2nd missionary journey	

His commitment

Luke 5:17-32

There can be little doubt that Matthew's response to the call he received from Jesus was immediate and wholehearted. Without appearing to hesitate, he left his former profession behind and committed himself to the work which Christ had called him to do with eagerness and enthusiasm. It is worthwhile noting that Matthew did not turn his back upon his fellow tax collectors or his friends after he had committed himself to Jesus, but sought to make them aware of the message and meaning which his new Master had brought into his life. He demonstrates a great evangelistic concern for his friends by inviting them to his home for a feast so that he can introduce them to Jesus (v.29). Matthew knew that the answer to life could not be found in gold, but in God – not in money, but in the Master.

"... you also must testify, for you have been with me from the beginning." (John 15:27)

FURTHER THOUGHT

To celebrate his new life in Christ, Matthew opened his home to hold a feast for his friends and acquaintances at which Christ was the guest of honour. This was one way Matthew could tell the world that he had accepted the Messiah. What ways have you taken to let others know of your commitment to Christ?

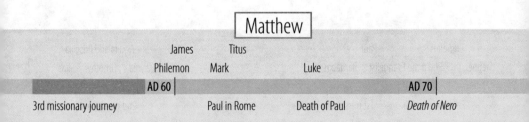

		Matthew		
	James	Titus		
	Philemon	Mark		Luke
	AD 60			AD 70
3rd missionary journey		Paul in Rome	Death of Paul	Death of Nero

DAY **226**   His commissioning

Mark 3:13-19

Once Jesus has brought together the team that is to accompany Him during His three-year ministry throughout Palestine, His next task is to commission them. This involves laying before them the broad outline of His ministry – to preach, teach, heal the sick and cast out demons. Matthew, along with the others, listens as Christ unfolds the full scope of their ministry. The key to Matthew's involvement – as indeed for the others – lies not so much in the words that Christ speaks to them, but in the fact that they have been chosen **"to be with Him"**. Matthew and the others, in order to become true disciples of the Master, must do more than listen to His words and copy His actions, they must assimilate His attitudes. And that can only be done by spending time with Him.

"You have made known to me the path of life; you will fill me with joy in your presence, with eternal pleasures at your right hand." (Psa. 16:11)

FURTHER THOUGHT

"Discipleship," as one preacher has pointed out, "is not just reading the Bible, attending Christian meetings, or even saying the Lord's Prayer. Discipleship is spending time with Jesus, lingering in His presence, gazing upon His face and getting to know Him." Are you such a disciple?

Cornelius		Paul			Aquila and Priscilla	
Stephen	Philip the Evangelist	Barnabas			Lydia Timothy Silas	
AD 40				**AD 50**		
Paul's conversion	1st missionary journey				2nd missionary journey	

Matthew 21:1-9; 25:34

Except for the references concerning Matthew's call, the feast he gave for his friends and his commissioning, along with the other eleven disciples, the Gospels are silent as to what Matthew said and did while he was in Jesus' company. Nevertheless it becomes clear that Matthew had caught the full focus of Christ's ministry in the words that he later wrote about Him, for Matthew's Gospel, as we said, presents Christ in a light that is not quite captured by any of the other Gospel writers. In it he presents Jesus as the Messiah, the one foretold by the Hebrew prophets, and traces the fulfilment of the Messianic prophecies. Matthew writes much also about the kingdom of heaven.

"... Has not God chosen those who are poor in the eyes of the world to be rich in faith and to inherit the kingdom he promised those who love him?" (James 2:5)

FURTHER THOUGHT

Every Christian is called by God to show Christ to the world in a special and distinctive way – to show some aspect of Him through our individual gifts and talents that, because of our uniqueness, only we can show. Have you discovered your own unique spiritual focus? If not, then give it some thought today.

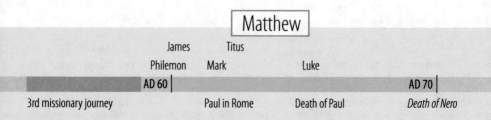

	Matthew		
James	Titus		
Philemon	Mark	Luke	
AD 60			AD 70
3rd missionary journey	Paul in Rome	Death of Paul	Death of Nero

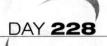

Matthew
Matthew: "A gift of God"

His emphasis
Matthew 13:1–52; 3:2; 4:17; 5:17

Matthew places great stress upon the need for repentance because of the coming of the kingdom of heaven, quoting the teaching of both John the Baptist (3:2) and of Jesus (4:17) in this respect. He records much of Jesus' teaching about the kingdom of heaven through the many parables Jesus related on this subject. The series of parables chosen by Matthew deals with the many different aspects of the kingdom message. Another emphasis which Matthew seems to bring out of his Gospel is the fact that not only did Christ fulfil Old Testament prophecy, but He also fulfilled the law (5:17). The early Christians reading Matthew's Gospel would have been familiar with the law, and doubtless would have been greatly helped to see how Christ fulfilled the demands of God's eternal law.

"... until the appearing of our Lord Jesus Christ, which God will bring about in his own time – God, the blessed and only Ruler, the King of kings and Lord of lords." (1 Tim. 6:14–15)

FURTHER THOUGHT
How beautifully Matthew contributed to the picture we have of Christ by emphasising the special aspect of His Kingliness. If it were not for this, then we might not so easily have grasped the fact that the One who is the Servant, the Son of God, and the Man Christ Jesus, is also the Lord of the universe – the King of kings!

Cornelius		Paul			Aquila and Priscilla
Stephen	Philip the Evangelist	Barnabas			Lydia Timothy Silas
AD 40				AD 50	
Paul's conversion		1st missionary journey			2nd missionary journey

His desire

Acts 1:1-14

The silence which hangs around the figure of Matthew in the New Testament is broken briefly in the Acts of the Apostles, where he is mentioned as being among the group of Jesus' followers who awaited the coming of the Holy Spirit in Jerusalem. It must be assumed that, after the death and resurrection of Jesus, the desire of Matthew to learn more of his Master did not diminish. Would he have been found among the waiting disciples if this was not so? There was great hostility against the disciples in Jerusalem, one must remember, and to maintain a witness to Jesus could have cost them their lives. Matthew's strong desire to know more of Christ resulted not only in a mighty baptism in the Spirit but, by reason of the Gospel he wrote, his ministry was extended to the ends of the earth (v. 8).

"Delight yourself in the Lord and he will give you the desires of your heart." (Psa. 37:4)

FURTHER THOUGHT

Archbishop William Temple once said: "Your knowledge and experience of Jesus will be as great as your desire for Him." Jeremiah expressed this in a different way: "You will seek me and find me when you seek me with all your heart" (Jer. 29:13). How strong is your desire for Jesus?

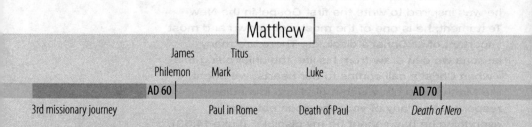

		Matthew		
	James	Titus		
	Philemon	Mark	Luke	
	AD 60			AD 70
3rd missionary journey		Paul in Rome	Death of Paul	Death of Nero

Matthew, the tax collector

Along the north end of the Sea of Galilee, there was a road leading from Damascus to Acre on the Mediterranean, and on that road a customs-office marked the boundary between the territories of Philip the tetrarch and Herod Antipas. Matthew's occupation was the examination of goods which passed along the road, and the levying of the toll.

Matthew, as a Jew, was condemned for impurity by the Pharisees, as he was prevented from fulfilling the requirements of the law, and was compelled to violate the Sabbath, which the Gentiles did not observe. His occupation itself associated him with men who, everywhere in the Empire, were despised and execrated for extortion and fraud.

Key Lesson – Matthew

Alexander Whyte, the great Scottish preacher of a bygone generation, said of Matthew: "When he rose up and left all to follow the Lord, the only things he took with him from his old occupation were his pen and ink. And it is well for us that he did, since he used them for such a good and wonderful purpose." After the record of his feast, Matthew disappears from history; he is heard of no more in the New Testament except, as we saw, as one of the group in Jerusalem after the Ascension. However, by virtue of the fact that he was inspired to write the first Gospel in the New Testament, he is one of the most well known and most important of all Christ's disciples. There are many lessons we can draw from his life, the chief being this – when Christ's call comes to our hearts, we ought, like Matthew, to obey with a glad and immediate response. For "any of you who does not give up everything he has cannot be my disciple" (Luke 14:33).

Mark

A praying mother

DAY **230**

Acts 12:1-16

John Mark was a relative of Barnabas and the son of Mary, at whose home some of the early Christians met. It is generally thought that Mary was a fairly wealthy widow – wealthy enough to have at least one servant and a house large enough to accommodate a group of praying Christians. The early Christians seem to have met in a number of different homes – those associated with James apparently meeting in another place (see v. 17). When King Herod imprisoned Peter, the early Christians met in this house to pray for his release. God answered their prayer and upon being given his freedom, Peter made his way to Mary's home, where he knew his fellow Christians would be gathered. Mark, it would appear, had the priceless blessing of a praying mother as he embarked upon a life of Christian service.

"... these I will bring to my holy mountain and give them joy in my house of prayer. Their burnt offerings and sacrifices will be accepted on my altar; for my house will be called a house of prayer for all nations." (Isa. 56:7)

FURTHER THOUGHT

The influences that flow from a home that is dedicated to prayer are beyond all telling. The prayer meetings in Mary's house not only brought release to Peter, but laid a solid understanding of God's presence and power in the heart of John Mark. Is your house a house of prayer?

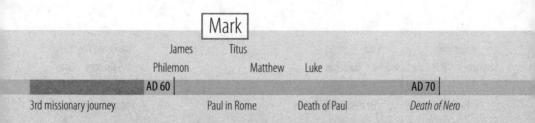

	Mark		
	James	Titus	
	Philemon	Matthew	Luke
AD 60			AD 70
3rd missionary journey	Paul in Rome	Death of Paul	Death of Nero

Mark

DAY 231

A traveller with Paul

Acts 12:19–13:5; 13:13

Although Saul of Tarsus had been genuinely converted and had committed his life to Jesus Christ, the Christians in the church at Jerusalem were still highly suspicious of him. Barnabas, the cousin of John Mark, intervenes and vouches for him to the leaders of the church. Paul is then welcomed into fellowship, and some time later he and Barnabas are commissioned by the church at Antioch to go on their first missionary journey. Mark sets out with them also to assist them in their travels but, for some reason, when they arrive at Perga he decides to abandon the trip and return to Jerusalem. Subsequent events reveal that Paul views this action of John Mark's with a good deal of disgust, and considers him a deserter in the cause of bringing Christ to the heathen world.

"... I do not consider myself yet to have taken hold of it. But one thing I do: Forgetting what is behind and straining towards what is ahead, I press on towards the goal to win the prize for which God has called me heavenwards in Christ Jesus." (Phil. 3:13–14).

FURTHER THOUGHT

No one can be quite sure as to the reason for John Mark's desertion. Some think it was cowardice; others that he was homesick. How tempting it is to sit in judgment on a person's apparent failure. Perhaps we ought to consider more carefully our Lord's words: "Do not judge, or you too will be judged" (Matt. 7:1).

	Cornelius	Paul			Aquila and Priscilla		
Stephen	Philip the Evangelist	Barnabas			Lydia	Timothy	Silas
	AD 40				AD 50		
Paul's conversion	1st missionary journey				2nd missionary journey		

Acts 15:35–41

Paul and Barnabas, having returned to Antioch from their first missionary journey, now plan a second one. The intention this time is to visit the churches which were founded during their initial travels. Barnabas wishes to take John Mark with them once again, but Paul thinks otherwise. In fact, so sharp is the disagreement between them that the partnership between Paul and Barnabas is broken and the planned itinerary divided. Paul teams up with Silas, and Barnabas takes John Mark and heads toward Cyprus, his homeland (Acts 4:36). How Mark behaved and acted on that journey with Barnabas we do not know, but all further references to him in the New Testament testify to his worth in the life of the Church – suggesting that Barnabas' confidence was not misplaced. There is little doubt that he profited much from his association with his cousin Barnabas, one of the leaders of the early Church.

"But you know that Timothy has proved himself, because as a son with his father he has served with me in the work of the gospel." (Phil. 2:22)

FURTHER THOUGHT

Some modern-day Christians make much of the principle of linking a younger Christian to an older and more experienced one. This certainly seemed to produce positive results in the life of John Mark. Perhaps we ought to implement this principle more in our church life. What do you think?

	Mark			
	James	Titus		
	Philemon	Matthew	Luke	
	AD 60			AD 70
3rd missionary journey		Paul in Rome	Death of Paul	Death of Nero

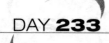

Mark

Mark: also known as John Mark

DAY **233** Faithful co-worker

2 Timothy 4:1–11

Although John Mark did not become a leading figure in the early Church, as did Paul and Barnabas, he did much in a supporting role to contribute to the growth and development of the Christian message in the first century. Despite the fact that his first attempt at missionary work seemed to end in failure, and later caused a serious rift between Paul and Barnabas, he came back to make a great impact upon the early Church – and later on the whole world – through the short but important Gospel which he wrote. One has only to read Mark's Gospel to see how effectively he condenses the account of Christ's life and ministry – a skill which he no doubt developed as he memorised or recorded the details of his journeys and contacts with the leaders of the early Church.

"For we are God's fellow-workers; you are God's field, God's building." (1 Cor. 3:9)

FURTHER THOUGHT

Someone said: "The people we meet are part of God's purposes for our lives." Are you aware of the fact that your family relationships, your education and the people you have rubbed shoulders with in the past are part of God's purposes in fitting you for the work that He has for you to do?

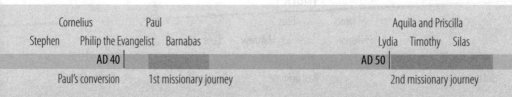

	Cornelius	Paul			Aquila and Priscilla		
Stephen	Philip the Evangelist	Barnabas			Lydia	Timothy	Silas
	AD 40				AD 50		
	Paul's conversion	1st missionary journey			2nd missionary journey		

Restored to Paul

Colossians 4:10-11; Philemon 24

It might be thought that Paul's point-blank refusal to take John Mark with him on his second missionary journey might have resulted in a permanent estrangement between him and the young disciple. Happily, however, this is not so. Paul, when writing to the Colossians, makes reference to Mark as one of his fellow-workers, and affirms that he is a comfort to him. Mark also teams up with Paul in sending greetings to the church of Colosse – yet another indication of the close relationship which now exists between them. Perhaps the final and most revealing comment on this issue is seen in Paul's letter to Timothy, when the apostle once again tells of Mark's great usefulness in the affairs of the gospel, and asks that Timothy should bring John Mark with him when next he visits him (2 Tim. 4:11).

" ... being confident of this, that he who began a good work in you will carry it on to completion until the day of Christ Jesus." (Phil. 1:6)

FURTHER THOUGHT

What if John Mark had given up when he learned how the apostle Paul viewed his initial failure? We would have had no Gospel of St Mark! Has some failure in your life caused you to remain indolent and inactive? Then in Christ's Name, rise up and get to work. Take the first step to recovery – today.

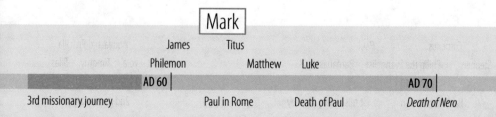

	Mark			
	James	Titus		
	Philemon		Matthew	Luke
	AD 60			AD 70
3rd missionary journey		Paul in Rome	Death of Paul	Death of Nero

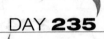

Mark

DAY 235 — Companion to Peter

1 Peter 5:1–13

John Mark was not only restored to full fellowship with Paul after his early failure in the ministry, but came to enjoy a close relationship with Simon Peter also (v. 13). Doubtless, his close relationship with Peter and Paul equipped him ideally for the task of writing his Gospel. One can imagine him listening intently to the stories which Peter had to tell concerning Jesus, asking questions, verifying the facts and making sure that he understood every detail. One can imagine, too, that in his conversations with Paul, the theologian, he would learn the deep spiritual insights which had to do with the deeper meaning of Christ's life here on earth. Many scholars believe Mark's Gospel was the first of the four to be written, and that it was a source document for the later writings of Matthew and Luke.

"Brothers, if someone is caught in a sin, you who are spiritual should restore him gently. But watch yourself, or you also may be tempted." (Gal. 6:1)

FURTHER THOUGHT

When we see how affectionately both Paul and Peter regarded John Mark, we can see how wonderful and complete was his spiritual recovery. Peter called Mark "my son", suggesting that he was one of Peter's converts. As an exercise, write out 1 Peter 5:13.

Cornelius	Paul		Aquila and Priscilla	
Stephen	Philip the Evangelist	Barnabas	Lydia	Timothy	Silas
AD 40			**AD 50**	
Paul's conversion	1st missionary journey		2nd missionary journey	

His Gospel theme

Mark 8:1–26; 10:45

I n Mark's Gospel, as in Isaiah's prophecy, Jesus is presented as the Servant. The Gospel recounts what Jesus did as He moved around from place to place in the three and a half years of His ministry in Palestine. Events, in general, are dealt with in chronological order – evidence of the orderly and methodical mind which John Mark possessed. In view of the fact that Mark emphasises the servanthood of Christ in his Gospel, the circumstances of Jesus' birth and childhood are omitted. He opens with an account of the ministry of John the Baptist, and moves briskly through the events of Christ's baptism to come to grips with the main purpose of his writing – an account of the public ministry of Jesus.

"Who, being in very nature God, did not consider equality with God something to be grasped, but made himself nothing, taking the very nature of a servant, being made in human likeness." (Phil. 2:6–7)

FURTHER THOUGHT

Mark presents Christ as the Servant, and his main theme can be discovered by focusing on Mark 10:45. Take a moment for a spiritual check-up, and ask yourself: How much of my life and ministry is spent in serving and ministering to others?

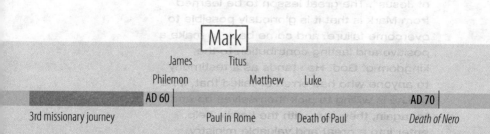

Mark

| James | Titus |
| Philemon | Matthew | Luke |

AD 60 | | AD 70

3rd missionary journey | Paul in Rome | Death of Paul | *Death of Nero*

John Mark

A change of name usually corresponds with a crisis in life. In Mark's case the name laid aside, John, was Jewish, and the name assumed or bestowed upon him, Mark (Marcus), was Roman. It is probable that the change marked his conversion from Judaism to Christianity, or his desire to spread his new faith among the Gentiles. His Gospel is obviously intended for the use of Gentile Christians, and, according to an old and reliable tradition, was written in Rome.

Key Lesson – Mark

"Very few Christians know unbroken progress in discipleship," says R.E.O. White, "so Mark ... has a special place in the hearts of those who know their own fallibility." He also points out that Mark lived what many might consider to be a very "ordinary" Christian life – no recorded visions, revelations, or unusual supernatural experiences – yet he was the one God used to write one of the most important books of the New Testament – the first and the closest to the actual events of all the "lives of Jesus". The great lesson to be learned from Mark is that it is gloriously possible to overcome failure, and come back to make a positive and lasting contribution to the kingdom of God. He stands as a testimony to anyone who has erred or failed that, if he or she is willing to pick themselves up and try again, they can, with the Lord's help, enter into a great and valuable ministry.

Luke

Luke: "Light-giving"

The author

Luke 1:1–14; Acts 1:1

Luke was a doctor, who accompanied Paul on one of his missionary journeys and later became the author of both Luke's Gospel and the book of Acts. Luke dedicated both of these documents to the "most excellent Theophilus" – a name meaning "loved of God" (Luke 1:3; Acts 1:1). No one seems to quite know who Theophilus was; some believe the reference to mean the Christian reader in general, while others believe it to refer to one of the early Christians whose name does not appear elsewhere in the New Testament. The strength of Luke's writings lies in the fact that he was an eyewitness to many of the events which he records, and that he collected much of his information from other eyewitnesses.

"You yourselves are our letter, written on our hearts, known and read by everybody." (2 Cor. 3:2)

FURTHER THOUGHT

A great writer once said that "the colour of our eyes creeps into the nib of our pen". By that he meant that our character flows out through what we write – and, of course, the same principle applies to what we say. In all that Luke writes and says, Christ is clearly evident. Is it the same with you?

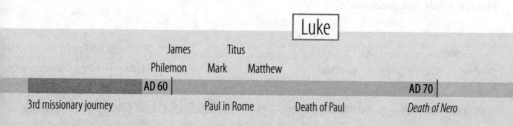

Luke

	James	Titus		
Philemon		Mark	Matthew	
AD 60				**AD 70**
3rd missionary journey		Paul in Rome	Death of Paul	Death of Nero

Luke

Luke: "Light-giving"

DAY 238   The doctor

Colossians 4:1–14

Hippocrates, who is regarded as the father of modern medicine, and who lived on the Greek island of Kos in the fifth and fourth centuries BC, founded a new approach to the treatment of sickness which has had great influence throughout the centuries. During the 500 years following his death, the insights he had recorded were added to by his successors, and by the first century AD there was a good deal of information readily available to bright young men who wanted to study medicine. Luke, it is safe to assume, must have been an intelligent young man, eager to study the effects of various remedies on human sickness, but it is obvious that as well as being intelligent, he was a caring and compassionate person. Paul refers to him as "our dear friend Luke, the doctor". Luke was the first in a long line of doctors who have combined Christian love and human skill in ministering to those with physical needs and problems.

"Each one should use whatever gift he has received to serve others, faithfully administering God's grace in its various forms." (1 Pet. 4:10)

FURTHER THOUGHT

In the Gospel of Luke, there are approximately fifty medical terms. One writer says: "Luke used more medical words than Hippocrates." Look up Luke 4:38, 8:43 and 14:2 to see just three of them. When reading through Luke's Gospel, keep your eyes open for others.

	Cornelius	Paul		Aquila and Priscilla	
Stephen	Philip the Evangelist	Barnabas		Lydia Timothy Silas	
	AD 40			AD 50	
	Paul's conversion	1st missionary journey		2nd missionary journey	

Companion of Paul

Acts 16:10–17

L uke first joins Paul at Troas, from where they set out for Macedonia in obedience to a vision which has been given to Paul. The question of whether Luke would have used his medical skills to assist Paul as they travelled together is one that is often debated among Christians. Some believe that as Paul seemed to possess so many spiritual gifts, he would have relied upon these to maintain his health, while others feel that he would have availed himself of Luke's medical knowledge and assistance whenever his health was in jeopardy. Perhaps the truth lies somewhere in the middle. There were times, no doubt, when Paul would have used his faith to combat physical problems (see Acts 28:3–5), and times when he would have availed himself of his companion's medical knowledge.

"Is any one of you sick? He should call the elders of the church to pray over him and anoint him with oil in the name of the Lord." (James 5:14)

FURTHER THOUGHT

How do you feel about this often debated issue of whether Paul would have relied upon faith and prayer to overcome sickness, or taken advantage of Luke's medical knowledge? Think it through, using Scripture if you can, and come up with your own conclusions.

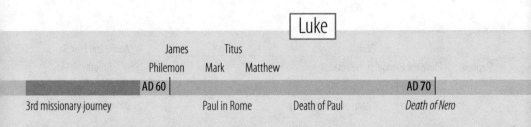

Luke

| James | Titus |
| Philemon | Mark | Matthew |

AD 60   AD 70

3rd missionary journey   Paul in Rome   Death of Paul   *Death of Nero*

DAY 240   Self-effacing
Acts 20:5-6; 21:1-17

One has only to read the writings of Luke to realise that he was obviously an intelligent and educated man. He clearly possessed literary, historical, theological and medical abilities, and comes across in his writings as deeply caring and warm-hearted. This, of course, is what one would expect of a good doctor. He appears also to have resolved any ego problems that his accomplishments might have brought him, for we never read such statements as "I was there and did this", or "I was part of this great event", but simply "we did" or "we saw". This is why many commentators refer to Luke as being self-effacing; he had learned to put his ego in its proper place – at the feet of Christ. The humble anonymity which he preserves in his writing is something we would do well to emulate.

"I have been crucified with Christ and I no longer live, but Christ lives in me. The life I live in the body, I live by faith in the Son of God, who loved me and gave himself for me." (Gal. 2:20)

FURTHER THOUGHT

It's important to realise that self-effacement is not self-belittlement. Many Christians get hung up over this issue. Can you discern the difference? Chat over the subject with a Christian friend today and see if you can identify some of the major differences.

	Cornelius	Paul		Aquila and Priscilla		
Stephen	Philip the Evangelist	Barnabas		Lydia	Timothy	Silas
	AD 40			AD 50		
	Paul's conversion	1st missionary journey		2nd missionary journey		

Loyal

The apostle Paul, while in prison at Caesarea, exercised his right as a Roman citizen and appealed to Caesar to override the verdict which had been reached in a lower court (see Acts 22:25 and 25:11). Paul was therefore dispatched to Rome in chains with a military escort, and during this journey Luke stayed with him, determined to support and care for him no matter what lay ahead. The great dangers through which they passed and the hardships they endured are graphically described in Luke's account of this journey. One would have hardly blamed Luke if he had turned away from this disaster-prone apostle, who seemed to go through so many difficulties one after the other, but not Luke. His loyalty knew no limits. He was a man bound, not only by a Hippocratic oath, but by an even greater loyalty – the loyalty of love.

"Be devoted to one another in brotherly love. Honour one another above yourselves." (Rom. 12:10)

FURTHER THOUGHT

Are you a loyal person? Can others depend on you when they are under stress or in difficulty? Loyalty has been defined as "assuming responsibility for the needs of another person". Check on yourself today, and try to evaluate the depth and degree of your loyalty.

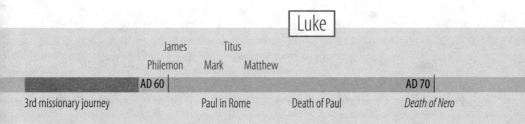

Luke

	James	Titus	
	Philemon	Mark	Matthew

AD 60			AD 70
3rd missionary journey	Paul in Rome	Death of Paul	*Death of Nero*

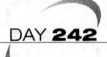

DAY **242**

A true friend

2 Timothy 4:1–13

I n one of his last messages, written under the shadow of execution (v. 6), the apostle Paul writes to Timothy asking for a warm cloak to be brought to him, as well as some scrolls and parchments. He also asks Timothy to bring John Mark with him when he comes, so that he can see him once again and renew their deep fellowship. It is obvious that Paul is feeling greatly in need of fellowship at this stage in his life as he lists the people who have departed from him, some no doubt for good and just reasons. Consider the words: "Only Luke is with me." What friendship! No matter what happened, Luke was a man who was willing to stay to the end.

"A friend loves at all times, and a brother is born for adversity."
(Prov. 17:17)

FURTHER THOUGHT

A publication once offered a prize for the best definition of a friend. Thousands of answers were received, but the one that was given the first prize was this: "A friend is someone who comes in when the whole world has gone out." Are you such a friend?

	Cornelius	Paul		Aquila and Priscilla	
Stephen	Philip the Evangelist	Barnabas		Lydia Timothy Silas	
	AD 40			AD 50	
	Paul's conversion	1st missionary journey		2nd missionary journey	

Luke 19:10; 5:24; 6:5; 6:22; 9:22

Luke probably wrote his Gospel somewhere around AD 60 during the time that Paul was imprisoned in Caesarea. He would then have had time to collect all his material and perhaps visit some of the places where Jesus had ministered. The vivid style of Luke's writings suggests that he was familiar with the setting of the events which he records, but which, of course, he did not witness personally. Luke, like the prophet Isaiah, presents Christ as Saviour and Lord, but his main emphasis is on His humanity. He refers to Jesus over and over again as "the Son of Man". Notice how he covers in great detail the genealogy of Christ, His growth into manhood, and the more human aspects of our Lord's life on earth. Notice, too, how he emphasises our Lord's care for the oppressed, the poor and the downcast. Luke tells it loud and clear that Jesus was truly human as well as divine.

"And being found in appearance as a man, he humbled himself and became obedient to death – even death on a cross! Therefore God exalted him to the highest place and gave him the name that is above every name ..."
(Phil. 2:8–9)

FURTHER THOUGHT

Sometimes the best way to remember something is to write it down. As your hand moves to express a particular thought in writing, your mind takes hold of it in a greater way. Write down now the words of Luke 19:10, which summarise the whole of Luke's Gospel.

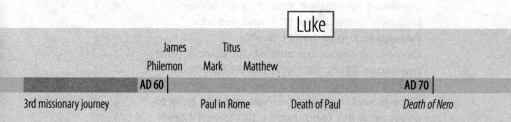

Luke

	James	Titus		
	Philemon	Mark	Matthew	
AD 60				AD 70
3rd missionary journey		Paul in Rome	Death of Paul	Death of Nero

The "beloved physician"

Here standeth Luke, Physician once, and still;
Healer of souls whom God delights to save;
Wise-eyed in helpfulness; in pity brave;
For all diseases using blessèd skill;
To halt, maimed, blind, beneficent; until
From town obscure by Galilean wave
Flashed forth the Day-Star, born of God, and gave
New life to suppliants with a sweet "I will."
At whose appearing Luke was straightly dumb,
Lost in the greater Light; nor found it hard;
But knelt and worshippèd; and afterward
For thy monition, O Theophilus,
Wrote large his gospel, and for help of us,
On whom the last days of the world are come.
E.C. Lefrox

Key Lesson – Luke

Does it surprise you to be told that Luke is the major contributor to the New Testament and provides, through the two books which he wrote, more information about the times of Jesus and the apostles than any other writer? Luke was an important figure, a Gentile and a second-generation Christian who, as far as we know, never actually met Jesus in the flesh. The main lesson we learn from Luke is drawn from the way he deliberately draws his pen through what someone has called "the perpendicular pronoun" – the letter "I" – and resorts instead to the pronoun "we".
Commentators often talk about Luke's "we" passages (Acts 16:10–17; 20:5–15; 21:1–18 and 27:1–28:16). Almost everything about Luke is self-effacing; he had learned how to overcome the tendency to put himself first and others second. And so must we!

5

John

DAY **244**

A chosen apostle

Matthew 10:1–6

When Jesus set out to gather His disciples at the beginning of His public ministry, He first called two pairs of brothers – Simon and Andrew, and James and John. There were as many boys named John in the olden days as there are today. The John we are looking at here is the son of Zebedee and Salome, and the younger brother of James. As John was one of the Twelve, he was chosen, not just to be a disciple of Jesus, but to be an apostle. The meaning of the word "apostle" is "one who is sent". A "disciple" is a general term, meaning a learner or a student, but the word "apostle" is much more precise. Notice the transition from verse 1, where the Twelve are called "disciples", to verse 2, where they are referred to as "apostles". All Christ's followers are called to be disciples, but not all are called to be apostles.

"It was he who gave some to be apostles, some to be prophets, some to be evangelists, and some to be pastors and teachers, to prepare God's people for works of service ..." (Eph. 4:11–12)

FURTHER THOUGHT
Some believe that after the Church was established in the first few decades after Christ, apostles and prophets were no longer needed and thus these ministries became obsolete. What do you believe about this? Are there apostles and prophets functioning in the Church today?

John

AD 70 |

Death of Nero   Destruction of Jerusalem

AD 80 |

Completion of the Colosseum in Rome

Destruction of Pompeii and Herculaneum

A hot-headed man

Luke 9:51–56

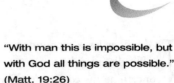

The Galilean fishermen, of whom John was one, were notoriously tough and volatile characters who would not hesitate to speak out plainly on any occasion which concerned them. Peter, for example, when confronted during Christ's trial by a young girl who accused him of being one of His disciples, lapsed into swearing and cursing (Matt. 26:74). John, too, seems to have had a similar disposition – at least during the early part of his relationship with Christ – when, along with his brother James, he blazed in anger at the Samaritans who would not give Jesus hospitality for the night. With good reason, it seems, Jesus had given the brothers the name "Boanerges" – sons of thunder (Mark 3:17). Another person who appears from his name to have been hot-headed – Simon the Zealot – was also chosen by Jesus to be an apostle.

"With man this is impossible, but with God all things are possible." (Matt. 19:26)

FURTHER THOUGHT

If you were about to found a church, would you choose hot-heads to assist you in your task? Yet Jesus seems not to hesitate to do it. Why? Was it because He saw them, not as they were, but as they could become? Worth pondering, don't you think?

DAY 246　　　An ambitious man

Matthew 20:20–28; Mark 10:35–37

No doubt as Jesus expounded to His disciples the truths concerning the coming kingdom, those who were more ambitious coveted for themselves a privileged position in the new regime. Peter, on one occasion, wanted to know from Christ what his reward would be for having left all to follow Him (Mark 10:28). Again, when travelling to Capernaum, the disciples were found arguing among themselves as to who was the greatest among them (Mark 9:34). It is evident from this, and other incidents in the lives of the disciples, that ambition was high on their list of priorities. James and John, probably encouraged by their mother, wanted the two top jobs in the kingdom, and are considered by many commentators to be the two most ambitious disciples.

"I press on towards the goal to win the prize for which God has called me heavenwards in Christ Jesus. All of us who are mature should take such a view of things. And if on some point you think differently, that too God will make clear to you." (Phil. 3:14–15)

FURTHER THOUGHT

There is nothing wrong with ambition, providing it is linked to the right goals. God has one ambition which supersedes all others. You can read about it in Romans 8:29: "For from the very beginning God decided that those who came to him ... should become like his Son" (TLB). Is that your ambition too?

John

AD 70

Death of Nero　　　Destruction of Jerusalem

AD 80

Completion of the Colosseum in Rome

Destruction of Pompeii and Herculaneum

292

John 21:1–20; 13:23; 19:26; 20:2

It seems from the record contained in the Gospels, that John became the closest to Jesus of all the disciples. John occupied the place of honour at the Last Supper, where he could engage in close and intimate conversation with his Master (John 13:23–26). This closeness between himself and Jesus is seen also as we study the Gospel which he wrote, for there we see signs of an intimate understanding of the ideas of the Lord that is not quite evident in the writings of Matthew. This close relationship between Jesus and John comes over most clearly in the moments prior to Jesus' death, when He selects John to be the one who will have the responsibility for the care of His mother, Mary.

"And we, who with unveiled faces all reflect the Lord's glory, are being transformed into his likeness with ever-increasing glory, which comes from the Lord, who is the Spirit." (2 Cor. 3:18)

FURTHER THOUGHT

What a remarkable change has taken place in John during the few years that he spent with Jesus! His zeal and pride were softened by the grace of the Lord Jesus, and weaknesses were turned into strengths. This is what should happen to all those who call themselves His disciples. Is this happening to you?

AD 90		AD 100	
	Revelation	Death of John	

DAY **248**

A special trio

Mark 5:37; Matthew 17:1; 26:37

During the three-year period in which Jesus talked and walked with His disciples, there were several occasions when He took three of them apart for a special purpose. The three who were singled out for this special favour were Peter, James ... and John. The first of these occasions was in the house of Jairus, when Jesus raised the ruler's dead daughter back to life. The second was on the Mount of Transfiguration when Jesus was transfigured before them. And the third was in the Garden of Gethsemane, when Jesus took them into the heart of the garden that they might be with Him during His deep spiritual struggle. It is interesting that all three occasions when Jesus took Peter, James and John apart were in some way connected with the theme of death.

"Jesus said ... 'I am the resurrection and the life. He who believes in me will live, even though he dies; and whoever lives and believes in me will never die." (John 11:25–26)

FURTHER THOUGHT

Question: Why did Jesus, on three separate occasions, take the trio into a situation connected with death? Answer: He wanted them to see that He was sovereign over death (in the house of Jairus), superior to death (on the Mount of Transfiguration) and subject to death (in the Garden of Gethsemane).

John

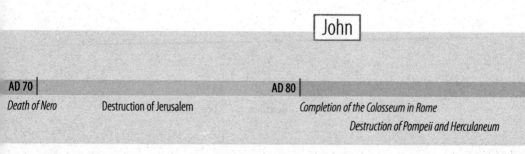

AD 70		AD 80	
Death of Nero	*Destruction of Jerusalem*	*Completion of the Colosseum in Rome*	
		Destruction of Pompeii and Herculaneum	

A caring friend

DAY **249**

John 19:27; 13:23; 1 John 2:9–10; 3:14–18; 4:7–11

A
lthough John was once a "son of thunder", it becomes obvious that his relationship with Jesus changed him from a proud zealot into a kind, deeply loving and considerate person. In fact, so amazing is the change in John that he seems altogether a different disciple to the one who teamed up with Jesus in the beginning. What produced such a dramatic change? We have already seen that it was the result of spending time in the presence of Jesus, listening to His words and imbibing His spirit. John was obviously a good learner, for what Jesus taught and demonstrated he not only saw and heard, but assimilated into his own person and put into daily practice.

"And the second is like it: 'Love your neighbour as yourself.'" (Matt. 22:39)

FURTHER THOUGHT

Christians have been defined as "people who care more for others than they do about themselves". Not an exhaustive definition perhaps, but an interesting one. How do you feel about such a definition? What is more – is such a definition true of you?

AD 90		AD 100	
	Revelation	Death of John	

DAY **250**   An active missionary

Acts 3:1–4:22

I n the early days of the Christian church in Jerusalem, it seems that the believers met to pray, not only in their homes, but also in the Temple (Acts 2:46). On one occasion when John and Peter were passing through the Beautiful Gate on the way to the Temple, they encountered a beggar asking for money. Peter and John were unable to give any financial help, but they gave him something better – healing and deliverance through the Name of Jesus. The healing of the lame man resulted in the immediate gathering together of a great crowd which, in turn, furnished them with the opportunity to present the claims of Jesus Christ to the people. As a result of their preaching, they were both charged not to preach any more, but they decided to disobey the authorities and continue their anointed witness to the Lord Jesus.

"Peter and the other apostles replied:
'We must obey God rather than men!'"
(Acts 5:29)

FURTHER THOUGHT

Many Christians are confused about how to relate to authority. Should we obey or disobey those who have the rule over us? The principle is this – we obey every law of the land except those which bring us into direct confrontation with the higher law of God and Christ.

John

AD 70

Death of Nero   Destruction of Jerusalem

AD 80

Completion of the Colosseum in Rome

Destruction of Pompeii and Herculaneum

296

"I am ..."

John	**6:35**	The Bread of Life
	8:12	The Light of the World
	8:58	Before Abraham was
	10:7	The Gate
	10:11	The Good Shepherd
	10:36	The Son of God
	11:25	The Resurrection and the Life
	14:6	The Way, the Truth and the Life
	15:1	The True Vine
Rev.	**1:8**	Alpha, Omega – the Beginning and the End
	1:17	The First and the Last

Key Lesson – John

There can be little doubt that John was one of the greatest of all the apostles. He was the writer of the fourth Gospel, the three epistles of John and the book of Revelation. In his Gospel, John presents a view of Jesus which is different from that of the synoptic Gospels ("synoptic" means "a like view"), in which the deity of Jesus shines through in majestic splendour. The main lesson we learn from examining John's life is the fact that when someone walks constantly with Jesus, assimilates His word, obeys His instructions, then his weaknesses are turned into strengths. It is not by coincidence that the "son of thunder" became the "apostle of love". Our weaknesses, in fact, have within them the potential for becoming our strengths. All it needs is for someone to move them on to the right track. Jesus is that "Someone". He did it for John – and He can do it for you.

Simon Peter

Simon: "Hearing"; Peter: "Stone" or "Rock"

DAY 251   A calling and confession

Matthew 4:18–20; 10:2; 16:16–19

Simon was a member of the fishing community at Bethsaida, beside the Sea of Galilee – a place from which Jesus also selected Philip and Andrew. With his brother Andrew, he was occupied in his work as a fisherman when Jesus called them to leave their settled and probably prosperous life (Matt. 19:27) to follow Him. Jesus gave Simon the surname Peter (Mark 3:16) – meaning "a rock". Simon Peter eventually became the foremost of the group of disciples and was their spokesman on the Day of Pentecost. He was the first disciple to acknowledge the divinity of Jesus, confessing Him to be the Messiah, the Son of God.

"... if anyone is in Christ, he is a new creation; the old has gone, the new has come!" (2 Cor. 5:17)

FURTHER THOUGHT

Ever noticed that in John 1:42, Jesus said to Simon, "You are Simon ... You will be ... Peter"? The natural was changed to the spiritual – with just one word. Today the Lord is saying the same thing to you: "This is what you are by nature, but this is what you shall be by My grace." Let that thought stimulate you toward greater spiritual heights.

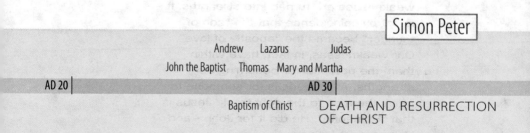

Simon Peter

| Andrew | Lazarus | Judas |
| John the Baptist | Thomas | Mary and Martha |

AD 20 | AD 30 |

Baptism of Christ   DEATH AND RESURRECTION OF CHRIST

An impulsive nature

Matthew 14:22-33; 17:4; John 18:10

The New Testament writers rarely give us any details of the physical appearance of the characters they portray, but they spend a good deal of time letting us know their character traits. Peter, it appears, had an impulsive nature which he demonstrates time and time again in the Biblical accounts. Here are a few examples: (1) he blurts out an inappropriate suggestion during the moments of Christ's transfiguration (Matt. 17:4); (2) objects to having his feet washed by Christ at the Last Supper (John 13:8); (3) strikes out wildly with his sword at the time of Jesus' arrest (John 18:10); and (4) leaps out of the fishing boat to swim to the risen Christ who is standing on the shore (John 21:7).

"... we also rejoice in our sufferings, because we know that suffering produces perseverance; perseverance, character; and character, hope."
(Rom. 5:3–4)

FURTHER THOUGHT

Did Jesus change Simon Peter's impulsive nature to one that was calmer and more tranquil? There can be little doubt that He did. Just look up 2 Peter 1:6 and note Peter's emphasis on patience. A close relationship with Jesus never fails to turn negative traits into positive ones.

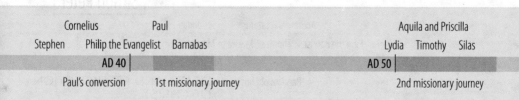

	Cornelius		Paul			Aquila and Priscilla		
Stephen		Philip the Evangelist	Barnabas			Lydia	Timothy	Silas
	AD 40					AD 50		
	Paul's conversion		1st missionary journey				2nd missionary journey	

DAY 253 — A tender heart

John 13:1-9

As Jesus and His disciples prepare to begin their meal in the Upper Room, no one appears to attend to the customary washing of feet – a service usually given by a slave to those coming into the house from a long distance. To the amazement of all present, Jesus rises from the table and begins to undertake the menial task of washing His disciples' feet. When He arrives at the place where Simon Peter is sitting and prepares to wash his feet, Peter's tender heart is deeply touched and he pleads with Jesus not to go ahead with this menial task. Peter has to learn, however, that he must submit to Jesus in everything if the relationship between them is not to be broken (v. 8b).

"But we see Jesus, who was made a little lower than the angels, now crowned with glory and honour because he suffered death, so that by the grace of God he might taste death for everyone." (Hebrews 2:9)

FURTHER THOUGHT

How would you have felt if you had been in that party of disciples and Jesus came to wash your feet? Appalled? Reluctant? Humbled? We must never forget that the Christian life involves us, not only in ministering to Christ, but equally letting Christ minister to us.

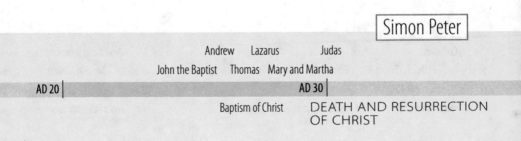

Simon Peter

The Rock

1. **His call – the first of the Twelve**

   "These are the names of the twelve apostles: first, Simon (who is called Peter) ..." **(Matt. 10:2)**

2. **His courage**

   "'Lord, if it's you,' Peter replied, 'tell me to come to you on the water.'" **(Matt. 14:28)**

3. **His confession**

   "'Who do you say I am?' Simon Peter answered, 'You are the Christ, the Son of the living God.'" **(Matt. 16:15,16)**

4. **His impulsiveness**

   "Then Simon Peter, who had a sword, drew it and struck the high priest's servant, cutting off his right ear." **(John 18:10)**

5. **His self-confidence**

   "But Peter insisted emphatically, 'Even if I have to die with you, I will never disown you.'" **(Mark 14:31)**

6. **His indifference**

   "... 'Simon,' he said to Peter, 'are you asleep? Could you not keep watch for one hour?'" **(Mark 14:37)**

7. **His denial**

   "But he denied it. 'I don't know or understand what you're talking about' ..." **(Mark 14:68)**

8. **His repentance**

   "Then Peter remembered the word Jesus had spoken to him ... And he broke down and wept." **(Mark 14:72)**

Simon Peter

Simon: "Hearing"; Peter: "Stone" or "Rock"

DAY **254**

A weak character

Matthew 26:33–35; 57–74

Jesus, of whom it was said that "He knew what was in a man" (John 2:25), told Simon Peter that, although his spirit was willing, his flesh was weak (Matt. 26:41). Peter seems to have been either unaware of this weakness or to have completely ignored it. At the Last Supper, he strongly professes his loyalty to Christ, and asserts that even if everyone else should desert the Master, he most certainly will not do so – even if it means dying with Him (Matt. 26:33–35). Peter stoutly maintains this attitude even though Jesus tells him that he will deny his Lord three times before many more hours have passed. What Jesus said came true, revealing how misplaced was Simon Peter's self-confidence and how weak his character really was.

"... For when I am weak, then I am strong." (2 Cor. 12:10)

FURTHER THOUGHT

Don't look too long at Peter's weaknesses – focus on your own. Are you aware of any weaknesses you may have? Are you able to recognise them and depend on God's power to overcome them? Remember, maturity is being able to recognise your weaknesses as well as your strengths.

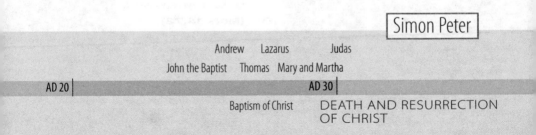

Simon Peter

Andrew   Lazarus   Judas

John the Baptist   Thomas   Mary and Martha

| AD 20 | | AD 30 | |

Baptism of Christ   DEATH AND RESURRECTION OF CHRIST

A repentant spirit

Matthew 26:75; Luke 24:12

When the crowing of the cock reminds Peter of Christ's words at the Last Supper concerning his threefold denial of Him, he breaks down and weeps bitterly. Unlike Judas Iscariot, whose remorse leads him to end his life, Simon Peter repents of his failures and seeks to rejoin the disciples. When, later, some women come to the place where the group is assembled bringing the news of Christ's resurrection, they are regarded as mistaken; but Peter and John, though to some extent disbelieving, run to the tomb to see for themselves (John 20:2–10). They then discover for themselves the thrilling fact that Jesus is no longer dead, but alive!

"The Lord is close to the broken-hearted and saves those who are crushed in spirit." (Psa. 34:18)

FURTHER THOUGHT

Someone has described the difference between remorse and repentance in this way: "Remorse says 'I am sorry', but repentance says 'I am sorry enough to quit.'" Keep that in mind so that the next time something occurs over which you need to repent, you will not stop at remorse – being sorry – but move on to repentance – being sorry enough to quit.

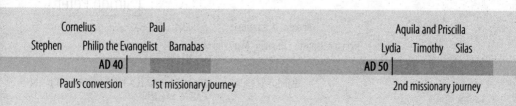

	Cornelius	Paul			Aquila and Priscilla		
Stephen	Philip the Evangelist	Barnabas		Lydia	Timothy	Silas
	AD 40			AD 50		
Paul's conversion	1st missionary journey			2nd missionary journey		

Simon Peter

Simon: "Hearing"; Peter: "Stone" or "Rock"

DAY **256**

A responsive will

John 21:1-17

Simon Peter and some of the other disciples return to Galilee and take up their old trade of fishing. However, although they spend a whole night on the lake, they catch nothing. As they return to shore, they are challenged by a stranger to cast their net on the right side of the boat. The stranger, of course, is Christ but, although not aware of this, they do as He commands and immediately the net is filled with fish. John recognises the stranger as the Lord, and as soon as Simon Peter hears this, he jumps into the lake and swims to the Master. After an early morning breakfast which Christ prepares for them, Peter is challenged three times as to how much he loves Christ.

"We love because he first loved us."
(1 John 4:19)

FURTHER THOUGHT

Simon Peter, it seems, was evasive in his response to Christ, even after his repentance and return to the disciples' company. Yet Jesus lovingly persists with His question "Do you love me?" until Simon Peter finally capitulates. Jesus is asking you the same question now – "Do you love Me?" What is your response?

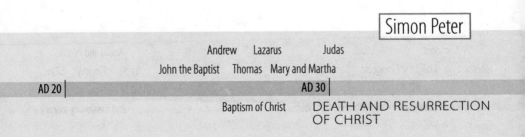

Simon Peter

| | Andrew | Lazarus | | Judas | |
| John the Baptist | Thomas | Mary and Martha | |

| AD 20 | | AD 30 |
| | Baptism of Christ | DEATH AND RESURRECTION OF CHRIST |

A bold witness

Acts 2:14–41

After the coming of the Holy Spirit, the Christian believers are endued with power as Jesus promised (1:8). Peter, who, prior to this, cowered with the other disciples behind closed doors for fear of the Jews, now becomes a fearless spokesman for the group. He accuses the crowd of complicity in the death of Christ, and asserts that Jesus was murdered by sinful men. How different is Peter's attitude now from that which he demonstrated during the night of Christ's trial. Through his inspired sermon, in which he testifies to Jesus as the Messiah who has now ascended into heaven, 3,000 people are brought to commit their lives to Christ.

"Do not get drunk on wine, which leads to debauchery. Instead, be filled with the Spirit." (Eph. 5:18)

FURTHER THOUGHT

What can be the explanation of how a cowardly, thrice-denying disciple was turned into a fearless and blazing witness for Christ? There is only one answer – the fullness of the Holy Spirit. Have you received the Spirit's fullness in your life? If not, then kneel and ask God to fill you to overflowing – today.

Cornelius	Paul		Aquila and Priscilla	
Stephen	Philip the Evangelist	Barnabas	Lydia	Timothy	Silas
	AD 40		AD 50	
Paul's conversion	1st missionary journey		2nd missionary journey	

Key Lesson – Peter

It has often been said that while most Christians admire Paul and revere John, every Christian loves Peter. Peter's blunders, limitations, impulsiveness and human frailty seem to endear him to everyone. He walks on the water with Jesus - and yet "follows at a distance" on land. Yet despite this, we still love him. Perhaps some of the greatest words that are recorded in Scripture are those used by Jesus when addressing the big fisherman: "You are ... you will be." We have already touched on them, but they deserve further comment, for they are the hinge on which Peter's life swings. They open up an understanding of the main lesson of his life, which is this: no matter what we are by nature, with Christ's help and sustaining grace, we can become the man or woman God wants us to be. Peter was a reed, tossed in the wind ... but he became a rock. Something similar can happen to you.

A hospitable home
Luke 10:38; Mark 14:3-9

DAY **258**

Martha and Mary lived with their brother Lazarus in Bethany, a small village about two miles from Jerusalem. Martha was probably the elder of the sisters and an active worker, while Mary appears to have been more contemplative. Both were devout Jewesses and, together with their brother Lazarus, had a great interest in Jesus' ministry. When visiting Jerusalem, as He frequently did, Christ must have greatly valued the hospitality which was always available to Him in the home of Martha, Mary and Lazarus. He who said, "The Son of Man has nowhere to lay his head" (Matt. 8:20), would, no doubt, have been deeply grateful for the hospitality of this home in Bethany.

"Offer hospitality to one another without grumbling." (1 Pet. 4:9)

FURTHER THOUGHT

Hospitality has been defined as "the art of making people want to stay without interfering with their departure". In the light of what you have read today, ask yourself these questions: Is my home a hospitable place? Am I a hospitable person? If not, why not?

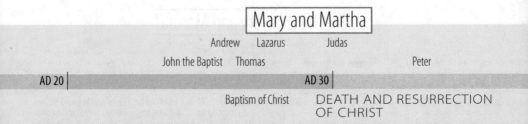

	Mary and Martha		
	Andrew	Lazarus	Judas
John the Baptist	Thomas		Peter
AD 20		AD 30	
	Baptism of Christ	DEATH AND RESURRECTION OF CHRIST	

DAY 259 — A special village

Matthew 21:17; Luke 24:50

The little village of Bethany, positioned as it is on the eastern side of the Mount of Olives, took on a special significance in Bible days. There were a number of reasons for this. First, it was adjacent to Jerusalem and provided an excellent retreat from the hustle and bustle of that busy city. Second, it was the first stopping place for travellers on the road to Jericho. Third, being flanked by the Mount of Olives, it was an attractive place to visit. Its greatest significance, of course, comes from its association with Christ, and to this very day, thousands of travellers and pilgrims stop at Bethany to visit the traditional sites on their way to Jericho and the Dead Sea.

"But you were washed, you were sanctified, you were justified in the name of the Lord Jesus Christ and by the Spirit of our God." (1 Cor. 6:11)

FURTHER THOUGHT

Have you ever considered how places, things and people become special, not because of what they are or contain in themselves, but by reason of their association with Christ? Jesus makes special everything He touches – including you.

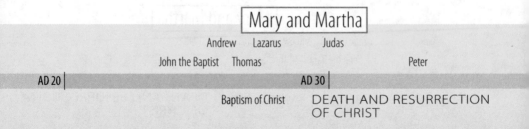

Mary and Martha

Andrew   Lazarus   Judas

John the Baptist   Thomas   Peter

AD 20 | AD 30 |

Baptism of Christ   DEATH AND RESURRECTION
OF CHRIST

At Jesus' feet

Luke 10:39

Although Martha and Mary were sisters, they were quite the opposite in temperament. Mary had a reflective personality, while Martha appears to have been an energetic, practical type of person. Mary would have revelled in the visits of Jesus, and no doubt would have listened to His words with great interest and concentration. Such was the power and wisdom contained in the words of the Master, that Mary delighted to sit at His feet and drink in the truth that He expounded so simply, yet so effectively. As Mary's spiritual life deepened under the teaching of Jesus, she became one of His most devoted followers, whose love for her Lord is widely discussed and constantly praised.

"When I saw him, I fell at his feet as though dead. Then he placed his right hand on me and said: 'Do not be afraid. I am the First and the Last.'" (Rev. 1:17)

FURTHER THOUGHT

What kind of temperament do you have? Are you an extrovert like Martha, or an introvert like Mary? Whatever your temperament, one thing is sure – like Mary, you need daily to "sit at Jesus' feet" if your soul is to be fed and your spiritual life developed.

Cornelius	Paul		Aquila and Priscilla
Stephen	Philip the Evangelist Barnabas		Lydia Timothy Silas
AD 40		AD 50	
Paul's conversion	1st missionary journey		2nd missionary journey

Mary and Martha

Martha: "Lady"; Mary: "Bitter"

DAY **261**

A family complaint

Luke 10:40–42

Martha is so preoccupied with the task of preparing a lavish meal for Jesus – the honoured guest – that she does not know where to turn. The sight of Mary sitting and listening to Jesus and ignoring the needs of the kitchen drives her to the point of distraction. Angrily, she reproaches Jesus for permitting what she feels is an unjust situation to continue, and hotly demands that He should tell Mary to get up and help her prepare and serve the meal. Jesus gently refuses to comply with her request, instead commending Mary for her devotion – making plain by His statement that He values spiritual fellowship much more than physical nourishment.

"There remains, then, a Sabbath-rest for the people of God; for anyone who enters God's rest also rests from his own work, just as God did from his." (Heb. 4:9–10)

FURTHER THOUGHT

Ever heard the term, "workaholic"? This is someone who is addicted to activity and work. Martha was probably such a person – she got her self-worth from what she did, rather than who she was. From where do you get your self-worth? From your inner being, or from your outer activity?

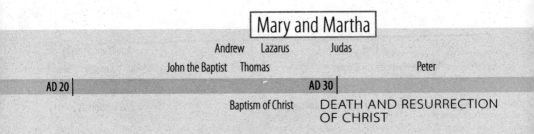

Mary and Martha			
Andrew	Lazarus	Judas	
John the Baptist	Thomas		Peter
AD 20		AD 30	
	Baptism of Christ	DEATH AND RESURRECTION OF CHRIST	

A family crisis

John 11:1–15

Jesus was quite a distance away from the family home of Mary, Martha and Lazarus when He received the message that Lazarus was seriously ill. The sisters' plea was that He should come at once and heal their brother of his sickness. Strangely, the Master decided to postpone His visit and "stayed where he was two more days" (v. 6). How puzzling this must have been to the two sisters, who expected Jesus to immediately come to their aid. Jesus often did the unexpected, not because He delighted to be different, but because He understood the true nature of every event and sought to bring the greatest glory to God in everything.

"... being confident of this, that he who began a good work in you will carry it on to completion until the day of Christ Jesus." (Phil. 1:6)

FURTHER THOUGHT

Have you ever asked the Lord to help you with something and found, as Mary and Martha did, that He failed to immediately respond to your petition? It's a difficult time, isn't it? But remember, God's delays are not His denials. Mary and Martha got their answer, but in a different way than they expected.

Cornelius	Paul		Aquila and Priscilla	
Stephen	Philip the Evangelist	Barnabas	Lydia	Timothy	Silas
AD 40			AD 50	
Paul's conversion	1st missionary journey		2nd missionary journey	

Mary and Martha

Martha: "Lady"; Mary: "Bitter"

DAY 263   A devoted act

John 12:3-8

Someone has described this incident as "the loveliest scene in the whole of the Gospels". As the shadow of the cross falls across Jesus' path, Mary's sensitive spirit perceives that a deep crisis is near. Therefore, as Jesus reclines at table in the house of Simon the Leper, Mary brings out an expensive bottle of perfume and pours the whole of the contents over His feet. The aroma fills the whole house, but Judas questions the wisdom of her action, calling it an act of extravagance. Jesus defends Mary's action, however, and sees it as an act of deep devotion which greatly encourages Him as He moves towards the ordeal that lies before Him on the hill of Calvary.

"Worship the Lord in the splendour of his holiness; tremble before him, all the earth." (Psa. 96:9)

FURTHER THOUGHT

One great preacher said of Christ: "God's Anointed should be our anointed." He means, of course, that just as God has poured on Him the "oil of joy" (Psa. 45:7), so should we pour upon Him the perfume of our highest adoration and affection. Do as Mary did, and worship Jesus - extravagantly.

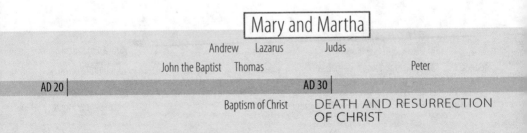

	Mary and Martha	
Andrew	Lazarus	Judas
John the Baptist	Thomas	Peter
AD 20	AD 30	
	Baptism of Christ	DEATH AND RESURRECTION OF CHRIST

Worship or service

I cannot choose; I should have liked so much
To sit at Jesus' feet – to feel the touch
Of His kind, gentle hand upon my head
While drinking in the gracious words He said.

And yet to serve Him! – Oh, divine employ –
To minister and give the Master joy,
To bathe in coolest springs His weary feet,
And wait upon Him while He sat at meat!

Worship or service – which? Ah, that is best
To which He calls us, be it toil or rest –
To labour for Him in life's busy stir,
Or seek His feet, a silent worshipper.

Caroline Atherton Mason

Key Lesson – Mary and Martha

Martha and Mary seem to belong together – hence the reason why we have not dealt with them separately. Most people refer to them as "Mary and Martha", but it seems that Jesus placed Martha first, then Mary, then Lazarus. The two sisters were of opposite temperaments – Martha the practical one, and Mary the devotional one. Martha loved to do things; Mary just loved to be. The happy person is the one who has both of these characteristics – practicality and devotion – but with devotion slightly in the ascendancy: "Mary has chosen what is better" (Luke 10:42). Perhaps Scripture links these two women closely together so that we might have a glimpse of the value of both temperaments (for each is valid in its own right); but, at the same time, it subtly suggests the desirability of allowing God to fuse into us by His Spirit both characteristics – practicality and devotion.

Lazarus

Lazarus: "Without help"

DAY 264 · A sickness contracted

John 11:1–3

Lazarus was a close friend of Jesus. We know that from the statement: "Lord, the one you love is sick" (v. 3). Little else is known about Lazarus – neither his occupation, his age, nor his parentage. There is no record of any statement he made. He is indeed a shadowy figure. Early Christian tradition believed that Lazarus was a fairly rich man, a view somewhat reinforced by the fact that his sister, Mary, anointed Jesus with an expensive ointment. The first reference to him we have in Scripture is when he falls seriously ill, causing his sisters such anxiety that they send a message to Jesus to come and heal him. What the sickness was we do not know, but it was serious enough to cause his death.

"This was to fulfil what was spoken through the prophet Isaiah: 'He took up our infirmities and carried our diseases.'" (Matt. 8:17)

FURTHER THOUGHT

Matthew Henry, the famous Bible commentator, says: "It is no new thing for those whom Christ loves to be sick." If you are sick at this moment, don't view it as a sign of God's punishment or disapproval. Take hold of the fact that He loves you – yes, really – and desires to do you good.

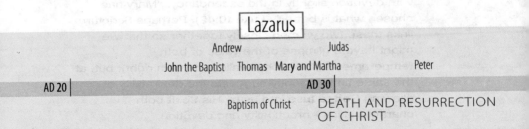

Lazarus

	Andrew	Judas	
John the Baptist	Thomas	Mary and Martha	Peter
AD 20		AD 30	
	Baptism of Christ	DEATH AND RESURRECTION OF CHRIST	

God's glory declared

John 11:4–5

hen Jesus receives the news of His friend Lazarus' sickness, He responds by stating: "This sickness will not end in death. No, it is for God's glory so that God's Son may be glorified through it" (v. 4). This statement introduces us to one of the great mysteries of the universe – the sovereignty of God. Jesus is saying that what has happened to Lazarus has been allowed by His Father so that the Son might have an opportunity to demonstrate His power to raise the dead. Jesus evidently saw this situation – and, for that matter, every other crisis situation – not so much as an obstacle as an opportunity.

"For we do not have a high priest who is unable to sympathise with our weaknesses ... Let us then approach the throne of grace with confidence, so that we may receive mercy and find grace to help us in our time of need." (Heb. 4:15–16)

FURTHER THOUGHT

How different our days would be if we could see every emergency or crisis from God's point of view! What we regard as a block, God sees as a blessing; what we view as a setback, God sees as a springboard. Ask God right now to help you to see all your trials and difficulties from His point of view.

Cornelius	Paul		Aquila and Priscilla
Stephen	Philip the Evangelist	Barnabas	Lydia Timothy Silas
AD 40			**AD 50**
Paul's conversion	1st missionary journey		2nd missionary journey

Lazarus

Lazarus: "Without help"

DAY 266 — A puzzling response

John 11:5–16

When Jesus received the news of Lazarus' illness, He appeared to imply that it was not serious and would not cause death (v. 4a). The disciples were well aware of the dangers that awaited them if they went near Jerusalem at this time; Thomas even expected that they might be killed (v.16). When Jesus delayed setting out for Bethany, the disciples probably concluded that Jesus did not consider Lazarus' illness serious enough to run the risk of imperilling their own lives. If this was so, then how puzzled they must have been when, two days later, Jesus informed them that He must now go to Bethany to raise Lazarus from death – a statement which appears to contradict His earlier response.

"Every good and perfect gift is from above, coming down from the Father of the heavenly lights, who does not change like shifting shadows."
(James 1:17)

FURTHER THOUGHT

The situation described in the passage today has puzzled many commentators. Did Jesus contradict Himself? The answer is found on the following page – but before you look, think it through yourself and see if you can come to any conclusions.

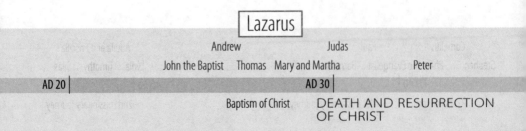

	Lazarus		
	Andrew	Judas	
John the Baptist	Thomas Mary and Martha		Peter
AD 20		AD 30	
	Baptism of Christ	DEATH AND RESURRECTION OF CHRIST	

A positive declaration

John 11:17-37

Martha's and Mary's urgent message to Jesus concerning their brother's illness failed to bring an immediate response – and, in the course of time, Lazarus died. Naturally the sisters are brokenhearted, and many of their friends come from Jerusalem and round about to mourn with them and console them (v. 19). When Jesus arrives, Lazarus' funeral has already taken place, and as the Master nears the home of Martha and Mary, Martha goes out to meet Him with the words: "Lord ... if you had been here, my brother would not have died" (v. 21). She quickly follows this with a positive affirmation: "But I know that even now God will give you whatever you ask" (v. 22).

"Trust in the Lord with all your heart and lean not on your own understanding ..." (Prov. 3:5)

FURTHER THOUGHT

How interesting that Martha, although saddened and hurt by the fact that Jesus had not arrived in time to heal her brother, still affirms her confidence in Him. Isn't this what faith is all about – being willing to accept reality, but believing at the same time in One who is greater than reality?

Cornelius		Paul			Aquila and Priscilla	
Stephen	Philip the Evangelist	Barnabas		Lydia	Timothy	Silas
	AD 40			AD 50		
Paul's conversion	1st missionary journey			2nd missionary journey		

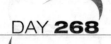
DAY 268   An unexpected miracle

John 11:38–44

Jesus' sorrow at Lazarus' death was so great that some of the people around Him said: "See how he loved him!" (v. 36). Others questioned why Jesus had not come earlier and healed him. When Jesus has had time to compose Himself, He stands in front of the tomb and asks that the stone which seals the entrance be removed. Martha protests: "But Lord, he has been dead four days. By this time he will be decaying ..." (v. 39, Phillips). Jesus reminds her of an earlier conversation, saying, "Did I not tell you that if you believed, you would see the glory of God?" (v. 40), and then proceeds to pray to His Father. Following this powerful prayer, Jesus commands Lazarus to return from the dead, and miraculously Lazarus walks out of the tomb.

"Jesus looked at them and said, 'With man this is impossible, but with God all things are possible.'" (Matt. 19:26)

FURTHER THOUGHT

Have you ever considered the fact that if Jesus had responded immediately to Mary's and Martha's request, all that would have been recorded here would have been a miracle of healing? The delay, however, gave rise to an even greater miracle – the miracle of resurrection. God often chooses not to respond to the lesser in order that He might do the greater.

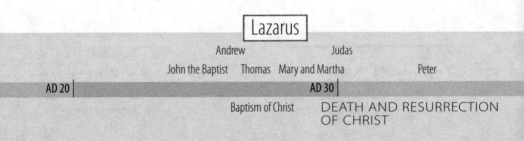

Lazarus				
	Andrew		Judas	
	John the Baptist	Thomas	Mary and Martha	Peter
AD 20			AD 30	
		Baptism of Christ	DEATH AND RESURRECTION OF CHRIST	

A mixed reaction

John 11:45-54

Many who stood around the tomb of Lazarus that day and saw him raised from the dead chose to believe in Jesus, but some went straight to Jerusalem to report to the Pharisees what they had witnessed in the little village of Bethany. The Jewish leaders decided that they must act decisively before the news of Lazarus' resurrection induced others to become disciples. This became the moment of decision for the Pharisees, for from this time they plotted how they could kill both Christ and Lazarus (see John 12:10). Why Lazarus? Because he was living proof of the power that Jesus of Nazareth demonstrated before the eyes of men.

"Immediately the boy's father exclaimed, 'I do believe; help me overcome my unbelief!'" (Mark 9:24)

FURTHER THOUGHT

Isn't it interesting how the acts of God produce completely different reactions in people? Some are brought closer to Christ as they see and feel His power, while others turn away from Him and move in the opposite direction. Why should this be? Talk it through with a friend today.

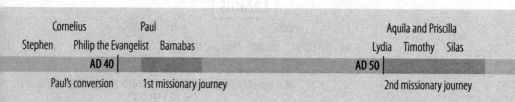

Cornelius		Paul		Aquila and Priscilla		
Stephen	Philip the Evangelist	Barnabas		Lydia	Timothy	Silas
AD 40				AD 50		
Paul's conversion		1st missionary journey		2nd missionary journey		

Lazarus

DAY 270   Fellowship enjoyed

John 12:1-2, 17-18

Just prior to the Passover, an event of great spiritual significance, Jesus joins the reunited family of Martha, Mary and Lazarus for a special meal. One can imagine the atmosphere in the home that day as Lazarus, the one who went down into death and remained there for four days, enjoys fellowship with the One whose power over death is indisputable. Martha, still busy and active, serves the meal, Lazarus reclines with Jesus at the table, while the other sister, Mary, sits at Jesus' feet. Many come to Bethany, not just to see Jesus, but also to meet the man whom Jesus raised from the dead (v.9).

"God, who has called you into fellowship with his Son Jesus Christ our Lord, is faithful." (1 Cor. 1:9)

FURTHER THOUGHT

In a sense, the special fellowship Lazarus enjoyed with Christ after his resurrection is similar to the fellowship we enjoy with Him. We were once dead (Eph. 2:1), but now we have been raised from spiritual death to enjoy eternal fellowship with Christ – not just at a table, but on a throne! (Eph. 2:6)

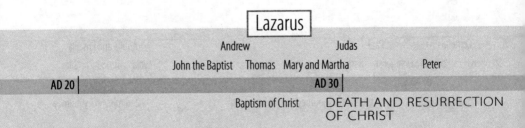

Lazarus

Andrew		Judas
John the Baptist	Thomas Mary and Martha	Peter

AD 20 | AD 30 |

Baptism of Christ   DEATH AND RESURRECTION OF CHRIST

The death of Lazarus

Jesus did not contradict Himself in this instance. How could He when He was the divine Son of God? Obviously His comment that Lazarus' sickness "will not end in death" had reference to permanent death. Jesus knew that Lazarus would die, but would not remain in death for more than a few days. Later, of course (we don't know exactly when), Lazarus experienced permanent physical death – and, like all others who have died, awaits the final resurrection.

The raising of Lazarus

The following factors enhance the importance of this miracle:

The number of days (4) between death and resurrection **(John 11:39)**

The number of witnesses involved **(John 11:45; 12:17f)**

The evident health of Lazarus after the event **(John 12:1f, 9)**

The evidential significance of the event among the Jews **(John 11:53; 12:10f)**

Key Lesson – Lazarus

It's interesting that we hear nothing of Lazarus in the New Testament until the time that he falls sick and is about to die. Although he is one of the most talked-about figures in history and one of the most preached-about personalities in the Gospels, not one word is recorded of anything he said. His ministry is a ministry of silence. In the few statements that are made concerning him, we catch a glimpse of a man who just wanted to serve and cared nothing for attention or praise. if he got attention, it was not of his own doing; he was content to have greatness "thrust upon him". The lesson of his life is that when we do not seek to be on "centre stage" we may very well end up there. But when we do, it must be due not to our own efforts – but His.

Judas Iscariot

Judas: "Praise"; Iscariot: "Of Kieroth"

DAY 271 — One of the Twelve

Matthew 10:4; Mark 3:19; Luke 6:16

We are told by Luke that Jesus spent a whole night in prayer prior to choosing His band of twelve disciples (Luke 6:12), and one of those He selected was Judas Iscariot – the man who later betrayed Him. During Jesus' public ministry, Judas travelled everywhere with Him and lived in close proximity to Him, but never seemed to share His spirit. Some have suggested that Jesus got His directions wrong in choosing Judas to be one of His disciples. This cannot possibly be so, however, for one of Christ's divine qualities was His ability to know what was in every man (see John 2:25). Whatever was His reason for choosing Judas, we can be sure it was not because of a mistake.

"You did not choose me, but I chose you and appointed you to go and bear fruit – fruit that will last. Then the Father will give you whatever you ask in my name." (John 15:16)

FURTHER THOUGHT

What do you think about the selection of Judas as one of the Twelve? Was it a mistake? Did Christ know Judas' traits, yet hope he would improve? Or did He permit it for a sovereign purpose? Think the matter through carefully, or talk it over with a friend, and come to a conclusion.

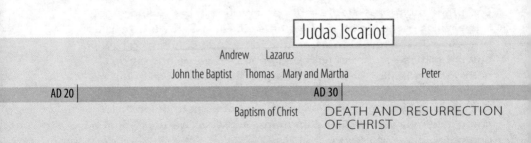

Judas Iscariot

Andrew   Lazarus

John the Baptist   Thomas   Mary and Martha   Peter

AD 20

AD 30

Baptism of Christ   DEATH AND RESURRECTION OF CHRIST

Hypocrite

John 12:4–6; Matthew 26:14–16

Having chosen Judas to be one of the disciples, Jesus gives him a position of trust as the keeper of the common purse. He proved, however, to be unworthy of that trust, taking for himself the money which had been donated to support Jesus and the disciples. Judas' greed and hypocrisy were also shown by his willingness to betray the Son of God for the price of a slave (Ex. 21:32), and in his pretended concern for the welfare of the poor when he criticised Mary of Bethany for anointing Jesus' feet with costly ointment. His continued presence in the apostolic band must have daily involved him in hypocrisy as his heart became increasingly turned away from Jesus.

"Why do you call me, 'Lord, Lord,' and do not do what I say?" (Luke 6:46)

FURTHER THOUGHT

Billy Sunday, the quaint old preacher, used to say: "Hypocrites in the church? Yes, and in the home. Don't hunt through the church for a hypocrite; go home and look in the mirror. Then see that you make the number one less."

Cornelius		Paul		Aquila and Priscilla	
Stephen	Philip the Evangelist	Barnabas		Lydia	Timothy	Silas
AD 40				AD 50	
Paul's conversion		1st missionary journey		2nd missionary journey	

Judas Iscariot

Judas: "Praise"; Iscariot: "Of Kieroth"

DAY **273**   Traitor

Luke 6:16; John 6:70; 13:10–11; 17:12

The Gospel writers, on almost every occasion when Judas' name is mentioned, refer to him as the betrayer of Jesus. The betrayal of Christ was indeed a heinous crime, and there can be no doubt that Judas acted as the instrument of Satan in perpetrating it. In fact, in one place Jesus describes Judas as a devil (John 6:70), and it appears that Satan entered into him following Jesus' final gesture of love at the Last Supper (John 13:27). He is also described by Jesus as "the one doomed to destruction" (John 17:12), and nothing good is ever said about him except, perhaps, that he was capable of feeling remorse after seeing the result of his evil crime.

"They claim to know God, but by their actions they deny him." (Titus 1:16)

FURTHER THOUGHT

Dr W.E. Sangster, when writing of Judas' betrayal of Christ, said: "Every Christian should periodically question his own soul: 'Am I really in this because of my devotion to my Lord? Would I stand if a crucial test came?'" Good questions to ask before you start the day!

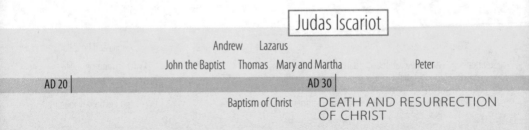

Judas Iscariot

Andrew   Lazarus

John the Baptist   Thomas   Mary and Martha   Peter

AD 20 | AD 30 |

Baptism of Christ   DEATH AND RESURRECTION OF CHRIST

Matthew 26:20-25; Mark 14:17-21

Jesus being the person He was – the divine Son of God – knew both the strengths and weaknesses of every one of His disciples. He took steps also to alert them to the evil possibilities that lay deep in their hearts. When Peter insisted that he would never deny Him, Jesus tried to prepare him for the next hours by telling him that he would deny Him, not just once or twice, but three times. He does something similar with Judas Iscariot on the eve of His betrayal, as if He wants to give him an opportunity to repent of his evil intentions. As we know, however, Judas is so bent on evil that he remains unmoved even when treated as an honoured guest at the Last Supper.

"Having loved his own who were in the world, he now showed them the full extent of his love." (John 13:1)

FURTHER THOUGHT

How grateful we ought to be for the love of Christ that pleads with us when we are bent on some course of action that will dishonour His name. Where would we be now if, at our first fingering of sin, He had not pleaded with us ... where would we be?

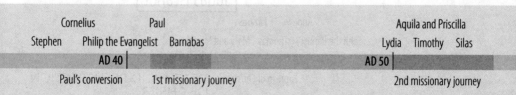

	Cornelius	Paul			Aquila and Priscilla		
Stephen	Philip the Evangelist	Barnabas			Lydia	Timothy	Silas
	AD 40				**AD 50**		
	Paul's conversion	1st missionary journey			2nd missionary journey		

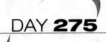

Judas Iscariot

Judas: "Praise"; Iscariot: "Of Kieroth"

DAY 275 — Betrayal accomplished

Matthew 26:47-56; Mark 14:43-50

Following the raising of Lazarus from the dead, the high priest and the Jewish leaders were deeply concerned that Jesus might recruit more followers to His cause, and determined to put Him to death. Jesus' high level of popularity at this time, however, meant that they must go about their plans with great care and caution. Judas' offer of betrayal was an opportunity that was too good to miss. His knowledge of Jesus' movements would enable him to lead the soldiers to a place where they could arrest Him without too many of the populace being aware of it. In the Garden of Gethsemane, Judas greets Jesus with the word, "Rabbi!" followed by a spurious show of affection, which results in Christ's arrest.

"Wounds from a friend can be trusted, but an enemy multiplies kisses."
(Prov. 27:6)

FURTHER THOUGHT

A kiss is usually the symbol of love and affection. But was ever the symbol of love so utterly prostituted as when Judas kissed Christ into the soldiers' arms? Such is the nature of evil – it twists the highest into the lowest, the best into the worst.

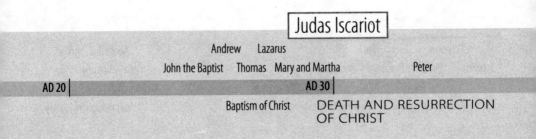

Judas Iscariot

	Andrew	Lazarus		
John the Baptist	Thomas	Mary and Martha		Peter
AD 20		AD 30		
	Baptism of Christ	DEATH AND RESURRECTION OF CHRIST		

Remorseful

Matthew 27:3–10

Once Christ has been condemned and it becomes obvious that He is to die on a cross, the full weight of what he has done bursts in upon Judas' conscience. Returning to the Temple, he pleads with the priests to take back the money, confessing: "I have betrayed innocent blood" (v. 4). They coldly reply that his problems are his own affair and that it means nothing to them. Judas then throws the thirty pieces of silver at their feet and, overcome by remorse, goes out and hangs himself. He has served the priests' unholy enterprise and, having no further use for him, they abandon him to the perdition which his rejection of Christ has made inevitable.

"If they have escaped the corruption of the world by knowing our Lord and Saviour Jesus Christ and are again entangled in it and overcome, they are worse off at the end than they were at the beginning." (2 Pet. 2:20)

FURTHER THOUGHT

In discussions among God's people, the issue is often raised: If Judas had gone to Jesus and asked Him for forgiveness, would he have received it? Knowing what you know of the forgiveness of God, what do you think?

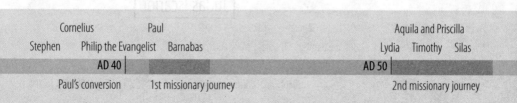

Cornelius Paul Aquila and Priscilla
Stephen Philip the Evangelist Barnabas Lydia Timothy Silas
AD 40 AD 50
Paul's conversion 1st missionary journey 2nd missionary journey

Judas Iscariot

Judas: "Praise"; Iscariot: "Of Kieroth"

DAY 277

Replaced

Acts 1:15–26

As a result of Judas' suicide, the number of the disciples is reduced to eleven. Peter quotes prophecies from the Scripture which, under the inspiration of the Holy Spirit, he applies to Judas. These Scriptures (Psalm 69:25; 109:8) show that the vacant office should be filled by a suitable person – the qualifications being that he should have accompanied the apostles during the time of Jesus' public ministry, and that he was a witness of the resurrection. Two candidates are selected and, after prayer, lots are cast. The one on whom the lot falls is Matthias, who then becomes the new twelfth apostle. Nothing more is said of Matthias as an individual, only corporately as one of the Twelve.

"For he chose us in him before the creation of the world to be holy and blameless in his sight." (Eph. 1:4)

FURTHER THOUGHT

The one thing above all others to which the apostles were asked to attest was the resurrection of Christ from the dead. Why was that so supremely important? Know the answer? If you don't, then look up 1 Corinthians 15:17: "If Christ has not been raised, your faith is futile; you are still in your sins".

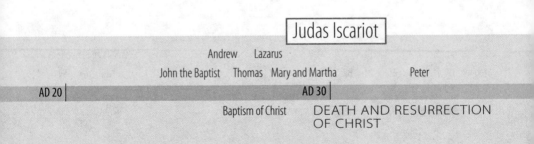

Judas Iscariot

Andrew   Lazarus

John the Baptist   Thomas   Mary and Martha   Peter

AD 20

AD 30

Baptism of Christ   DEATH AND RESURRECTION OF CHRIST

Judas

Another apostle bore this common Jewish name, but "Judas" now means the betrayer of Jesus. His sin has stamped the word with such evil significance that it has become the class-name of perfidious friends who are "no better than Judas". Iscariot is understood to be equivalent to ish-Kerioth, that is, "man of Kerioth". Kerioth was a town in south Judea. The other disciples were from Galilee. The southern Jews regarded the northerners with a certain superiority. Is it possible that some of this spirit of superiority alienated Judas from his fellow disciples? If it did, it is psychologically probable that Judas would attribute the lack of sympathy to them. They would appear reserved and unsociable, and in his own view he would seem the injured one. Such blindness is almost invariably characteristic of the pride which causes estrangement.

Key Lesson - Judas

Any lesson we draw from the life of Judas must, in the nature of things, be a negative one. In other words, we see in him, not a picture of how to do things, but of how not to do things. The reasons for Judas' actions have perplexed Christians from the first. The Gospels offer several "explanations", suggesting that one might not be sufficient to account for the behaviour of this unfortunate man. Without doubt, the main lesson we can draw from Judas is the danger of allowing personal interests to outweigh the interests of Christ and His cause. John the Baptist cried: "He must become greater; I must become less" (John 3:30). Unfortunately Judas Iscariot never came through to that important discovery - and as a result, lost not only his life, but his eternal soul.

Thomas

Thomas: "Twin"

DAY **278**

Chosen

Matthew 10:3

"Thomas the Twin", as he was known, was one of the twelve apostles. Nothing is known of his twin brother (or sister) and, assuming that he or she was alive at the time the Gospels were written, it does not appear that this twin became a follower of Jesus. Commentators believe that Thomas must have been a man of independent judgement for him to break such a close filial relationship to become a disciple of Christ. Was he chosen because of his independence or in spite of it? We will never know – except that he was chosen. Thomas appears to have been a brave and zealous man with an enquiring mind. If he didn't understand something, he did not hesitate to ask for an explanation.

"But God chose the foolish things of the world to shame the wise; God chose the weak things of the world to shame the strong." (1 Cor. 1:27)

FURTHER THOUGHT

Have you ever pondered as to why before the creation of the world (Eph. 1:4) the Lord chose you to be one of His present-day disciples? Was His choice based, as some believe, on the fact that He foresaw that you would accept Him – or, as others believe, on the fact that some are predestined to salvation and others not? What do you think?

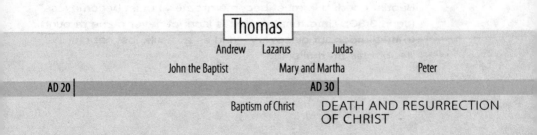

	Thomas		
Andrew	Lazarus	Judas	
John the Baptist	Mary and Martha		Peter
AD 20		AD 30	
	Baptism of Christ	DEATH AND RESURRECTION OF CHRIST	

John 11:16

We have already dwelt on the story of the raising of Lazarus from the dead, but we return to this passage today to focus on the thoughts that were going on in Thomas' heart as Jesus contemplated returning to Jerusalem. Remember, the Jews had earlier accused Christ of blasphemy (John 10:33) and had prepared to stone Him as prescribed by the law of Moses (Lev. 24:16). Despite the obvious ill feeling against Him that existed in some Jewish circles, Jesus decided to return to the Jerusalem area and visit Mary and Martha at their home in Bethany. Thomas' declaration of loyalty is significant and quite moving: "Let us also go, that we may die with him".

"Many a man claims to have unfailing love, but a faithful man who can find?" (Prov. 20:6)

FURTHER THOUGHT

Isn't it sad that we have picked out a bad patch in Thomas' life and labelled the whole of it because of that one mistake? Yes, he displayed doubt, but he displayed loyalty too. Make a decision today to take off any "labels" you may have attached to your friends and acquaintances.

Cornelius	Paul	Aquila and Priscilla
Stephen Philip the Evangelist Barnabas		Lydia Timothy Silas
AD 40		AD 50
Paul's conversion 1st missionary journey		2nd missionary journey

Thomas

DAY 280

Challenging

John 14:5

Jesus has just been teaching His disciples about His imminent departure to heaven, promising that after He has prepared a place for them, He will return to take them to their heavenly home. One of the statements Jesus makes is this: "You know where I am going and how to get there" (v. 4, TLB). Thomas strongly disagrees with this statement, and says: "No, we don't. We haven't any idea where You are going, so how can we know the way?" Thomas doesn't hesitate to challenge anything about which he is uncertain, and although some may regard his approach as rude or impertinent, obviously Jesus does not think so for He responds to him by making His point clearer still: "I am the way and the truth and the life" (v. 6).

"Since, then, you have been raised with Christ, set your hearts on things above, where Christ is seated at the right hand of God." (Col. 3:1)

FURTHER THOUGHT

Have you considered that if Thomas had not questioned Jesus' statement here, we might never have had that beautiful description of Jesus being Himself the Way? Once again, the point is brought home – never be afraid to ask searching or probing questions.

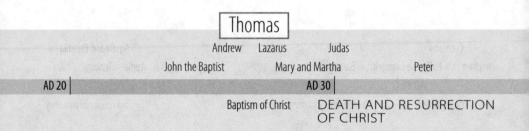

Absent

John 20:24

ollowing Christ's death and the apparent end of His ministry, the disciples became afraid of what the Jews might do to them, and so hid behind closed doors – petrified with fear. Suddenly, although the doors were locked and guarded against intruders, Jesus appeared in the midst of His disciples and greeted them with the words: "Peace be with you!" (v. 21). What a glorious revelation that must have been to those stunned and bewildered disciples – how it must have consoled their drooping spirits and elevated their faith. There is only one sad note to the story: Thomas was not with them when Jesus came!

"For God alone my soul waits in silence, for my hope is from him."
(Psa. 62:5 RSV)

FURTHER THOUGHT

Let your mind run over some of the reasons why Thomas may have missed that important meeting. Was it because he didn't expect Jesus to be there? Was he disappointed with the other disciples? Was it because it was dangerous to be present? Or was the real reason that there was something wrong with himself?

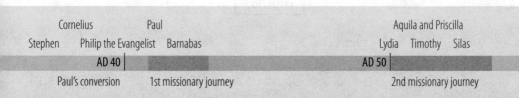

	Cornelius	Paul			Aquila and Priscilla		
Stephen	Philip the Evangelist	Barnabas			Lydia	Timothy	Silas
	AD 40				AD 50		
	Paul's conversion	1st missionary journey			2nd missionary journey		

Thomas

Thomas: "Twin"

DAY 282

Doubting

John 20:25

When Thomas, who was absent from that first post-resurrection meeting of Christ and His disciples, is told the thrilling news that Jesus is alive, he is utterly bewildered. The disciples insist that they have seen the very scars which the nails made on Jesus' body at the time of His crucifixion. Thomas, however, will not be swept off his feet by the testimony of others, and the independence of judgement we spoke of earlier comes again to the fore: "Unless I see the nail marks in his hands and put my finger where the nails were, I will not believe it". At least Thomas confesses his doubts – something many Christians are too "spiritual" to do.

"Jesus replied, "I tell you the truth, if you have faith and do not doubt ... you can say to this mountain, "Go, throw yourself into the sea," and it will be done. If you believe, you will receive whatever you ask for in prayer." (Matt. 21:21–22)

FURTHER THOUGHT

"Doubts," said Neil Strand, "can be valuable if they are recognised and confessed ... and if they force a man to search deeper and longer for answers." So, although the point has been made before - don't be afraid of doubts. For to pursue doubts is to discover some new and exciting beliefs.

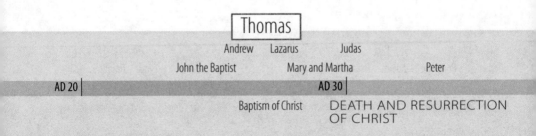

	Thomas		
Andrew	Lazarus	Judas	
John the Baptist	Mary and Martha		Peter
AD 20		AD 30	
	Baptism of Christ	DEATH AND RESURRECTION OF CHRIST	

John 20:26

Although no clear explanation is given to us in Scripture as to why Thomas missed that first post-resurrection meeting with the Lord, he appears to have been committed to staying in close touch with his fellow disciples – despite his doubts. We should not overlook that characteristic of Thomas. When next Jesus appears to the disciples, Thomas is present and experiences the wonder of seeing the risen Christ face to face. Jesus responds to Thomas' plea for physical proof in the most gentle and non-judgemental manner: "Put your finger here; see my hands. Reach out your hand and put it into my side. Stop doubting and believe."

"Immediately Jesus reached out his hand and caught him. 'You of little faith,' he said, 'why did you doubt?'" (Matt. 14:31)

FURTHER THOUGHT

Isn't it interesting that Jesus did not reject Thomas' attitude, but responded to it? How glad we should be that God accepts us as we are, not as He would like us to be. If He didn't – we would be sunk!

Cornelius	Paul			Aquila and Priscilla	
Stephen	Philip the Evangelist	Barnabas		Lydia	Timothy	Silas
AD 40				**AD 50**	
Paul's conversion	1st missionary journey			2nd missionary journey	

Thomas
Thomas: "Twin"

DAY 284

Believing
John 20:27-29

A s Thomas' doubts are removed by seeing for himself the physical evidence in Christ's hands and side, the unbeliever suddenly leaps beyond the other disciples and cries: "My Lord and my God!" Up until this time, none of the disciples had actually addressed Jesus as God. They had called Him "Messiah", "Son of God", "Son of the living God" – but not "God". This was probably one of the greatest and most revealing statements to have come from the group of disciples. And all the more significant because it came from a man who, up until the moment of seeing the physical evidence of Christ's wounds, was a doubter and an unbeliever.

"It is better to take refuge in the Lord than to trust in man." (Psa. 118:8)

FURTHER THOUGHT

The person who is afraid to face or express doubts, who represses them instead of confessing them, is indeed a troubled person. Some of the biggest doubters have become the greatest disciples. Why? Because they brought their doubts to Jesus and let Him deal with them in the way that only He can.

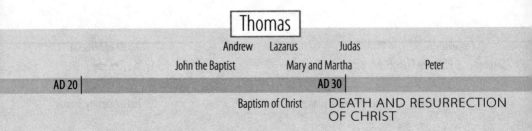

Thomas		
Andrew Lazarus	Judas	
John the Baptist	Mary and Martha	Peter
AD 20	AD 30	
Baptism of Christ	DEATH AND RESURRECTION OF CHRIST	

Thomas

"Old Father Morris," says his American biographer, "had noticed a falling off in his little village meeting for prayer. The first time he collected a tolerable audience, he took occasion to tell them something concerning the meeting of the disciples after the resurrection. 'But Thomas was not with them,' said the old man in a sorrowful voice: 'why, what could keep Thomas away? Perhaps,' he said, glancing at some of his audience, 'Thomas had got cold-hearted, and was afraid that they would ask him to make the first prayer; or perhaps,' he continued, looking at some of the farmers, 'he was afraid the roads were bad; or perhaps,' he added, after a pause, 'he thought a shower was coming on.' He went on summing up common excuses, and then he added, 'But only think what Thomas lost, for in the middle of the meeting the Lord Jesus came and stood among them!' "

Key Lesson – Thomas

Multitudes of Christians have been grateful that the Bible has turned a spotlight upon Thomas and his doubts. Those who have stuggled with doubts – or perhaps still do – find great comfort in the fact that Thomas, the doubter among the disciples, came through to radiant conviction and great spiritual achievement. Tradition claims the Thomas travelled to many countries preaching the gospel, and finally landed in India where, after founding a church, he was martyred. We cannot be absolutely sure about this, but this is what many of the early Church writers, such as Eusebius, believed. The main lesson of Thomas' life is surely this – those who wrestle with doubts can, with Christ's help, come through to a glorious certainty of faith and great spiritual effectiveness. Christ has great sympathy with those who cry out to Him, "I believe; help my unbelief!" – and He will.

Andrew

DAY 285

Fisherman

Matthew 4:18

Andrew was Simon Peter's brother and a member of the fishing community from which Jesus drew several of His disciples. Together with their partners, James and John, they plied their fishing trade on the Sea of Galilee with some success. Excavations at Capernaum, the main fishing village on the Sea of Galilee in Bible days, reveal that some of the houses were large – implying that fishermen were able to make a good living from their fishing business. A fisherman's task in Bible days was a strenuous one, and demanded total commitment. Successful fishermen were known to be reliable and industrious men – good qualities for disciples, too.

"Now it is required that those who have been given a trust must prove faithful." (1 Cor. 4:2)

FURTHER THOUGHT

As commentators have often pointed out, when Jesus selected His disciples, He chose men who were already busily engaged in a task and, to some extent, successful at it. In doing this, did Jesus follow the principle outlined in Luke 16:10? It would seem so. What do you think?

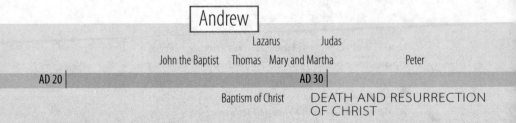

Andrew		
	Lazarus	Judas
John the Baptist Thomas	Mary and Martha	Peter
AD 20	AD 30	
	Baptism of Christ	DEATH AND RESURRECTION OF CHRIST

A new vocation

Matthew 4:19–20

As Jesus walks along the shore of Galilee, He catches sight of Andrew and Peter at work in their boat, letting down their fishing net. The Master speaks to them and informs them that He wants them to change their vocation and become His disciples. No doubt they knew at once what was involved in this challenge – a different lifestyle, constant travelling, hours of instruction – but they seemed not to hesitate. Christ's call came to them in words with which they could easily identify: "Come, follow me and I will make you fishers of men." The word "make" in the Greek is a strong one, indicating that Christ would impart to them His own spiritual strength and power.

"The fruit of the righteous is a tree of life, and he who wins souls is wise." (Prov. 11:30)

FURTHER THOUGHT

Do you know what the word "disciple" means? It means to be a learner, one who follows a master - assimilating his master's words, absorbing his teaching and following his lifestyle. On that basis - are you a disciple?

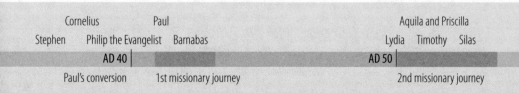

	Cornelius	Paul			Aquila and Priscilla		
Stephen	Philip the Evangelist	Barnabas			Lydia	Timothy	Silas
	AD 40				AD 50		
	Paul's conversion	1st missionary journey			2nd missionary journey		

DAY **287**

A change of leader

John 1:35–40

A ndrew, prior to his call to join the group of Christ's disciples, was a devoted disciple of John the Baptist. One day, when he was in the company of John and another disciple, a carpenter from Galilee passed by and John pointed Him out as "the Lamb of God". Andrew and the other disciple immediately left John and went after Jesus to get to know Him better. We are not told who the other disciple was, but we do know that something began in Andrew's heart that prepared him for the direct call of Christ. There had been many great spiritual leaders in Israel, but none so great as Jesus; others could proclaim Him, but none could equal Him.

"Then Jesus said to his disciples, 'If anyone would come after me, he must deny himself and take up his cross and follow me.'" (Matt. 16:24)

FURTHER THOUGHT

It's surprising how many Christians follow an earthly leader more willingly than they follow their heavenly Leader. There were some like this in the church at Corinth (see 1 Corinthians 1:12). It is important to respect God's chosen leaders, but not to idolise them and make them equal with Christ. Remember – a leader proclaims Christ, but does not equal Him.

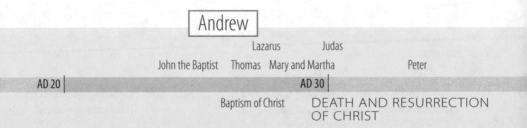

Andrew

Lazarus   Judas

John the Baptist   Thomas   Mary and Martha   Peter

AD 20 | AD 30 |

Baptism of Christ   DEATH AND RESURRECTION OF CHRIST

Introduces the family

John 1:41–42

Having left John the Baptist to seek Jesus and get to know Him more intimately, Andrew is so thrilled with his first encounter with Christ that he hastens to find his brother, Simon Peter, and joyfully introduces him to Jesus. Although a seemingly simple act, that introduction made a great impact, not only on Simon Peter personally, but on the ages to come. Simon Peter became the one to whom Christ gave the keys of the kingdom, and through his thrilling, Spirit-anointed sermon on the Day of Pentecost, opened its gates to thousands of newly converted souls. Little did Andrew know what impact that simple introduction was to have.

"'Go into all the world and preach the good news to all creation.'"
(Mark 16:15)

FURTHER THOUGHT

When you introduce someone to Jesus, you just can't tell what the outcome of that introduction will be – nor what the future may hold for that person. Have you ever introduced anyone to Christ? Ask the Lord to help you do this – today.

	Cornelius	Paul		Aquila and Priscilla		
Stephen	Philip the Evangelist	Barnabas		Lydia	Timothy	Silas
	AD 40			**AD 50**		
	Paul's conversion	1st missionary journey		2nd missionary journey		

Andrew

Andrew: "Manly"

DAY 289

A willing helper
John 6:8-9; 12:21-22

As Jesus preaches and teaches the people on the shores of Galilee, great crowds are drawn to Him. On this occasion, being some distance from the nearest town and because the people are hungry, a problem arises as to how they are going to be fed. Philip points out that even if it were possible to buy food, the cost would be too great. Andrew, overhearing these words, brings a young boy to Jesus who has with him five small loaves and two fishes. Jesus blesses the small supply and, miraculously, enough food is distributed to meet everyone's need. Later, when some Greeks ask Philip if they can be introduced to Jesus, he appeals to Andrew for help. No doubt by this time Andrew had clearly revealed what seems to be his uppermost characteristic – that of being a willing helper.

"And in the church God has appointed ... apostles ... prophets ... teachers ... workers of miracles ... those having gifts of healing, those able to help others, those with gifts of administration, and those speaking in different kinds of tongues." (1 Cor. 12:28)

FURTHER THOUGHT

Let your mind dwell on this characteristic of Andrew for a moment – that of being a willing helper – and ask yourself: Is that selfsame characteristic to be found in me? And remember, the thought is not just of being a helper, but a willing helper.

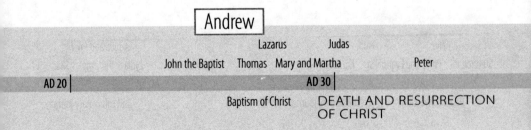

Andrew

Lazarus   Judas

John the Baptist   Thomas   Mary and Martha   Peter

AD 20

AD 30

Baptism of Christ   DEATH AND RESURRECTION OF CHRIST

A good learner

Mark 13:1–8

Jesus spent a good deal of His time teaching His disciples and preparing them for their future ministry in His Church. On this occasion, when one of the disciples remarked to Jesus how well-built and how magnificent were the Temple buildings, the Master turned to them and predicted their utter destruction. This prediction disturbed the disciples somewhat, and four of them – Peter, James, John and Andrew – approached Christ privately and asked Him to tell them precisely when the event would take place, and what would be the signs that would precede it. Andrew, no doubt, learned a lot from Jesus, not just by listening to what He said, but by asking Him pointed questions.

"Take my yoke upon you and learn from me, for I am gentle and humble in heart, and you will find rest for your souls." (Matt. 11:29)

FURTHER THOUGHT

Good learners are not people who merely sit and absorb the words of their teacher, but who are alert enough to ask sharp, incisive questions. Are you a questioning person? Never be afraid to ask a question – it could mean the difference between understanding and confusion.

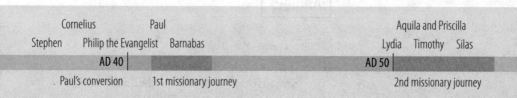

Cornelius   Paul   Aquila and Priscilla

Stephen   Philip the Evangelist   Barnabas   Lydia   Timothy   Silas

AD 40   AD 50

Paul's conversion   1st missionary journey   2nd missionary journey

Andrew

Andrew: "Manly"

DAY **291** — The place of prayer

Acts 1:13-14

After His resurrection, Jesus instructed His disciples to remain in Jerusalem and wait for the power of the Holy Spirit to descend upon them. Now that Judas is dead, the remaining eleven disciples – one of whom is Andrew – make their way, along with over 100 other followers of Christ, into the Upper Room. They wait in prayer for a period of ten days until at last, on the Day of Pentecost, the promised power is given. As the Holy Spirit falls, everyone in the room is filled with the Spirit and empowered to carry out Jesus' commission to them: "Go into all the world and preach the good news to all creation" (Mark 16:15).

"Then Jesus told his disciples a parable to show them that they should always pray and not give up." (Luke 18:1)

FURTHER THOUGHT

Someone has said that the place of prayer is the place of power. Have you discovered that secret in your own life? How would you respond if the Lord asked you today to spend ten days in prayer? Would you, even though you might not be able to take the time because of your duties and responsibilities, at least be willing?

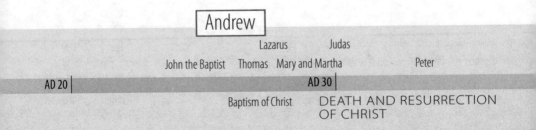

Andrew

| | Lazarus | Judas | |
| John the Baptist | Thomas | Mary and Martha | Peter |

AD 20 | AD 30 |

Baptism of Christ | DEATH AND RESURRECTION OF CHRIST

"... and the last shall be first"

"Oh, for a church of Andrews!" I do not know that many ministers would want a church of Peters; it would be too quarrelsome. I am quite willing for Thomas to go to the City Temple and Simon Zelotes to St James'. Let me have a church of Andrews – of simple, loving men, content to bring people to Jesus. Men like him are so valuable because everybody can be an Andrew. Not a greatly gifted man, but a greatly faithful man; not a man who would dispute with Peter as to who should be primate, or with John and James as to who shall sit on the left hand of Christ and who on the right, but a man who simply, humbly and lovingly does the work that lies nearest to him. He surely is of those last in the world's estimate who are first in the kingdom of God.
A. Hubleman

 ## Key Lesson
– Andrew

Andrew was the first recorded disciple of Christ – and his first action as a disciple was to seek out his brother, Simon Peter, and bring him to Jesus. This makes Andrew, not just the first disciple, but the first evangelist too. Some commentators refer to Andrew as "the overshadowed saint", in that he appears to be constantly overshadowed by his more ebullient and outgoing brother. Despite this, however, Andrew continues with his task of serving Christ, and excels as "a bringer of others to Jesus". First he brought his brother, then the lad with the loaves and fishes, and later the Greeks. What, then, is the main lesson of Andrew's life? Is it not this – that though overshadowed by his more energetic brother, he continues his ministry and service in a gracious and selfless manner? People may remember Peter for his great spiritual exploits, but in eternity there will be an equally great reward for Andrew – the man through whom the whole story of Peter began.

Stephen

DAY 292 First deacon and martyr

Acts 6:5; 7:59; 22:20

Stephen was the first of those selected by the apostles to do the work of a deacon and was, no doubt, one of the most outstanding men in the whole team. His name appears first in the list of deacons, causing many commentators to believe that he ranked as the foremost in the group. In his work as a deacon, Stephen would have had the task of ensuring that the widows were properly cared for, but much of his work was interrupted by the outbreak of violent persecution, particularly directed against the Hellenistic Jewish Christians – the group from which the deacons had been selected. Stephen was not only the first deacon in the early Church, but also its first martyr.

"Those who have served well gain an excellent standing and great assurance in their faith in Christ Jesus."
(1 Tim. 3:13)

FURTHER THOUGHT

Don't get the idea that becoming a deacon results in becoming a martyr! Spend a few moments today praying for the deacons or church workers in your community. The work of a deacon can be fraught with problems – your prayers could make a big difference.

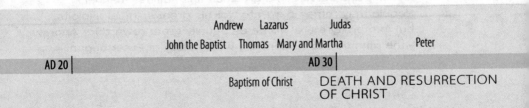

	Andrew	Lazarus		Judas		
John the Baptist	Thomas	Mary and Martha				Peter
AD 20			AD 30			
	Baptism of Christ		DEATH AND RESURRECTION OF CHRIST			

Full of the Holy Spirit

Acts 6:5; 7:55

Many commentators believe that Stephen is the central figure between Jesus and Paul. His life seemed to be so possessed by the Spirit, and the lineaments of Christ's nature were so clearly seen in his character, that it is not surprising the Christ-rejecting Jews put him to death. Expositors of Scripture have recognised in his name – meaning "crown" or "garland" – a prophecy of his greatness. Garlands or crowns were given by the ancient Greeks to those who rendered good service to their cities or brought them fame by winning in the national games. Stephen caught, for a brief time, the glory of His departed Lord – and reflecting it, was transformed into the same image.

"Don't you know that you yourselves are God's temple and that God's Spirit lives in you?" (1 Cor. 3:16)

FURTHER THOUGHT

Being "full of the Spirit" is one thing; maintaining that fullness is another. Do you know the secret of maintaining a Spirit-filled life? Turn to Ephesians 5:18–21 and you'll find out.

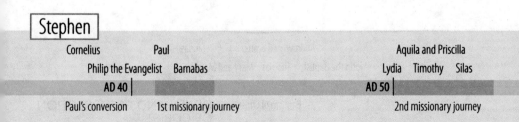

Stephen

Cornelius	Paul		Aquila and Priscilla
Philip the Evangelist	Barnabas		Lydia Timothy Silas
AD 40			AD 50
Paul's conversion	1st missionary journey		2nd missionary journey

Stephen
Stephen: "Crown"

DAY 294 — Full of grace and power

Acts 6:8

Stephen's character and abilities were of a high order. Not only was he Spirit-filled, but he was also a man of great faith and power. His ministry in and around Jerusalem was such that wherever he went, signs and wonders accompanied the preaching of the Word. So powerful was the impact of Stephen's life and service for God on the community that the Jewish leaders became fearful. No doubt they were already suffering in their consciences for what they had done to Christ, and Stephen's preaching made them feel even worse. Thus the Jews turn their attention once again to this threat of their security.

"Finally, be strong in the Lord and in his mighty power." (Eph. 6:10)

FURTHER THOUGHT

Did you notice the conjunction in the statement in Acts 6:8 – "full of God's grace and power"? Is it possible to be full of grace but have only a little power? Or to be full of power but have only a little grace? What do you think?

Full of light

Acts 6:9–15

The plan of the Jewish authorities to apprehend Stephen was quite different from the one used to take Jesus. There was no need to secure the services of the Temple guard, no need even to suppress any semblance of violence – the circumstances of the day enabled them to assume great boldness and, seizing a favourable moment, to come upon Stephen either when he was teaching in the synagogue or while he was transacting his duties as a deacon. Faced with false accusations, a conviction arises within him that this is a moment to bear witness to Christ – a conviction which gives indescribable grandeur and heavenliness to his countenance.

"Wisdom brightens a man's face and changes its hard appearance." (Eccl. 8:1)

FURTHER THOUGHT

Someone described some Christians as "people who have received the forgiveness of sins – only their faces don't seem to have heard about it yet!" That certainly was not the case with Stephen. How about you?

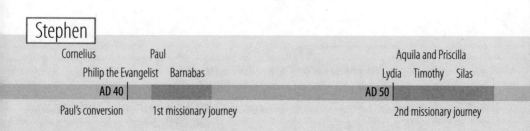

Stephen

Cornelius | Paul

Philip the Evangelist | Barnabas

Aquila and Priscilla

Lydia | Timothy | Silas

AD 40

AD 50

Paul's conversion | 1st missionary journey

2nd missionary journey

Stephen

Stephen: "Crown"

DAY 296

Full of truth

Acts 7:1-53

The speech which Stephen made prior to his martyrdom is one of the finest sermons in the whole of Scripture. Carelessly read, it may look like an epitome of the history of the Jewish people, a rambling attempt to reply to the false accusations of the religious leaders. But there is an important theme running through it – a theme with three parallel lines of attack. (1) What relation has locality to the true worship of God? His attackers said that he had spoken against "this holy place". (2) What relation has the Mosaic economy to time? His accusers said that he had blasphemed against Moses. Stephen says the ministry of Moses was transitory, not permanent. (3) What is it about truth that causes people to resist? The patriarchs were jealous of Joseph and resisted his words. Joseph had suffered for the truth – and Stephen was prepared to do the same.

"For since in the wisdom of God the world through its wisdom did not know him, God was pleased through the foolishness of what was preached to save those who believe." (1 Cor. 1:21)

FURTHER THOUGHT

Take a few moments to mark in your Bible, or on a separate piece of paper, where the three divisions of Stephen's sermon occur. Indicate where each begins and ends.

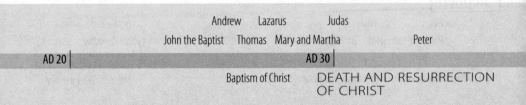

	Andrew	Lazarus		Judas		
John the Baptist		Thomas	Mary and Martha			Peter
AD 20				AD 30		
			Baptism of Christ	DEATH AND RESURRECTION OF CHRIST		

Full of compassion

Acts 7:54-60

Stephen's sermon is cut short by the mob who are out for his blood, and he is taken to a spot outside the city. The place, his mode of death, the stones thrown by the witnesses, were all in exact accordance with ancient precedent and Mosaic statutes (see Leviticus 24:13–16). By such formalities they sought to represent their evil work as a solemn enactment of national law upon a blasphemer of Jehovah. Stephen's death, however, was his last act of imitation of his Lord. Christ prayed to God; Stephen prayed to Jesus. Christ said: "I commit"; Stephen said: "Receive". Christ prayed for His accusers; Stephen similarly prayed for his – "Lord, do not hold this sin against them."

"I die every day – I mean that, brothers – just as surely as I glory over you in Christ Jesus our Lord." (1 Cor. 15:31)

FURTHER THOUGHT

Three comparisons have been drawn above between the death of Christ and the death of Stephen. Other similarities also exist between the deaths of Jesus and Stephen – can you identify them?

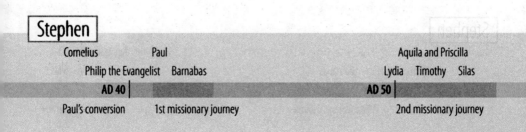

Stephen				
Cornelius	Paul		Aquila and Priscilla	
Philip the Evangelist	Barnabas		Lydia	Timothy	Silas
AD 40			**AD 50**	
Paul's conversion	1st missionary journey		2nd missionary journey	

DAY **298**   Focus of love and hatred

Acts 8:1-2

ollowing Stephen's death, the early Church mourned with great sadness its very first martyr. Devout men lovingly took away the body of Stephen and expressed their grief with "great lamentation" (RSV). In Stephen's death, as in Christ's, both love and evil are seen in clear focus. Sin is seen for the evil and damnable thing it is – while, at the same time, love is seen for what it is – forgiving, reconciling, redeeming. It has been a conviction of the Church for centuries that the conversion of Saul of Tarsus was the fruit of Stephen's prayer. The quenching of Stephen's light was the kindling of a brighter light for the illumination of the world.

"I tell you the truth, unless a grain of wheat falls to the ground and dies, it remains only a single seed. But if it dies, it produces many seeds."
(John 12:24)

FURTHER THOUGHT

Both the cross of Christ and the death of Stephen bear eloquent testimony to the fact that when evil does its worst, God does His best. Can you trace any evidence of this truth in some incident or situation in your own life? It's a thought worth pondering throughout the day.

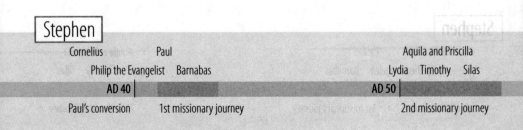

Stephen						
Cornelius		Paul			Aquila and Priscilla	
	Philip the Evangelist	Barnabas			Lydia Timothy Silas	
AD 40				AD 50		
Paul's conversion		1st missionary journey			2nd missionary journey	

The first martyr

When Dr Joseph Parker was quite a young man he was accustomed to discussing matters of faith outside the great ironworks on Tyneside in the north of England. One day someone challenged him to say what God had done for Stephen. He had, after all, been stoned to death. He answered: "What did God do for him? He gave him the power to pray for forgiveness for those who stoned him."

Key Lesson – Stephen

A commentator writing on the life of Stephen says: "To few men it is given to make their mark upon history in a very short time." How true. Stephen had a lowly beginning in Christian service, but his gifts and abilities made room for him to make as great an impact upon the life of the early Church as some of the apostles. As someone put it: "One can never keep a good deacon down." Although Stephen's career was brief - he appears and disappears within the space of two chapters – such was the effect of his life that he was honoured by a feast day in the Christian calendar next to Christ's own. The lesson to be learned from Stephen's life is this – don't be too assertive in displaying the talents and gifts you may think you have. God will see that whatever abilities you have will make room for themselves. You concentrate on deepening your ministry – God will concentrate on widening it.

Philip the Evangelist

Philip: "Lover of horses"

DAY 299

A deacon

Acts 6:1-7

The twelve apostles, as we saw, were all men who had known Jesus during the time of His public ministry, and were witnesses to His resurrection. Because of this, they had a special place and ministry in the early Church, teaching and sharing with others the things that Jesus had shared with them. As the Church grew, however, the administrative tasks became so great – management of the offering, distribution of food to widows, and so on, that they decided to appoint seven men (deacons) to take over this work and thus enable them to concentrate on the work of ministry. Philip, who was also an evangelist, was one of those appointed.

"You, my brothers, were called to be free. But do not use your freedom to indulge the sinful nature; rather, serve one another in love." (Gal. 5:13)

FURTHER THOUGHT

Whether they are called deacons or go under another name, every local church needs gifted people to take over administrative and other tasks so as to free others to exercise their gifts. Spend a few minutes now praying for those who do the administrative work in your church. They need as much grace and wisdom as your minister!

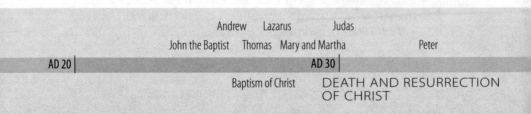

Andrew   Lazarus   Judas

John the Baptist   Thomas   Mary and Martha   Peter

AD 20 | AD 30 |

Baptism of Christ   DEATH AND RESURRECTION OF CHRIST

Anointed by God

Acts 8:1-8

The basic qualification for being a deacon in the early Church was that he should be a man who was full of wisdom and of the Holy Spirit. We do not know when Philip received his own personal experience of the Spirit, but the evidences of that infilling are recorded for us in detail. When persecution breaks out against the Christians in Jerusalem, they are scattered into different regions round about and the effect of this is more widespread evangelism. When Philip visits Samaria and preaches Christ, many are converted as well as healed – and such is the effect of his anointed ministry that the city is filled with overflowing joy.

"Then the disciples went out and preached everywhere, and the Lord worked with them and confirmed his word by the signs that accompanied it." (Mark 16:20)

FURTHER THOUGHT

Some think that we cannot expect evangelistic preaching today to be accompanied by such physical manifestations as were present in Philip's ministry. Others say that it can happen today, but only with those evangelists who are led into this type of approach. What do you think?

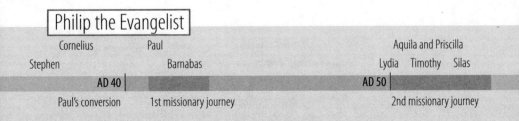

Philip the Evangelist

Cornelius	Paul		Aquila and Priscilla
Stephen	Barnabas		Lydia Timothy Silas
AD 40		AD 50	
Paul's conversion	1st missionary journey		2nd missionary journey

Philip the Evangelist

Philip: "Lover of horses"

DAY **301**

Met a magician

Acts 8:9–23

Magicians have existed for centuries. In ancient Egypt, you remember, there were those who duplicated by their magical arts some of Moses' supernatural signs (Ex. 7:8–12). In Samaria, where Philip was preaching, there was a magician called Simon who had built up a great reputation among the people by his practice of magical arts. Philip's anointed message, together with the supernatural evidence that accompanies it, convinces Simon of the truth of the gospel, whereupon he professes conversion and is baptised. When the apostles Peter and John arrive and lay hands on the converts for them to receive the Holy Spirit, Simon offers them money to be given the same power. Simon is sternly rebuked and told to repent of his wickedness which arises from a heart that is not right before God.

"For my own sake ... I do this. How can I let myself be defamed? I will not yield my glory to another." (Isa. 48:11)

FURTHER THOUGHT

Simon the Sorcerer reminds us of a certain type of person to be found in Christian circles whose longing is to gain honour for himself – or herself – rather than to do good to others. But no one can have the honour of an apostle without first demonstrating the spirit of an apostle.

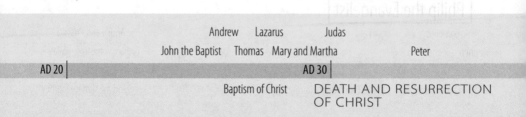

	Andrew	Lazarus		Judas	
	John the Baptist	Thomas	Mary and Martha		Peter
AD 20			AD 30		
	Baptism of Christ		DEATH AND RESURRECTION OF CHRIST		

Led by the Holy Spirit

Acts 8:26-39

As Philip continues his evangelistic mission in Samaria where he is ministering to thousands, he is bidden by an angel to leave the area and travel south to meet one man – an Ethiopian eunuch. The eunuch had been to Jerusalem to worship, and on his return journey along the Gaza road he was reading the prophecy of Isaiah as he sat in his chariot. The Spirit instructs Philip to run to the chariot and ask the man if he understands what he is reading. The eunuch confesses that he does not truly understand, whereupon Philip, beginning at the very point where he is reading, takes him on a spiritual journey through which he has a personal encounter with Christ.

"If man owns a hundred sheep, and one of them wanders away, will he not leave the ninety-nine on the hills and go to look for the one that wandered off? And if he finds it ... he is happier about that one sheep than about the ninety-nine that did not wander off."
(Matt. 18:12–13)

FURTHER THOUGHT

Imagine being taken away from a great crusade where hundreds are being converted to witness to one man! You would most certainly have to be "led" to do that. Many Christians would fight such a "leading", saying that they were involved in a greater work and it wouldn't make sense to leave it. How about you?

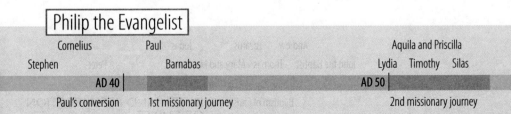

Philip the Evangelist				
Cornelius	Paul		Aquila and Priscilla	
Stephen	Barnabas		Lydia Timothy Silas	
AD 40			AD 50	
Paul's conversion	1st missionary journey		2nd missionary journey	

Philip the Evangelist

Philip: "Lover of horses"

DAY 303   Spreads the Gospel

Acts 8:40

His special assignment successfully completed, Philip is caught up by the Spirit and returns to his wider evangelistic work. Starting at Azotus (Ashdod), he travels northwards up the coast, preaching in every town until he reaches Caesarea, where he seems to have made his home. Philip's evangelism embraced both Jews and the half-Jewish Samaritans – this was a major step because "Jews do not associate with Samaritans" (John 4:9). It marked a turning point in carrying out Jesus' command to the disciples to witness "in Jerusalem, and in all Judea and Samaria, and to the ends of the earth" (Acts 1:8).

"There is neither Jew nor Greek, slave nor free, male nor female, for you are all one in Christ Jesus. If you belong to Christ, then you are Abraham's seed, and heirs according to the promise." (Gal 3:28–29)

FURTHER THOUGHT

Someone has said that "great doors turn on little hinges". How true. Philip's mission to the Samaritans was the precursor to the opening of the door to the Gentile nations by Peter. And that – if you are not a Jew – includes you. Spend a few moments reminding yourself of the circumstances through which you became a Christian – and give thanks!

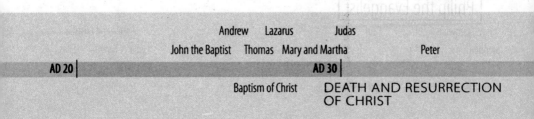

	Andrew	Lazarus		Judas		
	John the Baptist	Thomas	Mary and Martha			Peter
AD 20				**AD 30**		
		Baptism of Christ		DEATH AND RESURRECTION OF CHRIST		

Acts 21:8-9

Philip, we are told, had four unmarried daughters who lived with him in his home at Caesarea. His wife is not mentioned in Luke's account and may have been dead by the time Paul and his party – which included Luke – stayed in their godly and hospitable household. Many years prior to the great outpouring of the Spirit at Pentecost, the prophet Joel had predicted that when the Holy Spirit fell, one of the results would be that "your sons and daughters will prophesy" (Joel 2:28). All four of Philip's daughters had received this supernatural ability, and doubtless there were many in the early Church who had cause to thank God for the influence of the home and family of Philip.

"Unless the Lord builds the house, its builders labour in vain." (Psa. 127:1)

FURTHER THOUGHT

"The nearest thing to heaven," said Martin Luther, "is a good and godly home." The converse is also true – the nearest thing to hell is an evil and godless home. Pray for your own home and the homes of every Christian family in your community. A good and godly home is one of the greatest forms of evangelism in our modern times.

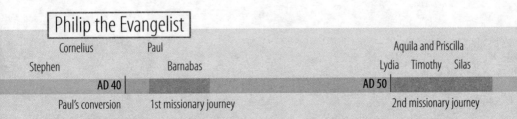

Philip the Evangelist					
	Cornelius	Paul		Aquila and Priscilla	
Stephen		Barnabas		Lydia Timothy Silas	
AD 40			AD 50		
Paul's conversion	1st missionary journey		2nd missionary journey		

Key Lesson
– *Philip* the Evangelist

Philip was one of the very first officers appointed by the Church, and so his life shows us what makes a good Christian leader. Chosen originally for his ability to deal with practical matters, he was just as willing to talk about his faith, even in difficult circumstances. When persecution scattered the Christians in Jerusalem, he went to preach to the Samaritans – people hostile to the Jews. Yet he cared just as much for an individual – the Ethiopian eunuch – as he did for the masses. Because he had studied the Scriptures he could explain to this man how the Old Testament prophecies had been fulfilled. The main lesson of Philip's life is that we should be faithful in the way we carry out the tasks God has given us to do, but at the same time be ready to act on the prompting of the Holy Spirit.

DAY **305**

Persecutor

Acts 8:1; 9:1-2

Saul was a Greek-speaking Benjamite Jew, the son of a Pharisee (Acts 23:6), who was born a Roman citizen in Tarsus, an important city in Asia Minor. He came to Jerusalem to be taught by Gamaliel, an eminent rabbi who was a prominent Pharisee and a member of the Sanhedrin. Paul proved to be an apt pupil, becoming a strict Pharisee who was intent on keeping the many requirements of the law (Phil. 3:6). As a young man, he witnessed the death of the first Christian martyr, Stephen, which caused him to see the faith as a serious threat to the Jewish religion. Against the restraints of his conscience, Saul became a zealous persecutor of the Church, pursuing the believers even beyond the borders of Palestine.

"Blessed are you when people insult you, persecute you and falsely say all kinds of evil against you because of me. Rejoice and be glad, because great is your reward in heaven ..."
(Matt. 5:11–12)

FURTHER THOUGHT

What made Paul react in such a negative way to the preaching and witness of the early Christians? The basic reason was fear. It is this which lies at the root of most wrong reactions. But fear of what? What do you think?

Andrew	Lazarus		Judas	
John the Baptist	Thomas	Mary and Martha		Peter
AD 20			AD 30	
	Baptism of Christ		DEATH AND RESURRECTION OF CHRIST	

Converted

Acts 9:3–31

Armed with letters of authority from the Sanhedrin to the Jews in Damascus to extend his ardent persecution of the Christians there (Acts 22:5), Saul was nearing the city when he was stopped in his tracks by the appearance of the risen Christ. Though Saul was physically blinded by the mysterious light which surrounded him, his spiritual eyes were now opened to the truth which he had been fighting so hard – namely, that Jesus Christ was the Son of God and the Saviour of the world. After three days of prayer and fasting, Saul's sight is restored when a local disciple, Ananias, comes and lays hands upon him in obedience to a vision. Saul immediately begins to preach the new truth he has discovered, and finds himself being persecuted for the very reason for which he has persecuted others.

"Except ye be converted, and become as little children, ye shall not enter into the kingdom of heaven." (Matt. 18:3 AV)

FURTHER THOUGHT

Saul, later called Paul, has been described as the "greatest Christian of all time". No other man, save Jesus of Nazareth, has left such an impression on history. Paul's conversion has been described by the critics as "an hallucination" or "a mild form of insanity". Well, it's a strange kind of insanity that produces a man who has done more to make people truly sane than any other man!

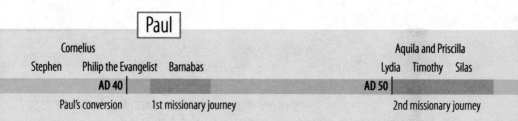

Paul		
Cornelius		Aquila and Priscilla
Stephen Philip the Evangelist Barnabas		Lydia Timothy Silas
AD 40		AD 50
Paul's conversion 1st missionary journey		2nd missionary journey

DAY **307**

Missionary

Acts 13:1-52; 14:1-28

Although Saul's Jewish background and training gave him a distinct edge in preaching the gospel to the Jews, the Lord called and commissioned him to be an apostle to the Gentiles (Acts 26:17–18). His first task was to become a pioneer missionary to the Gentiles living in the countries on the northern and eastern coasts of the Mediterranean. He travelled thousands of miles by land and sea, was constantly in danger, experienced shipwreck on three separate occasions and endured great hardship and persecution (2 Cor. 11:23–25). He travelled with a variety of companions, among whom were Barnabas, John Mark, Silas, Luke and Timothy. He was, without doubt, the world's greatest missionary.

"Therefore, if anyone is in Christ, he is new creation; the old has gone, the new has come!" (2 Cor. 5:17)

FURTHER THOUGHT

Our own conversions may not have been so dramatic as Paul's and yet think about it: weren't we equally ignorant of God and determined to follow our own ways? Do you thank Him for calling you to be His chosen instrument?

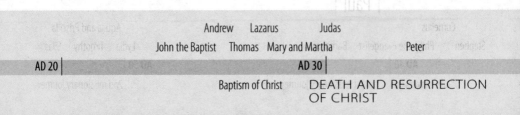

	Andrew	Lazarus		Judas		
	John the Baptist	Thomas	Mary and Martha		Peter	
AD 20				AD 30		
		Baptism of Christ		DEATH AND RESURRECTION OF CHRIST		

Persecuted

Acts 16:1-40

Paul's preaching and the many miracles which accompanied his ministry brought severe persecution from both Jews and Gentiles. Early in his Christian life, he had been smuggled out of Damascus to escape the murderous hatred of the Jews there. Later, at Lystra, he was stoned and left for dead by Jews who had pursued him from Antioch and Iconium. He also records in 2 Corinthians 11:24 that he was flogged five times by the Jewish authorities. The Gentiles, too, reacted violently when, as in the case of Demetrius at Ephesus (Acts 19:24) and the owners of the slave girl at Philippi (Acts 16:16), his words and actions directly affected their livelihoods.

"... how is it to your credit if you receive a beating for doing wrong and endure it? But if you suffer for doing good and you endure it, this is commendable before God." (1 Pet. 2:20)

FURTHER THOUGHT

Saul the persecutor becomes Paul the persecuted. Yet he was as determined to continue in the face of persecution as he was to cause it. Paul – as he was now called – was certainly not half-hearted about anything. A good trait – don't you agree?

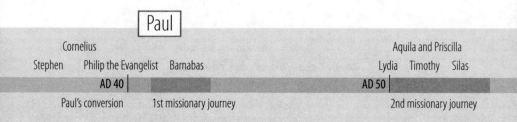

	Paul						
	Cornelius				Aquila and Priscilla		
Stephen	Philip the Evangelist	Barnabas			Lydia	Timothy	Silas
	AD 40				AD 50		
	Paul's conversion	1st missionary journey				2nd missionary journey	

DAY 309

Preacher

Acts 17:1-34

Paul was evidently a powerful preacher who proclaimed the gospel of Christ wherever he went. On one occasion, he is recorded as preaching all night (Acts 20:7–12). His general practice, when visiting a city, was to preach first to the Jews and then to the Gentiles. In most places, he was compelled to turn to the Gentiles because the Jews rejected his message. One welcome exception was at Berea, where the Jews eagerly listened to what he had to say, and examined the Scriptures to see if they confirmed his statements. When convinced of the truth of his arguments, many of them believed the gospel. As a result of Paul's preaching, many new churches were founded, and the Gentiles became a significant part of the Church which, in its formative years, had been exclusively Jewish.

"Yet when I preach the gospel, I cannot boast, for I am compelled to preach. Woe to me if I do not preach the gospel!" (1 Cor. 9:16)

FURTHER THOUGHT

Have you ever thought how important preaching is? This is how P. T. Forsyth defines it: "Preaching is the gospel prolonging and declaring itself ... It is an eternal, perennial act of God in Christ, repeating itself within each declaration of it."

Andrew	Lazarus	Judas		
John the Baptist	Thomas	Mary and Martha		Peter
AD 20		AD 30		
	Baptism of Christ	DEATH AND RESURRECTION OF CHRIST		

Church planter

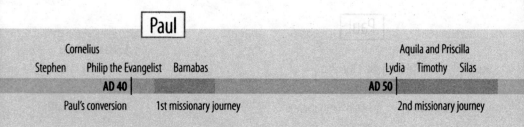

Acts 18:1–19:41

Paul was a pioneer missionary whose ambition was not to build on another man's foundation, but to preach the gospel in places where it had never been heard before (Rom. 15:20–21). He founded churches in Asia Minor and Greece. Paul was a master strategist when it came to church planting, selecting some of the major cities and sea ports as his targets. He took advantage of his Roman citizenship during his travels and, whenever possible, revisited his newly planted churches to help them become firmly established. Paul had a great love for his converts, and writes about his continual concern for their spiritual well-being (2 Cor. 11:28–29). Many of his letters were written to these churches, later becoming part of the canon of Scripture.

"Therefore go and make disciples of all nations, baptising them in the name of the Father and of the Son and of the Holy Spirit, and teaching them to obey everything I have commanded you. And surely I am with you always, to the very end of the age." (Matt. 28:19–20)

FURTHER THOUGHT

Not too many people are involved these days in the ministry of church-planting. Those who are, need our special prayers. Why not spend a few moments in prayer right now for someone you know who is involved in this ministry?

Paul					
Cornelius			Aquila and Priscilla		
Stephen	Philip the Evangelist	Barnabas	Lydia	Timothy	Silas
	AD 40			AD 50	
Paul's conversion		1st missionary journey		2nd missionary journey	

DAY **311**

Prisoner

Acts 24:1–27:44

Paul was imprisoned at Caesarea for two years under Felix, who sent for him often to talk with him, hoping that Paul would offer him a bribe to secure his release (Acts 24:26–27). When Felix was succeeded by Festus, the new governor called Paul before him and asked whether he would go to Jerusalem and have the charges brought against him by the Jews heard there. Paul responded to this by stating that he would exercise his right as a Roman citizen to appeal to Caesar to obtain the justice which was denied him in the provincial court. Later, after his arrival in Rome, Paul spends a further two years under house arrest, but continues to preach and teach without hindrance (Acts 28:31).

"As a prisoner for the Lord, then, I urge you to live a life worthy of the calling you have received. Be completely humble and gentle; be patient, bearing with one another in love." (Eph. 4:1–2)

FURTHER THOUGHT

Although Paul was often found in prison, he never regarded himself as a prisoner of Rome, but a "prisoner of Christ Jesus" (Eph. 3:1). Rome could bind his body with chains, but nothing could bind his spirit. Remember this the next time you feel "imprisoned" by your circumstances.

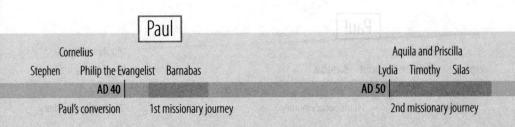

Paul						
	Cornelius				Aquila and Priscilla	
Stephen	Philip the Evangelist	Barnabas		Lydia	Timothy	Silas
	AD 40			AD 50		
Paul's conversion		1st missionary journey			2nd missionary journey	

The marks of Paul

Fruit-bearing
"The fruit of the Spirit is love, joy, peace, patience ..."
(Gal. 5:22, 23)

Burden-bearing
"Carry each other's burdens, and in this way you will fulfil the law of Christ."
(Gal. 6:2)

Seed-bearing
"A man reaps what he sows." **(Gal. 6:7).**
"Let us not become weary in doing good, for ...we will reap ... " **(Gal. 6:9)**

Brand-bearing
"I bear on my body the marks [or brands] of Jesus." **(Gal. 6:17)**

Key Lesson – Paul

To try to comment on the life of Paul in a few words is like trying to take a five-minute tour of the galaxy. His conversion to Christ was one of the most transforming experiences of history. Down the ages, millions have been converted through reading the account of his conversion or hearing a sermon on the theme. Indeed, as someone put it: "His conversion still converts." Out of the many wonderful lessons that we can draw from the life and character of the apostle Paul, the most important is that of whole-hearted commitment. There was nothing half-hearted about the great apostle. His commitment to Christ was so total and complete that someone said of him: "No other individual Christian has made such an impact upon history, or upon the thinking of the world." How does your commitment to Christ measure up against that of this unique and amazing man?

DAY 312

Generous
Acts 4:32-37

Barnabas was formerly known as Joseph, and was a Levite who hailed from Cyprus. After he was converted, he joined the group of believers who worshipped in Jerusalem. He was later given the surname "Barnabas", which means "one who encourages". No doubt the apostles saw in him the evidence of an encourager when they gave him this name, and his subsequent behaviour and attitudes show how appropriate and well-chosen it was. One of the very first actions which demonstrated Barnabas' ministry of encouragement was his willingness to sell a field which he owned in Cyprus and give the money to the apostles for distribution to those who were in financial need.

"... Whoever sows sparingly will also reap sparingly, and whoever sows generously will also reap generously." (2 Cor. 9:6)

FURTHER THOUGHT

"A generous attitude," said someone, "is the basis of all sound human relationships." Are you a generous person? One well-known minister says he makes this his daily prayer: "Today, dear Lord, I intend to be the channel, and not the stopping place, of all Your generosity to me." Worth copying?

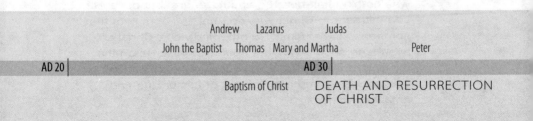

Andrew   Lazarus   Judas

John the Baptist   Thomas   Mary and Martha   Peter

AD 20 | AD 30 |

Baptism of Christ   DEATH AND RESURRECTION OF CHRIST

Acts 9:26-29

Three years after his dramatic conversion, Saul had to escape for his life from the Jews of Damascus, and he returned to Jerusalem where he tried to join the group of believers meeting there. For some strange reason, the disciples appeared to be afraid of him, suspecting an attempt by the Jews to infiltrate their fellowship. At this stage in Paul's history, Barnabas intervenes and takes him to the apostles, vouching for the genuineness of his conversion. He recounts to them how Saul boldly preached the gospel in Damascus, and it was as the direct result of Barnabas' intervention that Saul was able to continue his ministry in Jerusalem itself.

"Blessed are the peacemakers, for they will be called sons of God." (Matt. 5:9)

FURTHER THOUGHT

What a different place the Church would be if more people took on the role of mediator in times of conflict, tension or stress. It takes a person of special character to be a mediator – balanced judgement, objectivity and deep concern. Take a moment now to ask God to make you such a person.

	Barnabas			
Cornelius	Paul		Aquila and Priscilla	
Stephen	Philip the Evangelist		Lydia	Timothy	Silas
AD 40			AD 50	
Paul's conversion	1st missionary journey		2nd missionary journey	

DAY **314**   Missionary

Acts 11:19–23; 13:2; 15:36–40

B arnabas was highly regarded by the apostles in Jerusalem, and was sent by them to Antioch in Syria to oversee the evangelistic work going on there, particularly the work among the Gentiles. He rejoiced at the evidence of God's grace, and sought out Saul, who at that time was living in obscurity in his native Tarsus, to come and join him in the work of teaching and encouraging the new converts. After a trip to Jerusalem together in order to take a gift from the local churches for famine relief in Judea, Barnabas and Saul were commissioned by the church at Antioch and sent out on the first pioneering missionary journey to Galatia, calling at Cyprus on the way.

"Again Jesus said, 'Peace be with you! As the Father has sent me, I am sending you.'" (John 20:21)

FURTHER THOUGHT

How easily we forget that the reason why we have the gospel today is because a missionary came our way. Do you believe in missions? "Those who don't believe in missions," said one writer, "are usually the kind of people whose religion isn't worth propagating." Ouch!

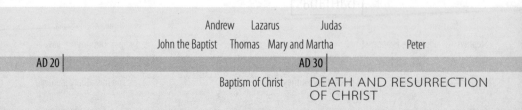

	Andrew	Lazarus	Judas	
John the Baptist	Thomas	Mary and Martha		Peter

AD 20 | AD 30 |

Baptism of Christ   DEATH AND RESURRECTION OF CHRIST

Spirit-filled

Acts 11:24

Like Stephen, Barnabas was a good man, full of the Holy Spirit and faith, and the sort of person who was able to contribute greatly to the growth and establishment of the early Church. He had many noble characteristics, but no doubt the greatest was his ability to open up to God and allow the Holy Spirit to flow through his life in service to others. Some commentators claim that much of the credit for Saul's rapid growth in the things of God must be placed at the feet of Barnabas. It certainly seems that the ministry of encouragement – the ministry in which Barnabas specialised – had a tremendous influence upon the apostle Paul (see again Acts 9:26–29).

"But you will receive power when the Holy Spirit comes on you; and you will be my witnesses in Jerusalem, and in all Judea and Samaria, and to the ends of the earth." (Acts 1:8)

FURTHER THOUGHT

Are you a Spirit-filled person? If not, why not? In seeking to become Spirit-filled, however, make sure that your desire is not to get possession of the Spirit, but for the Spirit to get possession of you. This refinement of purpose is decisive, for if you just want to use God rather than be used by Him – it won't work.

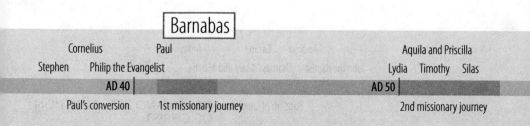

Barnabas

Cornelius	Paul		Aquila and Priscilla
Stephen	Philip the Evangelist		Lydia Timothy Silas
AD 40		**AD 50**	
Paul's conversion	1st missionary journey		2nd missionary journey

DAY 316

Inspirer

Acts 11:25–30

After being introduced to the believers in Jerusalem by Barnabas, and almost immediately being driven out of the city by the hostile Jewish religious leaders, Saul spent some ten years of his life back in his native city, Tarsus. We are not told what he did there, but Barnabas did not forget him, and once again gave him an encouraging and inspiring word. As a result of Barnabas' meeting with Saul, the newly converted disciple worked with him in Antioch for a full year, during which time Barnabas, the "encourager", no doubt built into Saul's life a solid foundation which would stand him in good stead when he later took up his calling as the apostle to the Gentiles.

"Consider him who endured such opposition from sinful men, so that you will not grow weary and lose heart." (Heb. 12:3)

FURTHER THOUGHT

How desperately the Church needs men and women like Barnabas, whose influence inspires and encourages.
"A pat on the back," says Ronald Scheer, "though only a few vertebrae removed from a kick in the pants, is miles ahead in results."

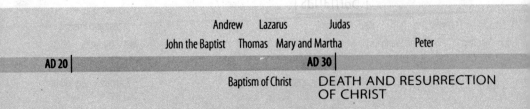

		Andrew	Lazarus		Judas		
	John the Baptist	Thomas	Mary and Martha			Peter	
AD 20				**AD 30**			
		Baptism of Christ		DEATH AND RESURRECTION OF CHRIST			

Acts 15:1–35

The first believers in the early Church, were, of course, Jews, but later large numbers of Gentiles were added to the Church, particularly in Antioch. Certain men came to Antioch from Jerusalem, teaching that circumcision was essential for salvation (v. 1) – a teaching that was hotly contested by Paul and Barnabas. The local church decided that the dispute must be resolved at the highest level – the Council at Jerusalem. A delegation is sent, headed by Paul and Barnabas, to meet the leaders of the Jerusalem church, who welcome them most warmly. Paul and Barnabas present their case that circumcision is not necessary for Gentile believers, and after listening to both sides of the argument, James gives a judgement in favour of the view of Paul and Barnabas.

"A man is not a Jew if he is only one outwardly, nor is circumcision merely outward and physical. No, a man is a Jew if he is one inwardly; and circumcision is circumcision of the heart, by the Spirit, not by the written code ..." (Rom. 2:28–29)

FURTHER THOUGHT

God has appointed a clear strategy for resolving arguments and difficulties in the Church. No spiritual problems or difficulties among believers ought to be taken to a secular court. Are you aware of this strategy? If not, you can read all about it in Matthew 18. Study the steps carefully – and follow them when necessary.

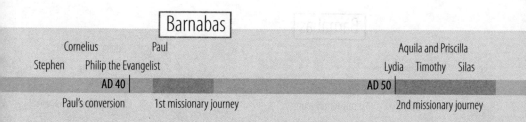

Barnabas

Cornelius	Paul		Aquila and Priscilla
Stephen	Philip the Evangelist		Lydia Timothy Silas
AD 40		AD 50	
Paul's conversion	1st missionary journey		2nd missionary journey

DAY **318**   Self-supporting

1 Corinthians 9:6

In general, the apostles did not support themselves financially, but expected the churches to whom they ministered to provide for their daily needs of food and shelter. Paul gives the justification for this approach to the Christian ministry (1 Cor. 9:14), but says that, for special reasons, he and Barnabas had not laid claim to their rights in this matter (9:12, 15). In another section of Scripture, we read that Paul supported himself by working as a tentmaker (Acts 18:3), but nothing is said anywhere in the New Testament as to how Barnabas achieved financial independence. No doubt Barnabas was led by the Spirit to adopt this exceptional stance toward the ministry.

"In the same way, the Lord has commanded that those who preach the gospel should receive their living from the gospel." (1 Cor. 9:14)

FURTHER THOUGHT

The general principle laid down in Scripture is that those who are engaged in "full-time Christian ministry" should be supported by the believers to whom they minister. How adequately is your minister or spiritual leader supported? Don't overlook this issue – look over it. Maybe God has brought it to your attention for you to take some positive action.

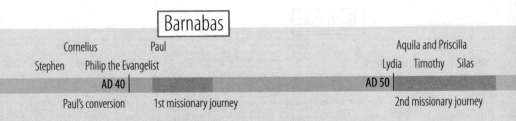

Barnabas		
Cornelius Paul		Aquila and Priscilla
Stephen Philip the Evangelist		Lydia Timothy Silas
AD 40		AD 50
Paul's conversion 1st missionary journey		2nd missionary journey

Barnabas – *missionary with Paul*

Barnabas is one of those minor characters of Scripture, who at once gain and lose by their closeness to a greater figure. He gains much from his relation to the gigantic figure of Paul, for it was in company with him that his best work was done. And yet, perhaps, he suffers more: for the friend with whom he walks is so colossal that we forget all when we see him. A mountain in Scotland would be a hillock in Switzerland. A Thames in England would be an obscure rivulet if it poured itself into the Amazon.

Crowned with immortal jubilee
This day, thy soul set free,
From earth to Heaven thou didst pass,
O holy Barnabas.

He, for whose sake, at whose dear call,
Thou gavest up thine all:
He shall thine all, thy treasure be
Lasting eternally.

'Mid fasting, prayer, and holy hands,
Lo! 'mid the saints he stands,
The Spirit's high behest to bear,
Christ's Heav'n-sent messenger.

To what barbaric shores away
Did ye that light convey,
When from God's chosen race ye turn'd,
Who faith's glad message spurn'd?

Lord, when to us an offer'd Guest
Shall come that Spirit blest,
Let not our hearts Heaven's bounty slight
Deeming our darkness light.

Isaac Williams

Key Lesson – Barnabas

John Bunyan, we are told, modelled his character, Mr Greatheart – the companion, defender, guide and friend of all weaker pilgrims on the King's Highway – upon Barnabas. Barnabas is certainly one of the greatest of the early Christians, and tradition tells us that he founded churches in Cyprus and Milan. The outstanding lesson to be learned from Barnabas' life is, without doubt, the importance of the ministry of encouragement. The word translated "encouragement" in the New Testament is usually the same word used for the Holy Spirit – "Comforter", or "one called alongside to help". We are never nearer to the work and ministry of the Holy Spirit than when we involve ourselves in the task of encouraging. In a day when so many people are discouraged, how necessary – indeed imperative – is this vital ministry. Ask God to make you a true and effective "encourager" in His Church from this very day.

Cornelius

Cornelius: "A horn"

Roman Centurion

Acts 10:1

Although centurions were relatively low-ranking officers in the Roman army, commanding 100 men within a legion of 6,000, they played a crucial role in the day-to-day running of that army. Centurions like Cornelius generally rose from the ranks, being selected by merit, whereas the high-ranking officers were more likely to come directly from important Roman families. The Roman soldiers in Palestine acted as an armed police force, and how the inhabitants were treated largely depended on how the centurions reacted to local incidents, as they were the officers who were in closest touch with local communities and what went on in them.

"To them God has chosen to make known among the Gentiles the glorious riches of this mystery, which is Christ in you, the hope of glory." (Col. 1:27)

FURTHER THOUGHT

A centurion, according to historians, was chosen for character and courage. One must not demean these qualities in anyone, but what are character and courage without conversion? Character can help us to live nobly in this world, but it is not the key by which we enter heaven. Then what is the key? Christ!

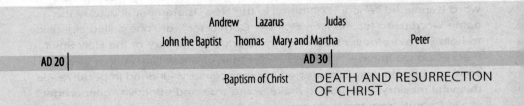

Andrew   Lazarus   Judas

John the Baptist   Thomas   Mary and Martha   Peter

AD 20

AD 30

Baptism of Christ   DEATH AND RESURRECTION OF CHRIST

Acts 10:2

Cornelius was a centurion of the Italian Regiment, and was, according to Scripture, a "God-fearing" man. The Italian Regiment was made up of Gentiles who attended the local synagogue, but who were not proselytes – that is, those who were circumcised and received fully into the Jewish faith. Centurions are spoken of favourably in Scripture; for example, we are told that a centurion built the synagogue in Capernaum (Luke 7:2–5), and Jesus described this man as having outstanding faith (Luke 7:9). The devotion which Cornelius had for God was expressed, according to the light that he possessed, in prayer and giving generously to the poor. Such was the deep devotion that underlay these acts that his prayers and sacrifice were highly pleasing to God (Acts 10:4).

"Blessed are they who keep his statutes and seek him with all their heart." (Psa. 119:2)

FURTHER THOUGHT

St Francis de Sales has an interesting thought on the difference between a good man and a devout man. He says: "He is a good man who keeps the commandments of God, but he is devout who not only observes them, but does so willingly, promptly and with a good heart."

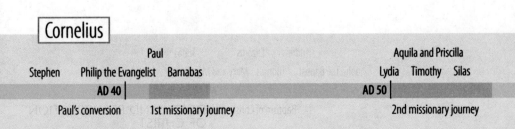

Cornelius						
		Paul			Aquila and Priscilla	
Stephen	Philip the Evangelist	Barnabas			Lydia Timothy Silas	
	AD 40				AD 50	
	Paul's conversion	1st missionary journey			2nd missionary journey	

Cornelius

Cornelius: "A horn"

DAY **321**   Heavenly vision

Acts 10:3-7

Not only was Cornelius a devout and sincere seeker after God, but so too, it appears, was his whole household. When Cornelius saw a vision of an angel who instructed him to send messengers to fetch Simon Peter from Joppa, he was able to take into his confidence a soldier and two of his servants and entrust them with this important mission. No doubt, after the initial fear of seeing the angel had abated, Cornelius would have been filled with joyful expectation at what lay in store for him and his household, following the arrival of Simon Peter.

"... he will delight in the fear of the Lord. He will not judge by what he sees with his eyes, or decide by what he hears with his ears; but with righteousness he will judge the needy ..." (Isa. 11:3–4)

FURTHER THOUGHT

Many of the Jewish disciples in Jerusalem would have been astonished if they knew God had given a vision to Cornelius who, in their eyes, was nothing more than a pagan. But how dramatically this event underlined the truth of what Samuel the prophet said many years before: you can read about it in 1 Samuel 16:7.

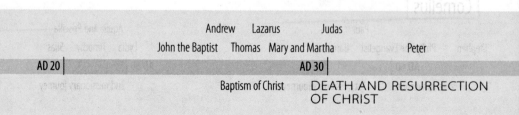

	Andrew	Lazarus		Judas		
	John the Baptist	Thomas	Mary and Martha			Peter
AD 20				AD 30		
		Baptism of Christ		DEATH AND RESURRECTION OF CHRIST		

Obedient response

Acts 10:8-21

I n this chapter of Acts, something intriguing and momentous is about to happen, and Peter has to be prepared for it, because it runs counter to his preconceived ideas and Jewish background. God is about to welcome the first Gentiles into His family, and as Simon Peter is the one chosen to administer this event, his bigoted attitudes towards Gentiles coming into the Church have to be changed. Just as Cornelius received a vision while in prayer, so also does Simon Peter. In the vision, he sees all manner of four-footed animals and is told to kill and eat those that are unclean under the law. When he protests, God tells him not to call common what He has made clean. This vision is repeated three times, presumably to drive the message deep into Peter's heart.

"Peter and the other apostles replied: 'We must obey God rather than men!'" (Acts 5:29)

FURTHER THOUGHT
It's interesting to note that, despite being perplexed over the vision, Peter is willing to make the attempt to do what God asks. It was thinking of this occasion in Acts that caused Nathaniel Emmons to write: "Obedience to God is the most infallible evidence of sincere and supreme love to Him."

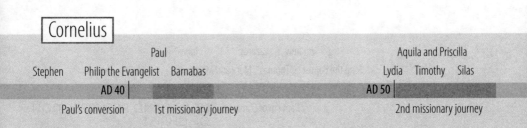

Cornelius						
		Paul			Aquila and Priscilla	
Stephen	Philip the Evangelist	Barnabas			Lydia Timothy Silas	
	AD 40				AD 50	
	Paul's conversion	1st missionary journey			2nd missionary journey	

Cornelius

Cornelius: "A horn"

DAY 323 — Righteous man

Acts 10:22-24

As we said earlier, all the centurions mentioned in the New Testament are favourably described, and appear as just and fair-minded men. Take another example – on the long journey to Rome, Paul was well-treated by the centurion, who allowed him to visit his friends and receive their hospitality (Acts 27:3). Cornelius, like the centurion at Capernaum, was highly regarded by the Jewish community in which he lived, and was known to be an honest and upright man. He must have been a man of outstanding character and reputation to break down the many barriers that inevitably existed between the representative of an occupying power and a subjugated population.

"Masters, provide your slaves with what is right and fair, because you know that you also have a Master in heaven." (Col. 4:1)

FURTHER THOUGHT

Do you hold any leadership role or have any responsibility for managing the affairs of others? One of the first requirements for this is that you are "righteous". This is, in fact, a Biblical requirement. Turn to 2 Samuel 23:3 and see!

Andrew	Lazarus	Judas
John the Baptist	Thomas Mary and Martha	Peter
AD 20	AD 30	
	Baptism of Christ	DEATH AND RESURRECTION OF CHRIST

Humble spirit

Acts 10:25-29

Cornelius' sense of expectation over the impending visit of Simon Peter knows no bounds, and he calls together all the members of his household to await the apostle's arrival. When, at last, Simon Peter enters his home, Cornelius falls before him in great humility, but Peter encourages him to stand, saying: "I am only a man myself" (v.26). Cornelius introduces Simon Peter to the audience in his house with great skill and understanding. Peter begins his message by stating that, although it is unlawful for a Jew to associate with or visit a Gentile, God has shown him that he should not call anyone common or unclean. This great apostle showed a humble spirit too!

"Therefore, whoever humbles himself ... is the greatest in the kingdom of heaven." (Matt. 18:4)

FURTHER THOUGHT

John Ruskin's comments on humility are worth more than a few moments of meditation. Think about them today: "The first test of a truly great man is humility. I do not mean by this, doubt of his own power; really great men have a curious feeling that greatness is not in them, but through them."

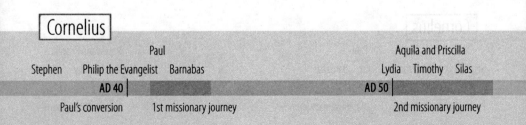

Cornelius

		Paul				Aquila and Priscilla		
Stephen	Philip the Evangelist	Barnabas				Lydia	Timothy	Silas
	AD 40					AD 50		
	Paul's conversion	1st missionary journey				2nd missionary journey		

Cornelius
Cornelius: "A horn"

DAY 325   Earnest seeker

Acts 10:30-48

It is obvious, in reading the story of Cornelius, that wherever there is a seeking heart, God is there to hear and answer. The chapter begins with a man praying, and ends with a great outpouring of the Holy Spirit. Peter preaches to this earnest and expectant congregation a clear message of salvation, showing that God accepts those of every nation who fear Him and do what is right (vv. 34–35). During Peter's sermon, the Holy Spirit falls on Cornelius and all his household, much to the amazement of the Jewish believers who accompanied Peter. When Peter sees with his own eyes the evidence of God's approval of the Gentiles, he commands them to be baptised, and thus confirms the entrance of the first Gentiles into the Church.

"Do not get drunk on wine, which leads to debauchery. Instead, be filled with the Spirit." (Eph. 5:18)

FURTHER THOUGHT

Whatever knowledge or understanding a person has of God, that understanding and knowledge is greatly deepened and enhanced by a personal experience of Pentecost. On which side of Pentecost are you?

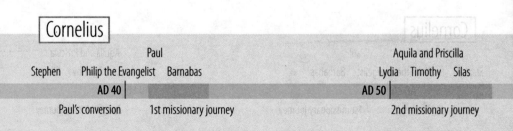

Cornelius						
		Paul			Aquila and Priscilla	
Stephen	Philip the Evangelist	Barnabas			Lydia	Timothy	Silas
	AD 40				AD 50	
	Paul's conversion	1st missionary journey			2nd missionary journey	

Cornelius – a Roman centurion

A centurion was the commander of 100 men in a Roman legion. The number of centurions in a legion was 60, the legion always comprising 60 centuries. The ordinary duties of the centurion were to drill his men, inspect their arms, food and clothing, and to command them in the camp and in the field. Centurions were sometimes employed on detached service, the conditions of which in the provinces are somewhat obscure. Men like Cornelius (Acts 10:1; 27:1) may have been separated from the legion to which they properly belonged for the discharge of special duties. They and other centurions mentioned in the Gospels and the Acts (Matt. 8:5; Mark 15:39, 44, 45; Luke 23:47) are represented by the sacred writers in a favourable light.

 ## Key Lesson
- Cornelius

The account of Cornelius is a milestone in the life of the infant Church. It is important to notice that Cornelius' pre-Christian religious experience is not condemned, denied or despised, but brought to fullness through the preaching of the gospel and the power of the Holy Spirit. Cornelius is led forward to a higher standard of conduct in Christ and to accept Him as the Lord of the universe. But what is the main lesson that we must draw from the life of this "good pagan"? Is it not this: that whenever God sees in our hearts a desire and a hunger for Himself, He will go to the utmost lengths to meet it? An epitaph to this good and just man might well be the words of Jesus: "Blessed are those who hunger and thirst for righteousness, for they will be filled."

DAY 326

Chosen

Acts 15:22, 40–41

We first read of Silas when he was chosen, as a leading member of the church in Jerusalem, to accompany Paul and Barnabas to Antioch in Syria with a letter from the Jerusalem Council giving a ruling on how much Moses' law was to be observed by the Gentile Christians. Silas appears to have been an inspiring preacher, who strengthened the young church during his stay at Antioch. Later, when Paul required a new travelling companion for his second missionary journey – having parted from Barnabas in a dispute over John Mark – he chose Silas, who was also a Roman citizen and so could claim the same privileges as Paul when travelling with him.

"His master replied, 'Well done, good and faithful servant! You have been faithful with a few things; I will put you in charge of many things. Come and share your master's happiness!'" (Matt. 25:23)

FURTHER THOUGHT

Before being chosen for the task of accompanying Paul and Barnabas, Silas had already, as the saying goes, "proved his soul". When we are faithful in the small tasks that God has given us then, in due course, we shall be selected for the bigger ones.

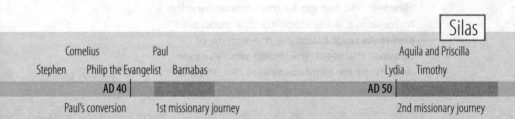

		Silas
Cornelius	Paul	Aquila and Priscilla
Stephen	Philip the Evangelist	Barnabas	Lydia	Timothy
AD 40		AD 50
Paul's conversion	1st missionary journey	2nd missionary journey

Imprisoned

Acts 16:19-24

When Paul and Silas arrived in Philippi, they were followed day after day by a slave girl who was possessed with an evil spirit, and repeatedly called out that Paul and Silas were God's servants come to proclaim the way of salvation. One day Paul decides to put up with these remarks no longer, and commands the evil spirit to come out of the girl. Following her deliverance, the girl is no longer able to tell people's fortunes, and thus her masters are deprived of a source of income. Angry at this, they bring Paul and Silas before the magistrates and accuse them of disturbing the peace and preaching heresy. The magistrates err, however, by allowing them to be beaten and thrown into prison without giving them a proper hearing and reaching a formal verdict as was required under Roman law.

"The apostles left the Sanhedrin, rejoicing because they had been counted worthy of suffering disgrace for the Name." (Acts 5:41)

FURTHER THOUGHT

For most of us, the world today seems a far cry from the time when Christians were thrown into prison for simply preaching the good news concerning Jesus Christ. Will such times ever return? Some believe they will. Could you face such a situation as this? Think it through.

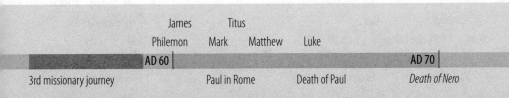

	James	Titus			
	Philemon	Mark	Matthew	Luke	
		AD 60			AD 70
3rd missionary journey		Paul in Rome	Death of Paul		*Death of Nero*

DAY 328

Rejoicing

Acts 16:25-39

Despite being severely flogged and thrust into the stocks with their wounds untreated, Paul and Silas pray and sing hymns to God. Their prayers move God's hands, and an earthquake takes place which throws open the prison doors, giving all the prisoners the opportunity to escape. Such is their amazement, however, and the conviction that God is present among them, that they make no attempt to escape. The jailor, when he sees what has happened, listens to Paul's and Silas' preaching and is converted, whereupon he invites them to his home where food is provided for them and their wounds washed. Later Paul and Silas demand an apology from the magistrates for their illegal treatment of two Roman citizens.

"Rejoice in the Lord always. I will say it again: Rejoice!" (Phil. 4:4)

FURTHER THOUGHT

Paul and Silas were a couple of jailbirds who knew how to sing in a darkened cage! They transformed prison gloom into a paean of praise. The Christian faith is never more splendid than when it is seen triumphing over circumstances and bringing praise from lips which, if natural reasoning had its way, would wail and groan.

Silas

Cornelius	Paul		Aquila and Priscilla
Stephen	Philip the Evangelist	Barnabas	Lydia	Timothy
AD 40			AD 50
Paul's conversion	1st missionary journey		2nd missionary journey

Supportive

Acts 17:4-7

I n the debate that ensues with the Jews concerning whether or not Jesus is the Messiah, Paul appears to be the chief speaker, just as he was during the first missionary journey with Barnabas (Acts 14:12), and Silas backs up his arguments prayerfully and supportively. In the city of Thessalonica many Jews, as well as devout Greeks, are persuaded by Paul's and Silas' arguments and surrender their lives to the Lord Jesus Christ. The success of their preaching causes the Jews to become jealous, and they incite a riot centred on the house of Jason, probably a converted Jew, where they believe Paul and Silas are staying.

"Now that you have purified yourselves by obeying the truth so that you have sincere love for your brothers, love one another deeply, from the heart." (1 Pet. 1:22)

FURTHER THOUGHT

"Dependable and supportive people," said the great preacher James Hastings, "... their price is above rubies." Are you such a person? Can you function as well when you are away from the glare of the spotlight, as when you are in it?

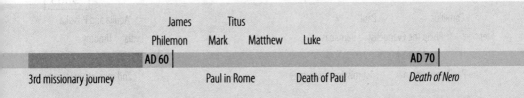

	James	Titus		
Philemon	Mark	Matthew	Luke	
AD 60				AD 70
3rd missionary journey		Paul in Rome	Death of Paul	Death of Nero

DAY 330

Fearless

Acts 17:10–15

Due to the rioting in the city of Thessalonica and the fierce hatred and bitterness of the Jews there, the believers send Paul and Silas away under cover of darkness to the nearby town of Berea. Here the Jews give an attentive hearing to what Paul and Silas have to say and, as a result, many come to accept Jesus as their Messiah. Soon, however, the Thessalonian Jews hear of this and come to Berea, stirring up trouble once again. Paul is sent away by the Berean believers, but Silas and Timothy stay on to brave the wrath of the rebellious Jews. Silas – and Timothy – were evidently fearless disciples of Christ, and able to act independently of Paul whenever the circumstances required.

"Surely God is my salvation; I will trust and not be afraid. The Lord, the Lord, is my strength and my song; he has become my salvation." (Isa. 12:2)

FURTHER THOUGHT

A well-known American preacher, Robert Schuller, is famous for coining the statement: "When the going gets tough – the tough get going." This effectively describes the attitude of Silas, for, when left to his own devices, his true character shone forth. It always will.

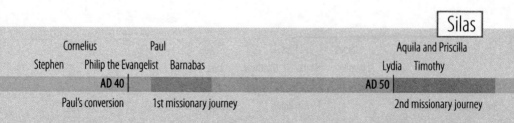

					Silas
	Cornelius	Paul		Aquila and Priscilla	
Stephen	Philip the Evangelist	Barnabas		Lydia	Timothy
	AD 40			AD 50	
	Paul's conversion	1st missionary journey		2nd missionary journey	

Acts 18:5

How different was Silas' reaction when faced with difficulties, compared to that of John Mark. It appears that John Mark drew back at the first sign of trouble, while Silas not only stayed in Berea to preach the gospel, but remained there for some considerable time. Much later, Silas and Timothy follow Paul to Athens, only to find he has gone to Corinth. When they eventually catch up with him they find him staying with two tentmakers – Aquila and Priscilla. Paul meets with great resistance from the Jews in Corinth and, as a result, turns his back on them and instead presents the gospel to the Gentiles – with positive results.

"Whoever can be trusted with very little can also be trusted with much ..." (Luke 16:10)

FURTHER THOUGHT

No greater statement could ever be made of someone than that he is "faithful". The word has two senses – "being full of faith" and "reliable". The one, of course, is the root of the other; for a man that is full of faith is a man who may be trusted to fulfil all that is expected of him.

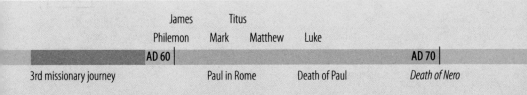

	James	Titus			
	Philemon	Mark	Matthew	Luke	
	AD 60				AD 70
3rd missionary journey		Paul in Rome	Death of Paul		Death of Nero

DAY **332**

Preacher

2 Corinthians 1:19; Acts 15:32

S ilas is presented to us in these passages as a leading member of the church in Jerusalem with a clear prophetic gift, who preached with great effect at Antioch, bringing many to Christ and strengthening the spiritual lives of the believers. His preaching ability is seen, too, in his travels with Paul and Timothy: all three of them, in fact, proclaimed the message that Jesus was the Messiah with tremendous power and spiritual effectiveness. Doubtless Silas, as well as all the other great preachers of the early Church, found tremendous joy and fulfilment in making known the good news that the One who was crucified on Calvary was none other than God's promised Messiah – the "suffering Servant" predicted by Isaiah.

"For we do not preach ourselves, but Jesus Christ as Lord, and ourselves as your servants for Jesus' sake."
(2 Cor. 4:5)

FURTHER THOUGHT

We ought not to forget, in these days of many innovations in the Church – dance, drama, and so on – that preaching is still the foremost way of presenting God's truth. Take a moment today to pray for those in your church who have been called by the Lord to a preaching ministry.

Silas

	Cornelius	Paul				Aquila and Priscilla	
Stephen	Philip the Evangelist	Barnabas			Lydia	Timothy	
	AD 40					AD 50	
	Paul's conversion	1st missionary journey				2nd missionary journey	

Silas – traveller with Paul

Paul chose Silas to accompany him on his second missionary journey when Paul and Barnabas parted company. As a leader of the church at Jerusalem and, like Paul, being a Roman citizen, he was an ideal choice as Paul's companion on this journey. Silas had prophetic gifts and had already risked his life for the gospel. He also had a literary role and is known by the Roman form of his name, Silvanus, in the pastoral letters he helped to write. (1 Thess. 1:1; 2 Thess. 1:1; 1 Peter 5:12).

Key Lesson – Silas

Many commentators refer to Silas as "Paul's shadow", but this is a very narrow and jaundiced view of a truly great and inspiring Bible character. It is true that, as someone put it, "he glides about in the dim background of the Acts", and that "he is never mentioned except in the company of someone else" – yet he is by no means an expressionless personality. He was gifted by nature, highly valued by more than one apostle, ready to speak, toil, travel and, if need be, suffer for Christ. The main lesson that can be learned from observing his life is that of the importance of dependability. He was content to take up whatever task was appointed to him by the Lord or by his colleagues, and to see the task through to the end. And he was willing to let others occupy the limelight. A truly priceless soul!

DAY **333**

Prayer

Acts 16:9–13

In the middle of one of his missionary journeys, Paul was given a vision of a man beseeching him to come over into Macedonia. Seeing this as a call from God to preach the gospel in that region, the apostle set out for Macedonia and came in due course to Philippi, the principal city in the area. On the first Sabbath day after his arrival in the city, Paul made his way to the riverside, where he found a group of devout women engaged in prayer. He and his companions take the opportunity to share with them the truths of the gospel of Christ, and by so doing, present the very first gospel message in the area which we now describe as Europe.

"... our gospel came to you not simply with words, but also with power, with the Holy Spirit and with deep conviction ..." (1 Thess. 1:5)

FURTHER THOUGHT

What an important moment was that first Sabbath day's meeting in Philippi! Out of it came the beginning of the propagation of the gospel in Europe. However busy you are today, pause now and again and give God thanks for sending His Word our way – your way.

Cornelius	Paul		Lydia
			Aquila and Priscilla
Stephen	Philip the Evangelist	Barnabas	Timothy Silas
AD 40			AD 50
Paul's conversion	1st missionary journey		2nd missionary journey

Worshipper

Acts 16:14

One of those present at the prayer meeting where Paul introduced the gospel was a woman by the name of Lydia. Lydia was born at Thyatira in the province of Asia, and had probably spent most of her life there. Her native city was famous for its dye-works, especially its purple dye, for this was a favourite colour of the nobility of that day. Lydia was a trader in either purple dye or cloth that had been dyed in that colour. It is commonly believed that she was a widow, but we have no clear evidence for that. What is clear, however, is that she was a devout woman, a Jewish proselyte, whose heart easily opened to the gospel as it was preached by Paul on that first Sabbath morning in Philippi.

"God is spirit, and his worshippers must worship in spirit and in truth." (John 4:24)

FURTHER THOUGHT

Eliezer, the servant of Abraham, tells how "being in the way, the Lord led me" (Gen. 24:27, AV). That is the principle illustrated by Lydia's conversion.

"Worshippers," said someone, "are people in the way – they put themselves in the way for God to lead them."

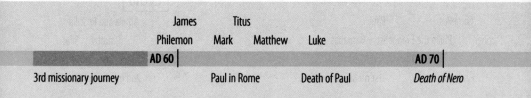

	James	Titus			
	Philemon	Mark	Matthew	Luke	
AD 60					AD 70
3rd missionary journey		Paul in Rome	Death of Paul		Death of Nero

DAY 335

Hospitable

Acts 16:15

L ydia showed evidence of the sincerity and earnestness of her confession of Christ in two ways. First, she willingly consented to be baptised, and also encouraged her household – either her children, or the workers in her business and perhaps her domestic servants – to take part in this act. Second, she extended the hospitality of her home to Paul and his companions. The hospitality she offered them was one of the first forms of service open to her, and she entered upon it without question or hesitation. The Living Bible paraphrase puts it thus: " 'If you agree that I am faithful to the Lord,' she said, 'come and stay at my home.' And she urged us until we did."

"Do not neglect to show hospitality to strangers, for thereby some have entertained angels unawares." (Heb. 13:2, RSV)

FURTHER THOUGHT
Hospitality, we must never forget, is one of the ministries which is urged upon us as Christians (1 Pet. 4:9). Mother Teresa said: "Let no one ever come to you without coming away better and happier. Be the living expression of God's kindness".

| Lydia |

Cornelius	Paul		Aquila and Priscilla
Stephen	Philip the Evangelist	Barnabas	Timothy	Silas
AD 40			AD 50
Paul's conversion	1st missionary journey		2nd missionary journey

Comforter

Acts 16:40

While staying in Lydia's home, Paul and Silas experienced severe persecution, being beaten and thrown into prison. The jailer was instructed to guard them carefully and so put them in stocks. The two missionaries prayed and sang hymns until an earthquake released them from their bonds. The terrified jailer expected all the prisoners to have escaped and was about to commit suicide when Paul assured him that everyone was present. After being released by the magistrates, Paul and Silas returned to the comforting hospitality of Lydia's home. When they had rested, they bade farewell to the Christians in Philippi and set out once more on their missionary travels.

"Therefore encourage one another and build each other up, just as in fact you are doing." (1 Thess. 5:11)

FURTHER THOUGHT

Did you know that the word "comforter" comes from the Greek, *parakaleo*, meaning "to come alongside and help"? It is a beautiful word, and is often used to describe the ministry of the Holy Spirit. This suggests that whenever we come alongside someone in need and help them, our ministry at the moment closely resembles that of the Holy Spirit Himself!

	James	Titus		
	Philemon	Mark	Matthew	Luke
AD 60				AD 70
3rd missionary journey		Paul in Rome	Death of Paul	Death of Nero

Key Lesson – Lydia

Lydia became the first convert in Europe because she was prepared for God to open her heart. Already a person of prayer, she was receptive to His message. But perhaps the main lesson of her life for us is this: we have the power to influence others. First, Lydia used her position of authority as head of her household to bring about the conversion of all who worked for her. And second, her immediate desire to share her material wealth by practising hospitality was copied by others and became traditional in the Philippian church (see Philippians 1:5; 4:10).

Aquila and Priscilla

Aquila: "Eagle"; Priscilla (Prisca): A Latin name

Refugees

Acts 18:2

Aquila and Priscilla were a Jewish husband and wife team, originally from Pontus in Asia Minor. They were living in Rome when the Emperor Claudius issued an edict expelling all the Jews from there, probably because of clashes in the Jewish community concerning the subject of Christianity. After leaving Rome, Aquila and Priscilla settled in Corinth but, like so many other Jews of the Dispersion, they were vulnerable to persecution and often moved from place to place. It is obvious from what the Scripture says about them that they turned their frequent journeys to good advantage in spreading and sharing the good news of the gospel.

" ... give thanks in all circumstances, for this is God's will for you in Christ Jesus." (1 Thess. 5:18)

FURTHER THOUGHT

How thankful we should be that God works all things together for good. In fact, C.H. Spurgeon said: "The Lord gets His best soldiers out of the highlands of adversity." Aquila and Priscilla learned how to turn their difficult circumstances to advantage. Have you learned that secret yet?

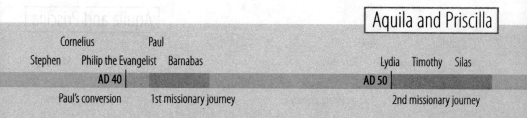

		Aquila and Priscilla
Cornelius	Paul	
Stephen	Philip the Evangelist	Barnabas		Lydia	Timothy	Silas
	AD 40			**AD 50**	
Paul's conversion	1st missionary journey		2nd missionary journey

Aquila and Priscilla

Aquila: "Eagle"; Priscilla (Prisca): A Latin name

Tent-makers

Acts 18:3

Aquila and Priscilla, like all Jews of whatever station in life, were trained in a craft. In their case it was tentmaking – the same trade as that of the apostle Paul. When Paul arrived in Corinth, he "became acquainted" with Aquila and Priscilla, "for they were tent-makers just he was" (TLB). We cannot be certain of Aquila's and Priscilla's spiritual condition at the time when the apostle joined them. Some think they were already Christians prior to Paul's arrival, while others believe they were converted under his dynamic ministry in Corinth. There can be no doubt, however, that Aquila and Priscilla would have been able to inform Paul about conditions in Rome, which would have been of great interest to this missionary strategist.

"A man that hath friends must shew himself friendly: and there is a friend that sticketh closer than a brother." (Prov. 18:24, AV)

FURTHER THOUGHT

If it is true that Paul's association with Aquila and Priscilla began on a business footing, it certainly did not stay on that level for long. Paul would soon have brought the conversation gently and tactfully around to Christ. And note the words "gently and tactfully" – they are important. For "to win some," as D.L. Moody once put it, "we must be winsome."

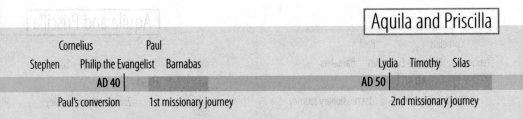

Aquila and Priscilla

Cornelius		Paul				Lydia	Timothy	Silas
Stephen	Philip the Evangelist	Barnabas						
	AD 40					AD 50		
Paul's conversion		1st missionary journey				2nd missionary journey		

Adventurers

Acts 18:18; Romans 16:3–4

It appears that Aquila and Priscilla risked their lives on Paul's behalf. We are not told anything about the circumstances, but Paul alludes to this fact when writing to the church in Rome. Aquila and Priscilla were a brave and adventurous couple who gained the gratitude of all the Gentile churches for their labours in the gospel (Rom. 16:4). It is quite clear that when, after spending a considerable time there, Paul left Corinth, Priscilla and Aquila accompanied him as far as Ephesus, where they remained when he returned to Antioch. It seems that eventually – possibly after the death of the Emperor Claudius – they returned to Rome, since Paul sends his greetings to them there (Rom. 16:3).

"... I do not consider myself yet to have taken hold of it. But one thing I do: Forgetting what is behind and straining towards what is ahead, I press on towards the goal to win the prize for which God has called me heavenwards in Christ Jesus." (Phil. 3:13–14)

FURTHER THOUGHT

"The worst thing that can happen to a Christian," says Edward Eddy, "is to lose a sense of adventure in spiritual things. To those who walk closely with Christ, every stumbling-block becomes a stepping-stone, every adversity an adventure. Without the recognition of this, one sinks down into despair." How do you interpret what is happening around you at the moment? As adversity – or an adventure?

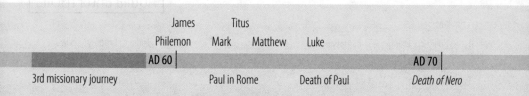

		James	Titus		
	Philemon	Mark	Matthew	Luke	
	AD 60				AD 70
3rd missionary journey		Paul in Rome	Death of Paul		Death of Nero

Aquila and Priscilla

Aquila: "Eagle"; Priscilla (Prisca): A Latin name

DAY 340

Teachers

Acts 18:24–26

During their stay in Ephesus, Aquila and Priscilla met up with another Jew from the Dispersion, known as Apollos. He was an eloquent speaker and had a good knowledge of the Old Testament. He had learned about Jesus but knew only of the baptism of repentance practised by John, being ignorant of the news of the descent of the Holy Spirit at Pentecost. Aquila and Priscilla heard him speaking boldly in the synagogue at Ephesus, but detected a lack of the Spirit's power and presence in his life. After taking him aside, Priscilla (as Chrysostom says) "was able to instruct him" – or, as Luke puts it, they "explained to him the way of God more adequately" (v. 26).

"... all of you who were baptised into Christ have clothed yourselves with Christ. There is neither Jew nor Greek, slave nor free, male nor female, for you are all one in Christ Jesus."
(Gal. 3:27–28)

FURTHER THOUGHT

Did you notice that Luke puts Priscilla's name first, suggesting she took the lead in the teaching ministry? Does this mean she was not fulfilling her Scriptural role? What do you think?

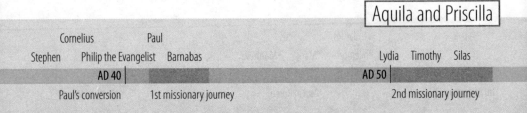

	Cornelius		Paul					Aquila and Priscilla
Stephen		Philip the Evangelist	Barnabas			Lydia	Timothy	Silas
	AD 40				AD 50			
	Paul's conversion	1st missionary journey			2nd missionary journey			

Church leaders

Romans 16:5

It is obvious that during their stay at Ephesus, Priscilla became the hostess of the new church there, as when Paul wrote from Ephesus back to Corinth, he sent the "warm" greetings of Aquila and Priscilla and "the church that meets at their house" (1 Cor. 16:19). In the letter to the Romans, we find a similar reference to "the church that meets at their house", which suggests that after returning to Rome, they again gave hospitality to meetings of the believers. Aquila and Priscilla flit in and out of the pages of the New Testament with the spotlight never focused clearly upon them. We would love to know more about this intriguing couple, but for some reason, the Holy Spirit is content to give us just a few glimpses into their spiritual actions and adventures.

"The greatest among you will be your servant. For whoever exalts himself will be humbled, and whoever humbles himself will be exalted." (Matt. 23:11–12)

FURTHER THOUGHT

Have you ever pondered what is the basic qualification for leadership in the Church of Jesus Christ? Is it just an ability to preach or teach? No. The basic qualification for leadership is a willingness to serve. Take a moment now to pray for the leader, or leaders in your church or community.

	James	Titus		
	Philemon	Mark	Matthew	Luke
AD 60				AD 70
3rd missionary journey		Paul in Rome	Death of Paul	Death of Nero

Priscilla – a question of background

Aquila came from Pontus, a remote province. Priscilla's origins seem different. Her name, appearing sometimes in its shorter form, as Prisca, is often met with in monuments in Rome.

One of the oldest of the catacombs at Rome is known as "the burial-place of Priscilla". The name Prisca has been found in association with an aristocratic family, some members of which were buried in this catacomb. From these facts it has been inferred that Priscilla was a member of this family, and that has been taken as the reason why, of the six places where she and her husband are mentioned in the New Testament, four have the wife's name first.

W. F. Adeney

Key Lesson – Aquila and Priscilla

Such a couple as Aquila and Priscilla – mentioned only six times in the New Testament, but always with warm appreciation – were obviously valued colleagues in the infant Church. Only twice is the husband, Aquila, mentioned first, from which commentators both ancient and modern infer that the wife was the more gifted personality. These two, yoked together in Christ, stand before us as a living picture of the way our earthly loves can be glorified if the light of heaven is allowed to shine into them. The main lesson that we learn from the lives of Aquila and Priscilla, however, is the fact that under God, they were able to turn their adversity into an adventure.

A godly mother

DAY **342**

2 Timothy 1:5; 3:14–17

Timothy's father was a Greek and his mother a Jewess, as was probably his grandmother Lois. Timothy was not circumcised as a baby – due, no doubt, to the fact that his father was a Greek – but received instruction, probably from his mother, Eunice, in the Hebrew Scriptures. Both Timothy's mother and grandmother are described by Paul as having a sincere faith which leads us to infer that they were Christian believers. Timothy appears to have had some physical problems – the apostle referring on one occasion to his "frequent illnesses" (1 Tim. 5:23) – but nevertheless he served the Lord with great sincerity and zeal, often in difficult and dangerous situations.

"The eye that mocks a father, that scorns obedience to a mother, will be pecked out by the ravens of the valley, will be eaten by the vultures." (Prov. 30:17)

FURTHER THOUGHT

Every Christian mother – and grandmother – ought to take encouragement from the success of Eunice and Lois with Timothy, who proved so effective a minister of Christ. Charles Dickens put it like this: "The virtues of mothers shall be visited on their children, as well as the sins of their fathers."

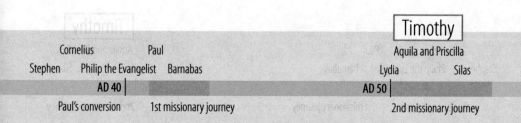

Timothy

	Cornelius	Paul		Aquila and Priscilla	
Stephen	Philip the Evangelist	Barnabas		Lydia	Silas
	AD 40			**AD 50**	
Paul's conversion		1st missionary journey		2nd missionary journey	

DAY **343**

Paul's "spiritual son"

1 Timothy 1:2; Acts 16:3

Timothy was born at Lystra, and was probably brought to Christ through Paul's ministry during his first missionary journey to that city. When Paul visited Lystra for the second time, he found that Timothy was highly regarded by the Christians there, and also by those at Iconium (Acts 16:2), so he invited Timothy to join him on his missionary journeys. At this time in Paul's ministry, Silas had replaced Barnabas, and Paul was doubtless looking for a replacement for John Mark also. A strong bond of love and affection developed between Paul and Timothy, causing the apostle to look upon Timothy as his "spiritual son" (1 Tim. 1:2; Phil. 2:19–22).

"You then, my son, be strong in the grace that is in Christ Jesus."
(2 Tim. 2:1)

FURTHER THOUGHT

In modern times, little emphasis seems to be laid on such terms as "fathers in Christ", or "mothers in Israel", yet such phrases were often used in times past to describe relationships within Christ's Church. Can the reason be that there are so few spiritual "fathers" and "mothers" in the Church of today?

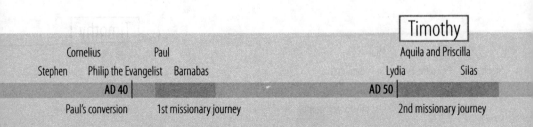

		Timothy
Cornelius	Paul	Aquila and Priscilla
Stephen	Philip the Evangelist	Barnabas	Lydia	Silas
AD 40		AD 50
Paul's conversion	1st missionary journey	2nd missionary journey

Ordained

1 Timothy 4:14; 2 Timothy 1:6

When Timothy joined up with Paul and Silas on their missionary travels, he entered into a completely new way of life which necessitated that he should become ordained. Ordination, in those days, required the ministry of the "laying on of hands", and Timothy is brought before the church for their approval and commendation, whereupon the elders lay their hands upon him, along with the apostle Paul, and he is set apart for the work of the ministry. We have no way of knowing whether or not the laying on of hands by the elders and the apostle took place simultaneously, but we can safely assume that both events happened at around the same time.

"Ye have not chosen me, but I have chosen you, and ordained you, that ye should go and bring forth fruit, and that your fruit should remain ..."
(John 15:16, AV)

FURTHER THOUGHT

Ordination is a highly debated issue in the Christian Church of today. Some are for it – others against it. What do you think? In the widest sense of the word, every Christian has been "ordained". Turn to Acts 13:48 (Authorised Version) and you'll see.

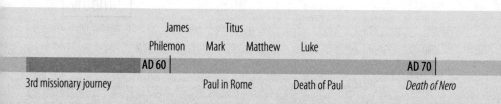

	James	Titus		
Philemon	Mark	Matthew	Luke	
AD 60				**AD 70**
3rd missionary journey		Paul in Rome	Death of Paul	*Death of Nero*

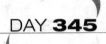

Timothy

Timothy: "Honoured of God"

DAY 345   Paul's companion

Acts 16:3; 17:14; 20:4-5

It becomes quite obvious in reading the story of Paul's travels that he took a great liking to Timothy. Travelling companions usually get closer to each other – or else farther apart; in this case, their friendship and fellowship deepened the more time they spent together. When they arrived in Berea, however, the party was split up as a result of the persecution that swept down upon the Christians there, and it was some time before Silas and Timothy caught up with the apostle Paul. They eventually met up again in the home of Aquila and Priscilla in Corinth. Timothy later accompanied Paul on the journey to Jerusalem to distribute the offering collected by the Gentile churches for their fellow believers in that city.

"He who walks with the wise grows wise, but a companion of fools suffers harm." (Prov. 13:20)

FURTHER THOUGHT

It's truly a wonderful thing when Christians who are teamed up together by Christ develop an increasing spiritual affection for each other. But it doesn't always happen that way. Some relationships are easier than others, but all, to some extent, have to be "worked at".

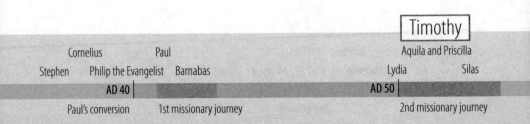

Timothy

	Cornelius	Paul		Aquila and Priscilla	
Stephen	Philip the Evangelist	Barnabas		Lydia	Silas
	AD 40			AD 50	
	Paul's conversion	1st missionary journey		2nd missionary journey	

Received instruction

1 Timothy 3:1–4:16

Paul took great pains over the well-being of the churches, and wrote letters to Timothy which, because of their enduring value for Christians down the ages, are included in the New Testament. He counselled Timothy on many things, not the least on the way to look after his health. Special directions were given also on how to become a good minister of the Lord Jesus Christ, and the qualifications Timothy should look for in those chosen to be leaders in the local churches. Paul's instructions to Timothy carry the spirit of a father talking to his son, and Paul's high opinion of Timothy show the latter to have been an attentive and obedient "son".

"Since my youth, O God, you have taught me, and to this day I declare your marvellous deeds." (Psa. 71:17)

FURTHER THOUGHT

How good are you at receiving spiritual instruction? Do you receive it with grace – or with a grudge? The way in which we take on board truth or instruction from Scripture says a lot about us. "We are," as someone put it, "what we respond to – nothing more and nothing less."

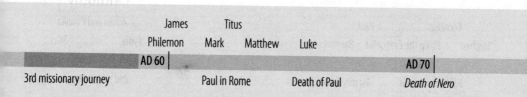

	James	Titus		
	Philemon	Mark	Matthew	Luke
	AD 60			AD 70
3rd missionary journey		Paul in Rome	Death of Paul	Death of Nero

DAY 347

Learned Scripture

2 Timothy 3:16

Here, in one of the great "3:16's" of the Bible, Paul reminds his "son" in Christ of the power that is resident in Holy Scripture. Although Timothy had been brought up by a Jewish mother and was doubtless well instructed in the Scriptures, he must now look at them through Christian eyes and learn how they show the way of salvation through faith in the Lord Jesus Christ.

Paul reminds Timothy that all Scripture is inspired – or "God-breathed" – and has fourfold influence in the life of believers: it is profitable for (1) teaching, (2) rebuking, (3) correcting and (4) training in righteousness. Timothy is also charged to preach the Word faithfully at all times (2 Tim. 4:1–2).

"Then you will know the truth, and the truth will set you free." (John 8:32)

FURTHER THOUGHT

We may understand Scripture from many different perspectives, but we do not fully understand it until we see that its main focus is Christ. Just as there is a road from every city, town and hamlet in Britain that leads to London, so there is a path from every Bible text that leads to Christ. Bible study is not effective until it finds that path.

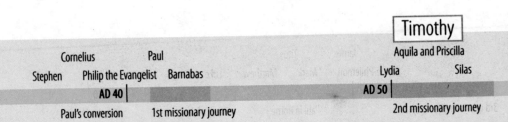

			Timothy
			Aquila and Priscilla
Cornelius	Paul		
Stephen	Philip the Evangelist	Barnabas	Lydia	Silas
	AD 40		AD 50	
Paul's conversion	1st missionary journey		2nd missionary journey

Imprisoned

Philippians 1:1; Colossians 1:1; Hebrews 13:23

Like many of the early Christians, Timothy experienced imprisonment for his faith. We do not know quite where or when he was imprisoned, but we do read of his release (Heb. 13:23). During Paul's lifetime, Timothy no doubt saw the inside of many Roman prisons – if only as a visitor – as Paul spent a good deal of his time incarcerated for the sake of the gospel. Timothy was evidently a great encouragement to Paul, and his name appears in the opening greetings to Philippians and Colossians – letters written by Paul from prison. One of Paul's last requests during his final imprisonment was directed to Timothy: "When you come, bring the cloak ... and my scrolls, especially the parchments" (2 Tim. 4:13).

"But even if you should suffer for what is right, you are blessed ..." (1 Pet. 3:14)

FURTHER THOUGHT

How would you feel if you were given a three-month prison sentence for telling the story of Christ? It doesn't happen today – well, at least not in the West. But, as many Christians predict, it could happen at some future date. You might not want to go to prison for Christ – but would you be willing?

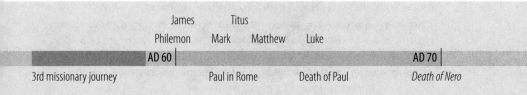

	James	Titus		
Philemon		Mark	Matthew	Luke
AD 60				AD 70
3rd missionary journey		Paul in Rome	Death of Paul	Death of Nero

Timothy – *teacher and evangelist*

It is not given to us to trace the history of Timothy's godly mother and grandmother except to say that they were of the Dispersion. It is highly probable that they were connected with the Babylonian Jews whom Antiochus settled in Phrygia three centuries before.

The marriage of a religious Jewess like Eunice was not uncommon among the Jews of the Dispersion as the husband would, no doubt, have been a proselyte. This mixed origin gave Timothy an intimate knowledge of both Jewish and Gentile worlds.

When Timothy became Paul's companion, Paul felt it prudent that he took on the full identity of the Jew through circumcision. Paul was not being inconsistent as he had previously argued against the need for circumcision, for that was in relation to salvation. In this instance, because much of his preaching was in the synagogues, he was concerned lest Timothy's presence should create a barrier in his being viewed as an uncircumcised heathen.

Key Lesson – Timothy

Many commentators regard Timothy as an enigma. His invaluable service to the infant Church is beyond question, but we know little or nothing about his age, his background or his special gifts. His ministry seems to have been that of a "link man", for he was always being sent here, there and everywhere – to Corinth, to Philippi, to Thessalonica, to come to Athens, to remain at Ephesus, and so on. "Among the widely separated infant churches," says one commentator, "he formed a living link of fellowship, counsel and encouragement between Paul and his converts, and between one congregation and another." The lesson we draw from his life is found in what must be one of the highest commendations ever given: "I have no-one like him, who takes a genuine interest in your welfare" (Phil. 2:20). Are you deeply concerned over the spiritual growth and development of those among whom God has placed you? If not, then pause right now, and listen ... learn ... and imitate.

Comfort

2 Corinthians 7:5–13

Paul and his companions were having a rough time – physically, mentally and spiritually – on their missionary travels in Macedonia, and the arrival of Titus and the good news he brought of the successful outcome of his delicate mission to the erring church at Corinth was a great comfort to them. Titus was evidently a strong character, possessed of great diplomacy and tact, who acted toward the churches in the same spirit as Paul himself (2 Cor. 12:18). Titus was Greek – some think he was Luke's brother – and was held in such high regard by Paul that an epistle was addressed to him. He mediated God's comfort to Paul and his companions when they so desperately needed it (v. 6).

"Praise be to the God and Father of our Lord Jesus Christ ... who comforts us in all our troubles, so that we can comfort those in any trouble with the comfort we ourselves have received from God." (2 Cor. 1:3–4)

FURTHER THOUGHT

Are you one of God's "comforters"? This is a ministry that we can all exercise - if we wish. God, it has been said, does not comfort us to make us comfortable, but to make us comforters. What are you doing with the "comfort" that has been given to you?

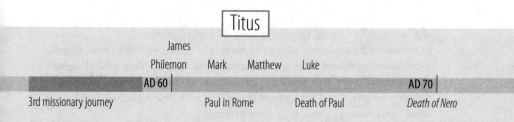

	Titus			
James				
Philemon	Mark	Matthew	Luke	
AD 60			AD 70	
3rd missionary journey	Paul in Rome	Death of Paul	*Death of Nero*	

Titus

Titus: A Greek name

DAY 350

Paul's protégé

2 Corinthians 2:13; 8:6

It is probable that Titus, like Timothy, was a young man when Paul chose him and discipled him. The great apostle guided his Christian growth by the spoken word and also by personal example. Paul obviously cared for everyone in the Christian Church, but he had a special regard for his own protégés.

When he temporarily lost track of Titus – not finding him at Troas as he expected – Paul could not rest, but moved on in search of him. Something of the manner in which Paul discipled Titus can be seen in the fact that when Titus had left an unfinished task at Corinth, Paul urged him to return there and complete it. Paul himself possessed great determination and staying power (Phil. 3:14), and obviously sought to inculcate this in his followers.

"Whoever serves me must follow me; and where I am, my servant also will be. My Father will honour the one who serves me." (John 12:26)

FURTHER THOUGHT

The concept of discipleship – that is, a younger Christian being taken under the wing of an older, more experienced Christian – is a topic of great debate in today's Church. How do you feel about it? Is it a valid Biblical principle? What are the dangers? If you have not already done so, think the issue through – and if you can, talk it over with a Christian friend.

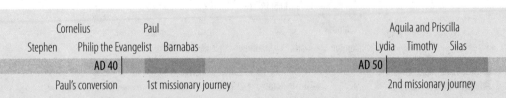

	Cornelius		Paul					Aquila and Priscilla	
Stephen		Philip the Evangelist	Barnabas				Lydia	Timothy	Silas
	AD 40						AD 50		
	Paul's conversion		1st missionary journey					2nd missionary journey	

414

Leader

Titus 1:1–16

Paul, when writing to both Timothy and Titus, calls them his true children (1 Tim. 1:2; Titus 1:4), and gives them similar and fatherly advice on how to carry out the oversight of a local church. Titus, who seems to be a more forceful character than Timothy, has been given a tough assignment in Crete. The Cretans have a bad reputation which Paul appears to agree with (1:12–13) and he counsels Titus to rebuke them sharply so that their faith may be sound. The qualities required of an elder or bishop are various, and only Christians of exemplary character would be able to meet the high standards set by the apostle. Both Timothy and Titus must have met these high standards, judging by the responsibilities placed upon them by Paul.

"Now get up and stand on your feet. I have appeared to you to appoint you as a servant and as a witness of what has been seen of me and what I will show you." (Acts 26:16)

FURTHER THOUGHT

Do you have a favourite definition of leadership? If not, perhaps you might like to make one up today. A definition of leadership given by the renowned Bible teacher, Bill Gothard, is this: "A leader is someone who sees farther into the future than those around him can." An interesting one – don't you agree?

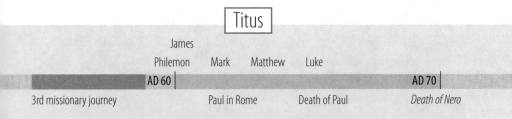

Titus

	James			
Philemon		Mark	Matthew	Luke
AD 60				AD 70
3rd missionary journey		Paul in Rome	Death of Paul	Death of Nero

Titus

DAY 352

Teacher

Titus 2:1-15

Teaching was to be a top priority in Titus' ministry, and it was to be done with authority (v. 15), backed up by an irreproachable personal example (vv. 7–8). He was not to permit his hearers to disregard what he had to say (v. 15). Paul obviously envisaged that Titus would enforce good discipline in a church which consisted of members drawn from a reprobate society and likely to defect from the faith if not firmly led. The hope of success lies in the grace of God (v. 11), which makes possible the living of self-controlled, upright and godly lives in the world, and the turning away from the habits of one's former life (v. 12).

"Let the word of Christ dwell in you richly as you teach and admonish one another with all wisdom, and as you sing psalms, hymns and spiritual songs with gratitude in your hearts to God." (Col. 3:16)

FURTHER THOUGHT

Do you ever get frustrated by the fact that the standards which God sets for believers seem so unbelievably high? Then don't fret – for He not only raises the standards to unbelievable heights, but He also provides the power by which we can attain to them.

	Cornelius	Paul			Aquila and Priscilla		
Stephen	Philip the Evangelist	Barnabas			Lydia	Timothy	Silas
	AD 40				AD 50		
	Paul's conversion	1st missionary journey			2nd missionary journey		

Wise

Titus 3:1–9

Paul further advises Titus not to get caught up in stupid controversies (v. 9), but to insist on wise behaviour from the members of the church. This should include obedience to the civil powers, readiness to engage in honest work, avoiding slander and quarrels, and showing gentleness and courtesy to everyone. He reminds Titus that salvation comes through God's goodness and mercy and by the ministry of the Holy Spirit. The accounts of the various missions which Titus successfully accomplished suggest that he was a wise man whose behaviour was modelled on Paul's own life and teaching.

"And he said to man, 'The fear of the Lord – that is wisdom, and to shun evil is understanding.'" (Job 28:28)

FURTHER THOUGHT

Have you ever considered what it means to be a "wise" person? A definition of "wisdom" which many Christians like is the one given in the J.B. Phillips' translation of Colossians 1:9: "That you may see things, as it were, from his point of view." So what is "wisdom"? Seeing things from God's point of view!

			Titus			
	James					
	Philemon	Mark	Matthew	Luke		
	AD 60					AD 70
3rd missionary journey		Paul in Rome		Death of Paul		Death of Nero

Titus
– young fellow-worker with Paul

Titus went with Paul and Barnabas to Jerusalem to lay questions before the apostles and elders there in reference to the Gentile converts (Gal. 2:1; cf Acts 15).

It seems probable that Titus returned from Jerusalem with Paul and Barnabas (Acts 15:22), and that afterwards he accompanied the apostle for a considerable time in his labours (2 Cor. 8:23).

Titus probably spent some time with the apostle in Ephesus, for the first epistle to the Corinthians was written at Ephesus, and was sent by the hand of Titus (2 Cor. 7:6–8).

We next hear of him as being left by the apostle in the island of Crete, that he might "straighten out what was left unfinished and appoint elders in every town" (Titus 1:5).

He was with Paul in Rome during his second imprisonment there although he did not remain with him until his trial (2 Tim. 4:10).

Key Lesson
– Titus

Titus has been called the most enigmatic figure in Christian history. He is never mentioned in Acts, and his story has to be largely constructed from a few scattered references and the letter written to him by Paul. What we do know for sure, however, is that he undertook a successful mission to Dalmatia (that is, the former Yugoslavia - see 2 Timothy 4:10). The main lesson we learn from Titus' life is the lesson of dependability. He was just the man to put in charge of a difficult job; just the man to have around when spirits were flagging or zeal was dying. In fact, many commentators refer to him as Titus the Dependable. Paul was greatly "comforted by the coming of Titus". We do not wonder at it!

Fellow worker

DAY **354**

Philemon v.1

During the apostle Paul's missionary journeys, many churches, both large and small, were established by him. However, the continuation and further development of these churches depended, humanly speaking, on the local believers who nurtured and discipled the groups of Christians meeting in different homes. Paul was the first to acknowledge the importance of appointing trusted Christians for the task of nurturing others – these were often spoken of as his "fellow workers" in the gospel. In introducing Philemon to us as a "fellow worker", we catch a glimpse of someone with a deep dedication and a firm commitment to the cause of the Lord Jesus Christ.

"Thus you will walk in the ways of good men and keep to the paths of the righteous." (Prov. 2:20)

FURTHER THOUGHT

Isn't it fascinating how, in just a couple of words – "fellow worker"– it is possible to get a vivid impression of a man's industriousness and character? What does this term conjure up in your mind? Spend a few moments thinking through just what might be involved. Could this phrase be used of you?

Philemon

	James	Titus		
	Mark	Matthew	Luke	
AD 60				AD 70
3rd missionary journey		Paul in Rome	Death of Paul	Death of Nero

419

Philemon

Philemon: "Affectionate"

DAY 355

A personal letter

Philemon vv. 1–3

Paul writes to Philemon from a prison cell in Rome. He sends greetings from Timothy and himself to Philemon, his wife Apphia, his son, Archippus (Col. 4:17), and to the members of the church in his house in Colosse. At the end of the letter, he sends further greetings from other fellow workers who are with him in Rome. Epaphras is mentioned first. He was probably known to Philemon because he was the evangelist who, under Paul's direction, founded the church in Colosse. Paul had a special request to make of Philemon, which he makes most tactfully and compellingly in this very personal letter.

"'This is the covenant I will make with them after that time, says the Lord. I will put my laws in their hearts, and I will write them on their minds.'" (Heb. 10:16)

FURTHER THOUGHT

This is the only letter of Paul's in the whole of the New Testament that is of a personal nature; the rest, without exception, are his official correspondence to the churches. Why should this personal letter be included in the canon of Scripture? Could it be because God wanted us to know how Paul faced the problem of slavery - one of the most difficult social problems of his time?

Cornelius		Paul		Aquila and Priscilla	
Stephen	Philip the Evangelist	Barnabas		Lydia	Timothy	Silas
	AD 40			AD 50	
Paul's conversion		1st missionary journey		2nd missionary journey	

Faith recalled

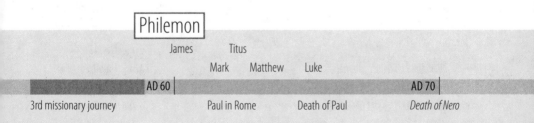

DAY 356

Philemon vv. 4-5, 10

Paul constantly remembered in prayer the Christians known to him, and thanked God for the good things about them which he knew from personal experience, or through the testimony of others who knew them. In Philemon's case, he singled out his love and faith towards Jesus Christ and his fellow believers. This, no doubt, convinced Paul that he could safely appeal to Philemon, rather than command him, to welcome back his runaway slave, Onesimus, whom Paul had led to Christ in Rome. This appeal of Paul to his old friend Philemon is, in fact, the central thrust of this short but appealing epistle.

" ... For everyone born of God overcomes the world. This is the victory that has overcome the world, even our faith." (1 John 5:4)

FURTHER THOUGHT

A man's nature, it has been said, is shown as much by the letters he receives as by those which he writes. This letter is almost as great a credit to Philemon as it is to the apostle Paul. What kind of letters do you receive? Be assured, your correspondents are saying something about you – if only between the lines.

Philemon

James   Titus

Mark   Matthew   Luke

AD 60   AD 70

3rd missionary journey   Paul in Rome   Death of Paul   Death of Nero

Philemon

Philemon: "Affectionate"

DAY **357**   Benevolence shown

Philemon vv. 6–7

Having highlighted Philemon's faith and love, Paul moves on to tell Philemon that he is praying that the sharing of his faith with others will spread the knowledge of all that is to be found and possessed in Christ. He recalls the joy and comfort he has drawn from Philemon's love, and how his benevolence has refreshed all the Christians with whom he has come in contact. It is a simple but beautiful expression of appreciation for Philemon's Christian contribution and not, as one commentator believes, "the buttering-up of Philemon before confronting him with the challenge of accepting back his runaway slave on a more Christian basis".

"Give to the one who asks you, and do not turn away from the one who wants to borrow from you." (Matt. 5:42)

FURTHER THOUGHT

The virtue which Paul especially highlights in Philemon's life is that of "benevolence". Some translations use the word "kindness", "hospitality" or "love". Someone put it like this: "God let His kindly rain fall on the evil and the good – we, too, ought to rain kindliness on all." How "kind" a person are you?

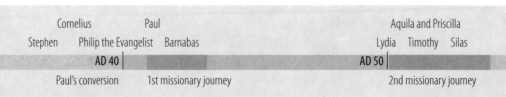

	Cornelius	Paul		Aquila and Priscilla		
Stephen	Philip the Evangelist	Barnabas		Lydia	Timothy	Silas
	AD 40			AD 50		
	Paul's conversion	1st missionary journey		2nd missionary journey		

An appeal to love

Philemon v. 9

Having commended Philemon for his attributes and qualities, as well as for his faith in the Lord Jesus Christ, Paul gets down to the main point of his letter, which is to plead the cause of the runaway slave, Onesimus, who has been converted to Christ under Paul's ministry in Rome. Paul explains that he would like to have kept Onesimus as his helper, but he would not do that without Philemon's consent, and thus he was sending Onesimus back to his master. He makes a special plea for Philemon to accept Onesimus back into his household, not as a servant, but as a brother in Christ.

"May the Lord make your love increase and overflow for each other and for everyone else, just as ours does for you." (1 Thess. 3:12)

FURTHER THOUGHT

How much easier it is to approach people over difficult and sensitive areas in the Christian life when you know that they are eager to do the right and loving thing. Do you experience this with others? But more important – do others experience this with you?

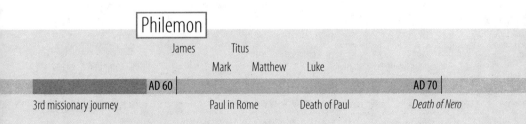

	Philemon				
		James	Titus		
			Mark	Matthew	Luke
		AD 60			AD 70
3rd missionary journey			Paul in Rome	Death of Paul	Death of Nero

423

Philemon

DAY 359   Obedience anticipated

Philemon v. 21

Paul makes an eloquent plea to Philemon, flowing from his own love for Onesimus which has developed during their short acquaintance in Rome, asking him to receive Onesimus, not just as a "dear brother", but as he would the apostle himself. He offers to repay personally any loss which Philemon may have suffered because of Onesimus' defection, but gently reminds Philemon of his own spiritual debt to the apostle as his spiritual father. Paul also explains that he needs some encouragement from Philemon since he is now in prison, and that his acceptance of Onesimus as a brother would be inspiring news indeed. Paul expects Philemon to do, not only what he asks, but far more.

"If you are willing and obedient, you will eat the best from the land ..." (Isa. 1:19)

FURTHER THOUGHT

"Expect the best of people," goes an old saying, "and you will get what you expect." Unfortunately, it doesn't always work out that way. How different things might be in our personal relationships, however, if we adopted the attitude of expecting the best from people, rather than the worst!

Cornelius		Paul		Aquila and Priscilla	
Stephen	Philip the Evangelist	Barnabas		Lydia Timothy Silas	
	AD 40			AD 50	
Paul's conversion		1st missionary journey		2nd missionary journey	

Hospitality claimed

Philemon v. 22

As a pioneer missionary, Paul depended a good deal upon the hospitality of his friends, and he confidently asks Philemon to prepare a guest room for him, as he hopes to be released from prison soon in answer to their prayers. He seems to have had no doubt that Philemon would do this, and that he would be welcomed with joy when he eventually arrived in Colosse. He was sure, too, that Onesimus would be part of the household again, and would be there to greet him if he had not been sent back by Philemon to serve him in Rome. The last three verses of the epistle are greetings from others and a final prayer for Philemon.

"Offer hospitality to one another without grumbling." (1 Pet. 4:9)

FURTHER THOUGHT

Was it faith - a divine assurance - or mere wishful thinking that led Paul to ask Philemon to prepare a room for him following his release from prison? Scholars have debated this question for centuries. What do you think?

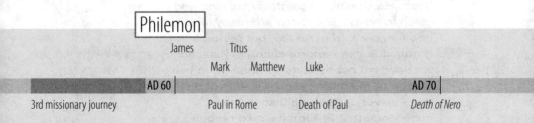

Philemon				
James	Titus			
Mark	Matthew	Luke		
	AD 60			AD 70
3rd missionary journey	Paul in Rome	Death of Paul		Death of Nero

Philemon
– letter to a prominent Christian

Jerome tells us that the letter to Philemon was rejected by many writers. From the absence of doctrinal teaching in this letter, they concluded that it was not by St Paul, or that, if it was his, it did not belong to the canon, since it contained nothing by which the Church might be edified. This decision arose out of a narrow view of the canon, and the primitive Church, as a whole, did not ratify the verdict.

Although it concerns a personal relationship, the letter is addressed not only to Philemon, but to "the church" (v. 2). It approaches the question of master-slave relationships which posed a problem for the whole of the Church. In Christ, the letter shows, earthly relationships are transformed – brotherhood is the context in which they must be worked out.

◎ Key Lesson – Philemon

Some of the Church Fathers argued that, as Paul's letter to Philemon contained no doctrinal teaching and was purely a personal and private letter, it ought not to be included in the canon of Scripture. However, the Holy Spirit overruled and, in so doing, has preserved for us a picture of a man with some very interesting character traits. He was benevolent, loving, kind and given to hospitality. There are many lessons one can draw from his life, but perhaps the greatest is this – approachability. Paul, as we saw, did not hesitate to open up to him on one of the most delicate issues of the day – slavery – but he did so in the confidence that Philemon would respond positively to his loving appeal.

James

James: "Supplanter" (English equivalent of the Hebrew Jacob)

Brother

DAY **361**

Matthew 13:55; Mark 6:3; Galatians 1:19

The name James appears approximately forty times in the New Testament, referring to three different men, but the James under consideration here is the son of Mary and Joseph, and thus the brother of our Lord Jesus Christ. Strictly speaking, of course, James should be referred to as the "half-brother" of Christ, for although they had the same mother, they did not have the same father. Jesus, as Scripture so clearly states, was conceived in Mary's womb by a miracle – "The Holy Spirit will come upon you, and the power of the Most High will overshadow you" (Luke 1:35). Jesus grew up among a family of four brothers – James, Joseph, Judas and Simon (Matt. 13:55) – and also several sisters, whose names are not given in Scripture.

"In the beginning was the Word, and the Word was with God, and the Word was God." (John 1:1)

FURTHER THOUGHT

The point that James was really a half-brother of Christ might seem trivial and unimportant to some, but for those of us who believe in the virgin birth, it is a vital issue. Much controversy rages nowadays over the divinity of Christ. Take a moment today to remind yourself of its truth and power.

James				
		Titus		
	Philemon	Mark	Matthew	Luke
	AD 60			AD 70
3rd missionary journey		Paul in Rome	Death of Paul	Death of Nero

James

James: "Supplanter" (English equivalent of the Hebrew Jacob)

DAY 362 — Sceptic

Mark 3:21, 31–32; John 7:5

It seems that during the three-year period of Jesus' ministry, James did not accept our Lord's Messiahship. In fact, we are told by John that none of Christ's brothers believed in Him. How strange that James and his brothers should be so sceptical of Christ's ministry when they were firsthand observers of His sinless life and His amazing miracles. Mary and Joseph also, at times, found Christ's behaviour and actions hard to understand (see, for instance, Luke 2:50). Later His brothers join their mother in seeking to restrain Christ – presumably because they, like Christ's friends, doubted His sanity (Mark 3:21). No wonder Jesus said: "Only in his home town and in his own house is a prophet without honour" (Matt. 13:57).

"Immediately the boy's father exclaimed, 'I do believe; help me overcome my unbelief!'" (Mark 9:24)

FURTHER THOUGHT

Are you a victim of scepticism from those who are closely related to you? Do they regard your Christian convictions as one stage removed from insanity? Only those who have experienced such alienation can measure its pain and poignancy. Take heart – Jesus knows exactly how you feel. He will provide special grace to help you in your hour of need.

Cornelius		Paul		Aquila and Priscilla	
Stephen	Philip the Evangelist	Barnabas		Lydia	Timothy	Silas
AD 40				AD 50	
Paul's conversion		1st missionary journey		2nd missionary journey	

Convert

Acts 1:14; 1 Corinthians 15:7

Although James was an eye-witness of Jesus' character and ministry, it is fairly clear that he did not become a convinced believer until after Christ had died on the cross and risen from the dead. This deduction – one shared by most evangelical commentators – is based on the fact that, following the resurrection, we are told that Jesus' brothers gathered with the disciples in the Upper Room. This view – that James became a convinced believer as a direct result of the resurrection – is further strengthened by the fact that in 1 Corinthians 15:7, reference is made to Christ's post-resurrection appearance to James. A new allegiance came into the hearts of James and his brothers following the resurrection. Years of scepticism and unbelief gave way to deep faith and conviction.

"... Jesus declared, 'I tell you the truth, no-one can see the kingdom of God unless he is born again'". (John 3:3)

FURTHER THOUGHT

The circumstances of James' conversion are never explained. We know that prior to the crucifixion and the resurrection he was an unbeliever, yet after those events he is seen among the believers. What is important is not so much the moment of a person's conversion, but the fact of it. After all, your birth certificate is not the greatest evidence that you are alive!

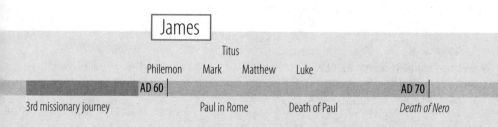

| James |
| Titus |
Philemon	Mark	Matthew	Luke
AD 60			AD 70
3rd missionary journey		Paul in Rome	Death of Paul	Death of Nero

James

DAY 364

Church leader

Galatians 1:19; Acts 12:17

After the outpouring of the Holy Spirit at Pentecost, a church was formed in Jerusalem, headed, so it seems, by James, the brother of our Lord. The degree to which James had been transformed becomes quite evident when we see the honour and respect the early Christians gave to him. It was in his capacity as leader of the church in Jerusalem that Saul of Tarsus conferred with him when he returned there after his encounter with Christ on the Damascus Road. It was James also, who presided over the famous "Jerusalem Council" and delivered the ruling, later conveyed to the churches by letter, that Gentiles coming into the Christian faith were not required to be circumcised or to keep the law of Moses.

"Obey your leaders and submit to their authority. They keep watch over you as men who must give an account. Obey them so that their work will be a joy, not a burden, for that would be of no advantage to you." (Heb. 13:17)

FURTHER THOUGHT

If you have time today, take a few moments to read the account of how James summed up the difficult situation that had arisen in the early Church in Acts 15:13–29. Take special note of his receptive understanding of the spirit of Scripture – and make up your mind to follow his pattern.

	Cornelius	Paul		Aquila and Priscilla	
Stephen	Philip the Evangelist	Barnabas		Lydia	Timothy	Silas
	AD 40			AD 50	
	Paul's conversion	1st missionary journey		2nd missionary journey	

Author and writer

James 1:1

Some scholars believe that the letter of James was not written by the brother of our Lord because of the way in which he introduces himself in the opening verse: "James, a servant of God and of the Lord Jesus Christ ..." They say that if it was written by James, the Lord's brother, then he would have affirmed this fact in his opening remarks. Such a view, however, does not take into consideration the tremendous impact which Christ's death and resurrection made upon James. The writer is so taken up with the fact of Christ's Lordship – "a servant of God and of the Lord Jesus Christ" – that by comparison, the fact that he was Christ's brother seems to be of no great importance. James rejoiced, not so much in his earthly relationship to Christ, but in his heavenly one.

"For by the grace given me I say to every one of you: Do not think of yourself more highly than you ought, but rather think of yourself with sober judgement, in accordance with the measure of faith God has given you." (Rom. 12:3)

FURTHER THOUGHT

James does not claim to be the Lord's brother, but, as someone put it: "Would he ever so claim?" His self-effacing attitude may cause problems for some scholars, but it really shows the true measure of the man. Remember, however, that self-effacement is not self-abasement. Do you understand the difference?

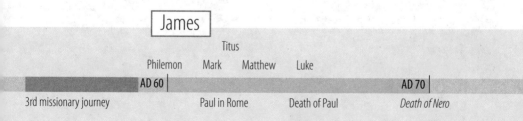

	James				
		Titus			
	Philemon	Mark	Matthew	Luke	
	AD 60				AD 70
3rd missionary journey			Paul in Rome	Death of Paul	Death of Nero

Key Lesson – James

Tradition states that James had a great reputation for being a man of prayer, and was referred to as "Camel Knees". Other early writers, such as Eusebius, say of him that he was a reasonable and fair-minded man. One writer refers to him as "James the Just". A close examination of James' letter shows a striking resemblance to the proverbial and epigrammatic style of Jesus, for in its five short chapters, some fifty echoes of Jesus have been counted – phrases like "a grapevine bear figs", "do not merely listen to the word", "moths have eaten your clothes", "you do not even know what will happen tomorrow" and so on. The lesson to be learned from James, therefore, is that the closer we live to Christ, the more effectively we will be able to echo His teaching and reflect His wisdom. Christ's priorities were James' priorities. We find in James the same deep concern with practical religion that Jesus spoke of so much in the Gospels. James not only echoed Christ's words, but His Spirit also. A brother indeed!